Three to Twenty-One Days—Esther's Progressive Prayer Fast

Breaking and Uprooting Generational Curses

Dr. Pauline Walley-Daniels

Foreword by: Dr. Ronald Cottle
Endorsed by: Susan Slusher

iUniverse LLC
Bloomington

THREE TO TWENTY-ONE DAYS—ESTHER'S PROGRESSIVE PRAYER FAST
BREAKING AND UPROOTING GENERATIONAL CURSES

Copyright © 2014 Dr. Pauline Walley-Daniels.

All rights reserved. No part of this book may be used or reproduced by any means, graphic, electronic, or mechanical, including photocopying, recording, taping or by any information storage retrieval system without the written permission of the publisher except in the case of brief quotations embodied in critical articles and reviews.

Unless otherwise indicated, all Scripture quotations taken from the King James Version of the Bible which is public domain.
Scripture references marked NKJV are from the New King James version of the Holy Bible. Copyright 1990, 1985, 1983 by Thomas Nelson, Inc.
Scriptures in bold or in italics are the emphases of the author.
Hymn lyrics are taken from the website: www.cyberhymnal.org.

iUniverse books may be ordered through booksellers or by contacting:

iUniverse LLC
1663 Liberty Drive
Bloomington, IN 47403
www.iuniverse.com
1-800-Authors (1-800-288-4677)

Because of the dynamic nature of the Internet, any web addresses or links contained in this book may have changed since publication and may no longer be valid. The views expressed in this work are solely those of the author and do not necessarily reflect the views of the publisher, and the publisher hereby disclaims any responsibility for them.

Any people depicted in stock imagery provided by Thinkstock are models, and such images are being used for illustrative purposes only.
Certain stock imagery © Thinkstock.

ISBN: 978-1-4917-1801-8 (sc)
ISBN: 978-1-4917-1802-5 (hc)
ISBN: 978-1-4917-1803-2 (e)
Library of Congress Control Number: 2013922653

Printed in the United States of America.

iUniverse rev. date: 12/19/2013

Contents

Dedication ix
Acknowledgments xiii
Foreword xv
Endorsement xvii
Testimony xix
Editorial Comment xxv
Introduction: The Quest for Fasting xxvii

Chapter 1: Esther's Progressive Prayer Fast 1

Chapter 2: The Realms of Fasting 18

Chapter 3: Strategies for Fasting 28

Chapter 4: Purpose of Progressive Prayer Fast 35

Chapter 5: Overview on Understanding Curses 40

Chapter 6: First Chapter of Esther 46

    Day One: Desire for Destiny Deliverance 49
    Day Two: The Nemesis of Generational Curses 69

Chapter 7: Second Chapter of Esther 95

    Day Three: The Discovery of a Royal Destiny 100
    Day Four: Fasting for Destiny Connections 112
    Day Five: The Power and Impact of Obedience 118
    Day Six: A Step into Royal Destiny 126

Chapter 8: Third Chapter of Esther 140

    Day Seven: The Repercussion of Disobedience 143
    Day Eight: The Discovery of Generational Curses 151
    Day Nine: An Unpleasant Inheritance 161

Chapter 9: Fourth Chapter of Esther 179

    Day Ten: The Cry for Deliverance 182
    Day Eleven: Marriage as an Instrument of Wisdom 189

Chapter 10: Fifth Chapter of Esther 204

    Day Twelve: Marriage as an Instrument of Deliverance 207

Chapter 11: Sixth Chapter of Esther 227

    Day Thirteen: The Struggle with Generational Curses 230
    Day Fourteen: Causes of Generational Curse 234

Chapter 12: Seventh Chapter of Esther 252

    Day Fifteen: Favor for Support to Uproot Curses 254

Day Sixteen: Request for Protection and
Preservation of Life 261

Chapter 13: Eighth Chapter of Esther 281

Day Seventeen: Repossession of Royal Destiny 284
Day Eighteen: The Empowerment of Esther
and Mordecai 289

Chapter 14: Ninth Chapter of Esther 305

Day Nineteen: Maintenance of Royal and
Divine Destiny 309
Day Twenty: Rest from Ancestral Enmity and
Generational Curse 317

Chapter 15: Tenth Chapter of Esther 337

Day Twenty-One: Proclamation of Final
Conquest and Victory 338

Reflection 357
About the Author 365
Bibliography 367
Appendixes 369
    Decision 371
    Rededication 373
    Pauline Walley Deliverance Bible Institute &
        Prophetic-Deliverance Theological Training Institute ... 375

About the Book 385

Dedication

Praise God from whom all blessings flow. One of the hardest things for me to do is exactly what I am doing on this page right now. Sometimes, after honoring certain people in a unique manner, they start to rebel and misbehave. Therefore, I have been careful with the information that is put into my writing, especially where individuals are concerned. However, be that as it may, we cannot allow other people's weakness to destroy our desire to appreciate some other persons for their contributions to our progressive life and endeavors. There are individuals who really deserve to be appreciated, but the fear of an opposite turnaround in one's relationship could be a real hindrance to publishing their names as part of an expression of appreciation. Instead of inking a name that might later turn a beautiful intention into a bitter pill, I considered another option that would pay off.

In retrospect, I have been raising a group of our church youths—the Overcomers Stars. Most of the members of Overcomers Stars joined our ministry when they were toddlers, while a few of them were born and raised here. One day the Lord inspired me to adopt the Overcomers Stars as my personal children and impart into them what I have as though they are my biological children. As time went on, each of them began to adopt me as their second mother and related to me affectionately, as the Lord had spoken.

It is a great joy to watch each member of this youth group grow up and now a majority of them are in college/university. Every weekend, we spend some time together, in the Word and on matters that affect our destiny. Having adopted them as my own children, they walk up to me very freely to hug, kiss, and chat with me. Besides, we are able to discuss school work, expectations, and everything regarding relationship and marriage.

Each parent refers to his or her children as "mine." I have a special pet name for each of them which also ignites jokes and sparkles of excitement whenever I address them by those names. Wow! I feel great and unique.

During the Mother's Day celebration in 2012, one of the youngest, nine-year-old Christian Kalu designed me a work of art with the inscription, "You're a cool adult, Mom; I am glad you're my mom. Love you." I was away on a mission field trip to Guyana, South America the week before Mother's Day. When I returned, the special poster with this unique inscription was placed on top of my desk. I was amazed and found it hilarious as bubbles of joy flowed out of my soul with continuous laughter. I was so excited at the expression of love from this young boy that I posted the card on the door of my office. Of course, everyone that came to my office gave a positive comment about that artistic impression of love coming out of a little boy. It's past Mother's Day now, but the card is still a point of attraction in my office.

Also, whenever we call a fast in the church, each of our toddlers and youths were encouraged to participate actively. The toddlers were taught to fast from one hour to three hours. At the age of nine years, Christian has been able to take a full-day fast during school holidays. When school is in session, he does the afternoon or evening fast for about three to six hours. Besides saying a prayer on his own, he knows how to have conversations with the Lord and get answers when he asks questions. Like the biblical Esther, Overcomers Stars have understood the meaning and importance of prayer and fasting. They have also learned to fast on their own in preparation for examinations and other matters that require divine intervention.

Considering this unique expression of love in our environment, why should other people's weaknesses nullify the gift of God in my life? It is an honor to be appreciative of other people's contribution to our lives. It is a blessing to let others know that "little is much when God is in it." It is an encouragement to let others know that they are connected to the fulfillment of our destiny. It is a joy to let others know that someone like you and me cares for them.

On this note, considering how the Overcomers Stars have responded to my adoptive motherly love, and accepted me as their spiritual mother and pastor, I hereby dedicate this book titled, *Esther's Progressive Prayer Fast*, to each and every one of them.

Acknowledgments

To God be the glory, great things He has done. His name be praised and exalted far above all others. Glory be to God in the highest! He deserves all the glory, honor, praise, and adoration. Amen!

Jehovah God deserves the glory for blessing me with unction to script volumes of words that flow from the well of wisdom. This unique inspiration has enabled me to hear and receive divine instruction and direction continuously as the living water never runs dry. Indeed, he is the Great God of Wonders.

Besides, he has appointed people to assist in the production of this work at various levels. Thanks to all members of Overcomers House who are always ready to test and prove the reality of the content of my writings before they are finally published. Thanks to everyone who gave their testimonies to support as proof producers of the message embedded in this book. Thanks to all the editors and publishers who support the publication of this material.

Praise the Lord for the iUniverse Editorial Board members who have also been of great encouragement to me. Their professional advice has kept me on my toes as they have shown great respect and special passion toward my works.

A special thanks to the ministers and leaders of Pauline Walley Evangelistic Ministries who have constantly used this book as the basic manual of prayer and fasting on regular basis. Thanks to the contributors who validated this work with their scripts—Dr. Ronald Cottle, the founder and president of Christian Life Educators Network and Beacon University in Columbus, Georgia; also Prophetess Susan Slusher, the dean of Christian International Equipping Network in Santa Rosa Beach, Florida.

I am forever grateful to my parents who taught me to read the Bible and pray. They also taught me to have faith in God through our Lord and Savior Jesus Christ, and to trust Him for everything in my life. Special thanks to my husband, Rev. Frederick Daniels, for allowing me to continue to do the will of God for my life and ministry.

May your needs be met! May the Lord open the windows of heaven and pour out his blessings upon you! May the face of Jehovah God shine upon you! I pray the blessing of the Most High God upon you all. Amen!

Foreword

Dr. Pauline Walley-Daniels is a prophetic apostle whose record of accomplishment as a leader in spiritual gifts is well known. Her school in New York has produced courses on the prophetic, apostolic, healing, deliverance, and much more. This study on the nature and power of fasting based on the life of Esther is another revelational work from her pen.

I recommend this book not just for those who practice regularly the ministry of the fast, but for all of the body of Christ who want greater spiritual power and authority for the miraculous in their lives and ministries. Every leader in the church needs to know how to harness the power of the fast as a weapon of spiritual warfare. The insights and practical guidelines, which Dr. Walley-Daniels shares in this book, are extremely helpful in that regard.

Read this book. It will help you to greater power and authority as a leader and as a man or woman of God.

Dr. Ronald E. Cottle
Founder-President
Christian Life Educators Network,
Apostolic Council of Transformational Servant-Leaders.

Endorsement

Dr. Pauline Walley-Daniels fights a good fight of spiritual warfare. In her book, *Esther's Progressive Prayer Fast: Breaking and Uprooting Generational Curses*, she presents powerful, effective prayers that are specific to the challenges individuals may face in fulfilling their destiny. Even if a person does not know how to pray for a specific area of freedom, Dr. Walley's prayers are so well formatted that one can follow along and receive freedom as they apply the prayers to their own lives. Readers will not only pray an effective prayer to fight against the enemy blocking the fulfillment of their destiny, but also will be given tools they can use to fight effective spiritual warfare in many situations throughout their lives.

Esther's Progressive Prayer Fast: Breaking and Uprooting Generational Curses presents revelation of the issues in the lives of many believers that keep them from believing and appropriating the fullness of God's plans for them. The book then builds upon the revelation by providing information, understanding, and tools to overcome those hindrances.

The guidelines to enter into warfare are clearly outlined in each chapter of the book. Prayer points are given, songs that raise the faith of the believer are suggested, and each related prayer is written out for one to follow. The reader is able to go beyond reading a textbook to entering into war against the enemy with a well-defined battle plan.

Dr. Pauline Walley-Daniels's passion to see that all believers fulfill their purpose and destiny is evident in this book, *Esther's Progressive Prayer Fast: Breaking and Uprooting Generational Curses*. When the material in this book is applied to believers' lives, they can effectively position themselves to rise up to the calling God has on their lives.

Susan Slusher,
Dean
Christian International Equipping Network
Santa Rosa Beach, Florida, USA

Testimony

Every year, Overcomers House Prophetic-Deliverance Church and its affiliates set themselves apart to do the Esther's Progressive Prayer Fast. Queen Esther declared the fast when she discovered that Haman, the enemy of the Jews, was plotting to destroy the Jews. It is a time when we (our church) go before God fasting and crying to Him for family members, for breakthrough and deliverance from any Hamanic decrees enacted against our lives and ourselves. Isaiah 58:6 (NKJV) states,

> Is this not the fast that I have chosen:
> To loose the bonds of wickedness,
> To undo the heavy burdens,
> To let the oppressed go free,
> And that you break every yoke?

This fast is taken very seriously, and every overcomer is encouraged to participate in the fast no matter his or her age. For this fast, we use the Word of God focusing on the book of Esther. In addition, we also use a book written by Dr. Pauline Walley-Daniels called the *Esther's Progressive Prayer Fast*, which includes prayers, declarations, decrees and instructions on how to receive and maintain deliverance from every kind of evil decree (*like the*

Hamanic decree) that was promulgated against our lives, as well as our family members.

My experience of this fast is one of victory. Reading the book of Esther repeatedly enlightened my eyes to how strategic and determined the enemy is and how we have to be strategic in defeating the enemy. The book authored by Dr. Pauline details the plot of the enemy, and brought home to me the struggles I was seeing in my life, especially in the area of marriage and finance. Through this fast, the Lord revealed to me how deadly negative decrees are, and how they go from generation to generation. I discovered that if negative utterances are not uprooted they can affect your life and frustrate not only one family member, but can also manifest through the generations.

I was determined like Esther when she discovered Haman's plot to destroy a whole nation to intervene through prayer and fasting to stop the enemy. I also was determined to recover everything that he had stolen from me, especially in the area of finances. I have begun to experience recovery in many areas of my life. Some things that I had lost, the Lord has restored them and I know that there are more to come. The eyes of my understanding have been enlightened to the enemy's devices along the line of relationships and finances. I have learned now how to always be on the offensive against the enemy and his devices. The Word of God declares that we should not be ignorant of the enemy's devices. "However, this kind does not go out except by prayer and fasting" (Matthew 17:21 NKJV). I praise God that through this Esther progressive prayer fast, I am experiencing restoration.

During this year's Esther's Progressive Prayer Fast, the focus was for God to totally restore every blessing that He had promised us, but it seemed long in manifesting, for whatever reason. Secondly, we were instructed by Dr. Pauline to focus our prayer on restoration of our family. The church really took this 2012 progressive fast seriously. I decided to follow the instructions and bring my family before the Lord. One case in particular: my second daughter was pregnant with her second child. During her prenatal checkup, the doctors kept giving her a negative report. They kept telling her that the results of the blood work showed that the baby had a high possibility of being born with some form of disability; also that the baby was very small for its gestational age.

I praise God for the knowledge I gathered from reading the preliminary book, *Esther's Progressive Prayer Fast* written by Dr. Pauline Walley-Daniels. This book detailed the strategies that Esther had used to bring deliverance to her people. In addition, each chapter ended with a prayer of declaration and decree. The book, *Esther's Progressive Prayer Fast* and the book of Esther in the Bible gave me the encouragement to use the same strategies that both Esther and Mordecai used when they discovered the negative decree that the enemy of the Jews had decreed against their lives.

Similarly, I began to make decrees and declarations concerning my daughter's pregnancy:

- I declared that this baby would be born normal with every organ intact.
- I declared that there should be no form of deformity.
- I declared that my daughter would not go through any type of long labor, but that she would experience a quick and uncomplicated delivery like Esther and the Jewish people experienced.

I also asked help from the members of the church to stand in agreement with me to pray and overturn the negative pronouncement that the doctors were making.

The church focused on the example of the three-day intensive fast that Esther had declared. They also focused on the specific request that she had presented to the Jewish people with regards to the negative decree that was sent out by the enemy of the Jews to totally destroy all the Jewish people. That devilish decree needed to be overturned, and this kind of decree demanded God's attention. According to Scripture, "God's ear is open to the cry of his people, and he is against those that do evil."

I spent three days in an intensive three-day fast, crying and asking God to overturn the entire negative pronouncement that the doctors were making against my grandchild. I was also instructed by Dr. Pauline to write my request and that at the end of the fast we would present it to God. God is truly a prayer-answering God. As we stood on His Word and cried, and presented our petition, He responded by overturning the negative pronouncement that both the medical laboratory and the doctors had given.

Evidenced by the healthy baby girl my daughter delivered, God did not only overturn the enemy's decree, he answered our prayer in a supernatural way. We were praying that she would deliver the baby like the Hebrew women in Exodus 1:19 (NKJV), which states that, "The Hebrew women are not like the Egyptian women; for they are lively and give birth before the midwives come to them." That was exactly what God did for my daughter. She delivered her baby three weeks earlier at the entrance of the hospital's emergency room, without the assistance of any medical personnel or doctor. Yet, she had no complications, and the baby is healthy and doing great in the name of Jesus.

I can say without a doubt that the effort and time God gave to Dr. Pauline to write down this instruction manual on the Esther's Progressive Prayer Fast is unique. The Lord gave her the wisdom to explain to the church how to recognize the negative decrees of the enemy against our lives. She explained in detail how our family members were affected by negative decrees through the generations. Dr. Pauline also showed how to uproot the curses by using the example of the Word of God with prayer to counteract the enemy's negative plans against our lives and destiny. Indeed, it is a great blessing given to her by God for the body of Christ. We have truly utilized this manual at Overcomers' House Prophetic Deliverance Church, and God has been faithful in answering our prayers.

Dr. Pauline, may God continue to bless and give you divine revelation on how to set his people free from the plans of the enemy. May you continue to be obedient to his voice! Amen!

Evangelist Renna Joseph
Director of Evangelism,
Pauline Walley Evangelistic Ministries
Bronx, New York

Editorial Comment

The Lord reminds us in His Word that if we need something, we should look for that thing, and we will find it. If we knock, that door will be opened; and if we just ask, we will get our answer.

Once again granted the special opportunity to edit Dr. Pauline's book, I thought to myself I've been learning about curses through Dr. Pauline's teachings and books, so why does the content continue to repeat itself? As I read and edited, I realized I was wrong. Yes, I was well aware that curses exist and can be passed on to the following generations from the past generations, BUT what I did not realize was exactly how far they can travel. The curses birthed from thousands of years ago still continue to manifest in the same exact power it had even till today. My understanding led me to believe that curses only reach maybe the fourth generation and stop.

For all of you who may still continue to believe that we are in no way connected to Abraham, Adam, Eve, and so forth, I suggest you read this book and trust me, the curses these people brought upon themselves, or spoke into the lives of others unknowingly will help you understand why we ourselves and the different nations of the world are faced with the challenges we see today.

Now, because this book focuses on the Biblical book of Esther, the curses highlighted in the book are taken from Esther's point of view. For instance, King Saul was ruler of Israel but lost the throne as a result of disobeying God's instructions. God does not accept such behavior and so dethroned Saul and crowned David king. After Saul died, his family could not inherit from him and this caused Saul's family to live in anger.

The anger caused them to curse David and his family. We later find out in the Bible that Mordecai is part of the lineage of Saul, meaning the curse of rejection was his portion. God sent Esther to break that curse entirely.

Are you that person that God has called to remove the curses within your lineage, as Esther was? Make yourself available to God and watch what He can do. Take a look back and see if you can remember some of the negative things pronounced. It's kind of hard, right? Especially, because we don't know everyone in our lineage personally. The answer is in prayer and fasting. God has revealed the avenue for solutions to Dr. Pauline, which is the wisdom and instruction presented in this book to help us in that aspect.

If you have purchased Dr. Pauline's recent books on curses, this one will not fail to intrigue you. If you have not done yourself a favor in adding to your book collection, it is never too late to start. In the process of doing so you will learn why we sometimes pray, fast, and get tired with no results. Unknowing to millions of us, the problem is so incredibly deep that not just any type of prayer and fasting will do. I know that many of us know about curses, but without the depth of understanding that God allows Dr. Pauline to spill on paper, it is baffling. That is just how mind-rattling God's wisdom is. She has simply asked, and God has given her the answers. Come on, let's take a ride!

Ruthy Kalu
Editorial Secretary
Pauline Walley Evangelistic Ministries
Bronx, New York

INTRODUCTION

The Quest for Fasting

Different types of fasting are mentioned in the books of the Bible. Different personalities approached their situations differently to attract the attention of Jehovah God. Each type of fasting adopted was effective. The people involved used fasting as a strategy to access the throne of heaven. They petitioned the Lord God with their cry until the gates of heaven were opened and their needs were met.

Similarly, people everywhere, irrespective of their belief systems, adopt different types of fasting as a strategy to persuade the Lord God of creation to hear their cry and attend to their needs.

- Some people see fasting as an instrument of persuasion.
- Some people use fasting as a method of self-denial.
- Some people use fasting as a symbol of repentance.
- Some people use fasting as an avenue of accessing the presence of God.
- Some people use fasting as a means to fulfill their personal needs.
- Some people believe that fasting is a spiritual exercise that every Christian must observe at a certain time and season.
- On the other hand, there are people who do not believe in fasting.

Thus, different people from different backgrounds have a different understanding of what fasting should be or should not be and how it ought to be observed.

This book is sequel to: *Strategic Deliverance Solutions: Discover and Destroy Ancestral Curses,* which discusses different types of curses. It also shows you how to detect a curse and eliminate it from your family and personal life.

In this book, *Esther's Progressive Prayer Fast: Breaking and Uprooting Generational Curses,* prayer and fasting are presented as instruments of war against destruction of human lives. Each chapter expounds on how the emergence of problems that may be considered minute could generate into problems that could haunt innocent people from a familiar descent. The book also reveals how a disagreement between two family members could create a kind of enmity that may separate them from each other unto eternity.

Fasting was, and still is the only strategic weapon that can be used to erase the plot of destruction caused by perpetual enmity. Fasting was employed to eradicate the nuisance that seeks destruction and termination of human lives.

This book opens with discussion on the Essence of Esther's Progress Prayer Fast. The twenty-one days of fasting are broken into segments of two or three days while a few have just a day each. This is to enable people who cannot go through a twenty-one-day fast at a stretch to do it on a weekly basis. One may concentrate on doing a segment of three days' fast on weekends or any day of the week for a period of seven weeks until the fast is concluded. Also you may pick the topic out of a segment according to your needs for concentration on the fast.

The book consists of a segment of two or three days of fasting. Each segment focuses on a chapter in the book of Esther with discussion and prayer points, and then a warfare prayer to conclude each segment of the fast. Each day provides you with a page for applicative reflection, whereby you jot down the various points that affect you so that you can deal with specific problems in order to achieve specific results.

Chapters one to six deal with the preliminary affairs that regard the application of fasting as well as what Esther's Progressive Prayer Fast is all about.

Chapter six focuses on the first chapter of Esther. The chapter is divided into two days of fasting based on the desire for destiny deliverance and the nemesis of generational curses.

Chapter seven focuses on the second chapter of Esther. The chapter is divided into four days with topical sections on the discovery of a royal destiny, a fast for destiny connections, obedience that attracts favor, and a step into royal destiny.

Chapter eight focuses on the third chapter of Esther. The chapter is shared among three topical days of fasting on the repercussion of disobedience, discovering generational curses, and Haman the descendant of Esau.

Chapter nine focuses on the fourth chapter of Esther. Here the chapter is split into two days of topical sections. The first day is on the cry for deliverance while the second day identifies marriage as an instrument of wisdom.

Chapter ten focuses on the fifth chapter of Esther. This chapter stands solo for day twelve of the fast as it pictures marriage as an instrument of deliverance.

Chapter eleven focuses on the sixth chapter of Esther. The chapter is shared between the thirteenth and fourteenth days of the fast with topics on the struggle with generational curses and causes of generational curses.

Chapter twelve focuses on the seventh chapter of Esther. This chapter is divided between the fifteenth and sixteenth days with topics on the favor for support to uproot curses as well as request for protection and preservation of life.

Chapter thirteen focuses on the eighth chapter of the book of Esther which is shared between the seventeenth and eighteenth days with topics on repossession of royal destiny and the empowerment of Queen Esther and her Uncle Mordecai.

Chapter fourteen is based on the ninth chapter of Esther. This chapter is divided between the nineteenth day that discuss the maintenance of royal and divine destiny, and the twentieth day on rest from generational torment and ancestral enmity.

Chapter fifteen is based on the tenth chapter of the book of Esther. This last chapter rounds up with the proclamation of final conquest and victory over unprecedented harassment that the Jewish people suffered in the Persian Empire.

The book concludes with a general reflective exercise that will enable readers to gain the purpose of reading the book. Its reflection will activate your intelligence and cause you to quickly grab the solutions that this book provides for you and those who are affected by the different situations that are similar to the ones mentioned.

This book is a journey into the secret place of your life—a place that is hidden from the view of humankind, but open to the eyes of the great Solution Provider. Enter in with rapt attention. Focus on purpose to achieve the optimum benefit of education, power, and authority to break loose from conglomerates of wicked conspirators and destiny destroyers.

God bless you as you read and enjoy this precious handbook that encourages prayer with fasting—Esther's Progressive Prayer Fast (EPPF).

*Our annual Esther's Progressive Prayer Fast is scheduled for the first week of July. You may check our website for further information. Thank you.

Reflection

The purpose of this book is to enable readers to make amendments wherever they have made some mistakes that have caused them to slump into a state of stagnancy, retrogression, and depression. For a person to gain full recovery and start off on a progressive pathway, it is important to reflect on the notes that one has jotted down on each chapter of this book. It is also important to do some specific reflections, because a general reflection may be productive but not effective. Reflection is a process of examining the lessons that you learned from reading or studying this book. For instance, it is wise to answer the questions below in order to experience the effectiveness of this book, as you may be expecting a real makeover in your life.

1. What have you learned?
2. How will you apply the lesson learned to your life?
3. How will you use the lesson learned to assist others?
4. What are the challenges or hindrances you are encountering?
5. Find out if God has ever spoken to you. What did God say, and what did you hear?
6. Are you in the right profession? Are you in the right place?
7. What is solution to you? Can you identify the solutions to some specific problems in your life?
8. Do you understand deliverance? What level of deliverance have you experienced so far?
9. What have you discovered about yourself?
10. What are the specific instructions and strategies that you want to adopt in order to overcome the ancestral challenges that confront some members of your family and yourself?

11. Asking for a deliverance solution means you want the Lord to intervene in matters that concern you. Do you really want His perfect will or permissive will for your daily endeavors?
12. What are the areas in which you need deliverance intervention?
13. Identify your challenges.
14. Identify your weak points and shortcomings.
15. Do you have a teachable spirit?
16. How often have you changed relationships because of hurt or anger?
17. Whenever you come across obstacles in the course of an aspiration, do you withdraw from active duty? What do you do to affect corrections in order not to fail again?
18. How do you react when someone points out your errors or weaknesses?
19. Do you often get angry, or do you work toward change?
20. How has the message in this book affected your life?
21. Give a brief summary on what the reading of this book meant to you.
22. Would you recommend the contents of this book to somebody?

Send your comments about how you feel about this book to the author. You may include the response to the questions answered above. Your words could be a healing balm to somebody in another part of the world.

Application

In order to achieve effective results in fasting, it is important that you identify the particular problems that need solution. Use the reflective questions provided to map out strategic solutions to the problems that affect your family members, environment, or anyone whom you intend to help besides yourself.

1. **List 3-5 lesson points that you have learned from today's reading.**

   _____
   _____
   _____
   _____
   _____

2. **Identify how the lesson affects you positively in 3-5 points.**

   _____
   _____
   _____
   _____
   _____

3. **Identify how you intend to use the lesson from today's passage to resolve your problem in 3-5 points.**

   _____
   _____
   _____
   _____
   _____

Breaking and Uprooting Curses

In the name of Jesus, and with the authority in the blood of Jesus, I bind and uproot the tree of curses planted against my life.
I speak to the tree of **generational and personal curses** that afflicts my life.
You shall no longer operate against my destiny.
I uproot you, **generational and personal curses,** out of my life right now.
In the name of Jesus, you tree of **curses** shall not prosper in my life.
Be uprooted out of my life and destiny right now, in the name of Jesus.
Be cast out of my life and go into the sea of destruction right now, in the name of Jesus.
I shall not see you, tree of **generational and personal curses,** again
And you shall not come by me, in Jesus's name.
I shall not invite you, tree of curses, again and you shall not harass me, in Jesus's name
I shall not entertain you, tree of curses, again and you shall not terrorize my life, in Jesus's name.
Let the blood of Jesus separate me from the tree of curses that steals the joy of my salvation.
Let the fire of the Holy Ghost destroy the **root of generational curses** that afflicts me.
The tree of generational curses shall no longer have access to me, in Jesus's name.
The tree of **curses** shall no longer manifest within and around me again, in Jesus's name.
I am washed and cleansed by the blood of Jesus Christ my Lord and Savior.
I am covered and sealed in the name of Jesus.
I am protected and guarded by the fire of the Holy Ghost. Amen!

Prayer Observations and Experiences

You may remember your dreams and some past occurrences while doing this prayer. You may also receive a revelation. It is important that you make notes for future reference.

Experiences

_____
_____
_____
_____
_____
_____

Observations

_____
_____
_____
_____
_____
_____

Revelations

_____
_____
_____
_____
_____
_____

CHAPTER ONE

Esther's Progressive Prayer Fast

Mercy Trotman's Encounter with Esther's Progressive Prayer Fast:

My name is Mercy Trotman.

- My Testimony: Isaiah 44:24-26; 2 Chronicles 20:20
- 2012: My year of Progressive Fertility and Productivity

As is the custom in Overcomers' House, Dr. Pauline Walley-Daniels (aka PWD) spends time in the Lord's presence before every new year to receive the theme/declaration for the next year. Each year's theme is like a continuation of the previous years. For instance, last year's (2011) theme and declaration was "The year of progressive fruitfulness and fulfillment." Of course we started the year with a lot of zest and expectation, looking forward to a new or any blessing that was not manifested in the previous year.

For my household and me, the first few months of 2012 surprisingly turned sour and challenging. My husband was going back and forth to the hospital and the nursing home. Both of my sons were also getting sick often. At some point, three of them were hospitalized at the same time in the same hospital for a long period of time (Montefiore Hospital). In view of this situation, when I went to our annual world convention "7th School of Prophetic-Deliverance World Convention," I really needed to experience my fertility and productivity. I needed to come out of the hardship and suffering with which the year started for me.

The presence of the Lord moved greatly in the convention. A lot of miracles and deliverances took place. People sent for their friends and family, and the next sessions were packed. In one of these sessions, Dr. Pauline was ministering corporately to us, and we were making some declarations. Then I fell into a trance, in which I saw a lady's hand with well-manicured fingers. The hand was resting on my left cheek in a comforting gesture. When I got out of the trance, I asked the Lord, "Whose hand was on my cheek?" Then the Lord revealed who it was, and rightly so. Once the Lord gave me the name, I identified the hand. I further asked the Father, "What is this lady's hand doing on my cheek?" He said, "She is highly deceptive." The Lord explained that the lady appears to be sympathetic of my situation, but goes behind to shoot arrows at me. I was also told that this particular lady practices witchcraft. The Lord further told me that He would change my current supervisor with whom I had worked for about five years.

Due to my husband and children's hospitalization, I missed many days of work, for which I provided documentation to my office. Upon returning to work, everything the Lord revealed to me began to unfold in a very theatrical manner. The doctors' notes that I provided at my office were disregarded. It felt like a coup d'état was launched against me with the primary aim to get me fired from the job.

- People had told me in the past that my then supervisor had threatened to get me fired.
- She accused me of absence without leave.
- She lied that I purposely made appointments for clients to come on the days that I would be absent from work.
- Even when she knew that I was encountering difficulties logging into my computer because the passwords were expired, and I needed new passwords, she would not assist me to obtain new passwords, but she was rather using every situation she could against me.
- Then she wrote me up stating that I did not want to input my time in the system.
- I was not completing my job timely, and that I did not account for the times that I was out of the office.
- Furthermore, I received the worst evaluation from her, as she stated that I only had completed 80 percent of my job for the last evaluation period.

In view of these accusations, I enlisted the assistance of a union representative who made sure that the situation was addressed in the light of what it was. He reminded everyone involved that my situation was recognized as a family hardship, and I was able to clarify and assuage all her lies. At this point, she became frustrated and subsequently antagonistic towards me. Then I understood the reason God said He would change my supervisor, so I requested to be transferred out of her unit. This move even got her more incensed, as she could not fathom the fact that I dared request for a transfer to another unit. This was an effrontery to her! Prior to my request, she was practically keeping malice with me. She would not respond to me. She would not discuss cases with me to ascertain the recommendation needed.

Eventually, I was reassigned to another unit. A few days after my transfer, my director summoned one of his deputies and myself to his office and served me with a notice of disciplinary charges, which encompassed criminal charges as well. This time around, I was accused of fraud, stealing, lying, etc. It was a miracle that I was not arrested. Although my accusers were not revealed, it was obvious that this was a case of retaliation and vendetta against me. My initial reaction was to laugh because I knew God would vindicate me. The moment I showed the accusation letter to my union representative, he confirmed that "these were pretty serious charges," which was practically beyond his jurisdiction. I had to take the rest of the day off work and go to my union office.

It was reported to me that after I had left the office to go sort out the accusations with the union representatives, this lady (my ex-supervisor) was dancing gleefully, and boasting that I thought I could get away with anything, and that I also thought I could mess with her. I informed Dr. PWD and Rev. Peace of the new development, they prayed with me and assured me that God would vindicate me, and in fact turn it around for my promotion. Dr PWD stated that God would fight for me as he fought for the biblical Esther and Mordecai. I held unto that promise.

I continued to read and pray with the book, *Esther's Progressive Prayer Fast,* authored by Dr. PWD, besides the Bible and other books. I started declaring that my name is in the Lamb's Book of Life, so it would not be in the hall of shame. The Lord gave me revelations of Scriptures to stand on. I received a lot of intercessory prayer from Dr. PWD, and all the leaders in Pauline Walley Evangelistic Ministries and Overcomers House Prophetic Deliverance Church. My whole church was praying for me. My mother, Missionary Comfort Ogba, and my older sister, Evangelist Ngozi Kalu, joined forces with the rest of my family to give me all the necessary support that I needed to overcome the false charges leveled against me on the job.

Considering the fact that the allegations made against me were false, I went for the hearing with the hope that the charges would be dropped. Unfortunately, after the hearing officer heard my side of the story, she still held on to the accusations brought against me. I was disappointed when she recommended my termination. So many brethren outside of my church were interceding for me. One of the intercessors enlisted to support me in prayer received a message that, "God said He would lift you [me] up gloriously." I strongly held on to that promise. In March of 2012, PWEM held a Women's Conference at Goshen, New York. During the conference, I received a revelation in which the Lord told me to pick up and rearrange my papers. My documents were scattered all over the place. In that revelation, I saw stains where I was sitting, and I saw myself wiping away the stains.

While praying with high expectation, I took some steps to encourage myself. One of the things I did was to write an assumed recommendation letter titled "My Expected End." This recommendation letter represented what I was trusting God to do for me: I was expecting to get a letter from my job, acquitting me of all the twelve charges, including violation of the penal code of the State of New York and the federal government. In fact, when I showed Dr. PWD this recommendation, she jumped up in excitement, thinking it was from my job. I then explained to her that I wrote the decision as a point of contact to believe God that my expectation for a favorable decision from my job would become a reality!

While I was preparing to go for the second and last hearing, my union warned me that my agency rarely overturns or changes their recommendation for termination, so they were certain that I would be terminated. They informed me of my options, which to me were not acceptable to say the least. As soon as I heard that my agency very rarely overturns the recommendation for termination, I started declaring that God would use me to set a new precedence in HRA, as I trusted the Lord to reverse the initial recommendation for termination. I made declarations from the book of Esther, Isaiah chapters 1 through 65, the Psalms, among other Scriptures. My prayer partners, friends, family members, and fellowship on the job were also praying. I was keeping prayer vigils on Friday nights to Saturday mornings with a few of my brethren at our church.

Amidst all these, I arrived at the second hearing without the slightest idea that I could have been stripped of my job on the same day. However, like in the case of Esther and Mordecai, the Lord raised an adviser who encouraged me to reschedule the hearing date so that I could gather more evidentiary documents to support my defense against all the charges leveled against me.

Obtaining these documents was another challenge, as the enemy stopped at nothing to frustrate me. Through all these, Dr. PWD and Reverend Peace were seeking divine instruction and direction from the Lord. In fact, at some point Dr. PWD told me that my name was Esther. She stated that this was my promotion in disguise. Upon submitting the additional documents, I did not hear from the disciplinary department for over a month.

On May 12, 2012, we had the Overcomers' House Divine Encounter, and Prophet Mark McLean from Jamaica was the guest speaker. When he prophesied to me, he stated that the Lord would vindicate me from the false accusations, and that the Lord had allowed all these trials and temptations because of what he has ahead of me. He further prophesied my promotion and many other good things. I was greatly encouraged; yet I did not receive any response from my job immediately.

Then in June 2012, we had our annual Esther's Progressive Prayer Fast. It was a fourteen-day fasting period with an intensive three-day dry fast as Esther did. During this fast, we had to make a list of our prayer requests. Of course, the expectation of vindication and total acquittal from all charges against me were at the top of my list.

A few days after the fast my sister, Evangelist Ngozi Kalu, came to visit me at home. On her way upstairs, she picked up my mail. I looked at the envelopes and spotted the one from my job. My heart started racing but before I opened it, I gave the Lord thanks for whatever I was getting ready to read or discover. Upon opening it I saw a copy of all the charges against me and then another page which stated that my case was handed over to the department of investigation which did a thorough investigation, and recommended that the agency DROP ALL THE CHARGES against me, because the accusations were unfounded. This page was concluded by a statement which said that I should not have been referred to the disciplinary unit in the first place. An excerpt from the memorandum sent to me on July 12, 2012, stated that, "based on the information that was presented to him, this case should not have been referred for disciplinary charges ..., an order is being forwarded to the Employee Discipline Unit to withdraw the charges."

So their recommendation was upheld by the deputy executive commissioner by dropping all charges against me. Praise the Lord, my name did not appear in the hall of shame, but rather, in the Lamb's Book of Life.

The King of Glory favored me, cherished me, and "extended His scepter" to me; when I came in, He overturned the evil decree promulgated against me. Now, my victory opened doors to double favors. I was transferred to another office with better professional satisfaction and fulfillment in February 2013. Seven months later, I received a promotion from Fraud Investigator 1 to Fraud Investigator 2 on my job. To God be the glory in Jesus's name! Amen!!!

Fasting as an Instrument of Petition

During the days of Esther, the people of God who lived in the territory of Persia went into fasting and mourning when they heard that destruction had been plotted against them. Wherever the news of the annihilation of the Jews was heard, the people broke down with fasting, crying, and wailing before the God of creation. The pangs of sorrow automatically switched their souls into the mode of agony, which motivated them to fast and wail without anybody's instruction or direction. They cried unto Jehovah God for deliverance from destruction. The matter at hand required divine intervention. Only the God of heaven could deliver them from the conglomerate of evil that was mounted against them. The initiative paid off well as fasting often attracts the presence of Jehovah God. The Lord heard their cries and intervened in a miraculous manner. The Lord prepared Mordecai as a stepping stone to create the offensive that would stir up the miracle. Esther would be the catalyst in the center of the mystery.

Fasting as a Weapon of War

When the news of the annihilation of the Jews got to Esther, the pattern of the fast moved into another dimension in the realms of the spirit. Thus, the fast shifted from an instrument of petition to a weapon of war, as Esther responded to the news with the statement, "If I perish, I perish." This was an expression of the anguish of her soul. It was a phrase that was determined to war against the spirit of destruction. It was a language of confrontation against the conspirators of evil.

The response of Esther to the devilish news propelled her to declare a fast that would equip her with wisdom to approach the king. Esther realized that unless she conquered the king's presence, and subdued the traditional laws of the palace, she would not be able to achieve her goal. She also needed to be empowered with divine authority to deliver her people from destruction.

Fasting as an Instrument of Favor

Esther declared three days' fast for favor before the king of Persia. Although the king was her husband, and she was the crowned queen of Persia, the matter at hand might ignite another war that could cause the destruction of her life, just as it had happened in the case of former Queen Vashti. Esther did not despise her position. She did not take her husband the king for granted. She recognized authority and gave honor to whom honor was due. Considering the application of the knowledge that she had acquired during her preparatory days, Esther wisely respected her legal grounds and authority.

Fasting as an Arena of Confrontation

Approaching the king of Persia at that era was like entering into the dungeon of death. Going into the presence of the king was confrontation with powers and principalities of darkness in the realms of the Persian territory.

- A warrant of death had been issued against the Jewish people living in Persia.
- The bloodthirsty demons had been released across the land.
- The rulers of darkness had been arrayed and positioned throughout the territory.
- The prince of Persia was seated on the throne of death, spitting evil as he drank from the cup of human destruction.

It was no small matter for Esther to assume that her marital position would grant her easy favor against the powers of destruction. The spirit of murder has no respect for anybody. The spirit of assassination is always bloodthirsty and highly destructive.

Esther needed divine wisdom and favor to confront not just her husband the king, but also the controlling forces that ruled over the palace. The powers and principalities of darkness that ruled over the corridors of politics also controlled the thinking faculties of the legislatures and judiciaries in Persia. The influence of the rulers and powers of darkness manipulated the mind and hearts of human authorities associated with the kingdom of Persia.

Jehovah God is righteous and just in all His ways. Although Esther decided to risk her life for her people to confront the powers of darkness, the just God of heaven granted her wisdom as she fasted for three days and nights without food or drink.

Fasting as an Arena of War

A study of Scripture shows that people are usually motivated to fast whenever they are confronted with some kind of evil. Confrontation is an act of war. Whenever you decide to fast, you are either initiating a war against an evil, or you are responding to a war coming from the camp of the enemy. The enemy is a restless warrior who constantly bombards our lives with different types of attacks. The kinds of attacks we face draw us into different types of wars that we fight consciously and unconsciously. Esther was unconsciously prepared as a warrior for the Jews. She was positioned by birth into the kingdom of Persia to deliver her people from destruction.

The Offensive

Fasting is a weapon that offends the enemy. Anytime we initiate a fast on legal grounds, the enemy is threatened. Fasting is legal when we focus on Scripture reading for our source of operation. Fasting without the Word of God is illegal operation. When you fast without the application of the Scriptures, the enemy can invade your environment with false revelations to frustrate your efforts.

- Whenever we initiate a fast as an instrument of praise, worship, and adoration to honor the Great God of Wonders, the enemy is automatically defeated and sent into hiding.
- Anytime we initiate a fast to seek divine leadership and direction for our daily endeavors, the works of the enemy are abolished and his strongholds are dismantled.

However, anytime we allow problems to push us into fasting, the enemy gains an advantage to frustrate our trust and belief in the Almighty God.

The strategies that the enemy uses to launch the offensive against us are numerous:

- He invades our environment with unexpected problems.

- He interferes with our plans and programs.
- He intrudes into our private affairs.
- He manipulates our weaknesses to his own advantage.
- He tortures us with bodily ailments.
- He accuses us constantly based on our ignorance.
- He harasses us with illegal matters.
- He bombards us with minor issues that distract us from progressiveness.

The Defensive

More often than not, Christians do not launch a conscious attack against the enemy. Rather, we wait for the enemy to offend us, and then we resort to fasting as a measure to curb the offensive attack from the enemy. Sometimes we don't realize that our challenges or difficulties are a type of arrows or missiles from the kingdom of darkness.

Unfortunately, we respond to the enemy's offensive by defending ourselves with fasting at a crucial moment. Sometimes we allow situations to get out of hand before we remember the need to fast and pray. Whenever we resort to fasting as a defensive, we struggle for strategies to quell the fiery darts of the enemy. In view of that, many people assume the negative, as they think that God is not able to solve their problems. Some even state that God has failed them, while others think that God is not interested in their cases. Regrettably, that kind of thought is part of the arsenal of arrows of frustration that the enemy uses to weaken our faith in the Lord.

Torments of Religious Pride

Kelly is an evangelical Christian who believed that if you don't touch the devil, no demon would bother you. He did not believe in praying against the devil. He thought casting out a demon was a myth.

Kelly had some friends who also believed that Christianity means peace and should not be associated with warfare. Therefore, he and some of his friends decided that they would not identify with any persons or group of people who pray a warring type of prayer whatsoever. Kelly and his friends would usually reprimand anyone whose prayer sounded violent or warring against the forces of darkness.

Kelly and his three friends were financially buoyant and great donors to their church and neighborhood. In view of their generosity, they were influential and well respected. However, they were spiritually dry and very ignorant about Scripture. They were more or less Christian moralists.

One day Kelly discovered that some of the people with whom he shared the same principles had suddenly deviated. One of them, Munsey, had to seek help for his son Jamie, who suffered horrors and nightmares. Jamie would scream out of his sleep and become violent. Sometimes he would run around the house screaming and yelling with a huge voice that did not sound like his natural voice. Jamie was scared of the night. His problem defied medical treatment because it was a spiritual attack on the family.

Munsey's wife, Showel, decided to seek assistance from a spiritual perspective. She sought help from different types of churches until she discovered the world of deliverance ministration. Then she started seeking help by reading books on deliverance. Eventually, she found one of my books titled, *When Satan Went to Church*. Showel was still reading the book when she called my office. When I picked up the phone, without enquiring who was on the line, Showel was so desperate for help she just started pouring out her heart. She said, "I'm reading a book here right now, titled, *When Satan Went to Church*. Please, I need your help right now. My son is horrified at night. He suffers massive attacks and screams out from his sleep. What can you do to help him?"

I invited her for a counseling session. During our interaction I discovered that Showel's husband, Munsey, had despised people who sought deliverance ministration as a measure of solving their mysterious problems. Hence, his own family was attacked. Showel convinced Munsey to support her in the process of deliverance so that their son could be made free.

Of course Munsey joined hands with Showel for another counseling session where I recommended Esther's Progressive Prayer Fast. This meant that we needed to do a series of fasting to discover the root of the problems involved. We were guided by **Psalm 35:13**, which says, "**But as for me, when they were sick, my clothing was sackcloth: I humbled my soul with fasting; and my prayer returned into mine own bosom**" and Daniel 9:3, "**And I set my face unto the Lord God, to seek by prayer and supplications, with fasting, and sackcloth, and ashes.**"

We would also need to do some more fasting to cast out the interfering demons, and uproot satanic strongholds from the family. The Lord Jesus said, "**Howbeit this kind goeth not out but by prayer and fasting**" (Matthew 17:21).

Munsey agreed to every recommendation needed to set his son and the whole family free from demonic harassment. Hence, his eyes were opened to understand the things of the Spirit. He started to realize the importance of the realms of warfare and confrontation. Of course, Munsey started seeking deeper knowledge on the act and process of deliverance. Soon after, Kelly heard the news that one of his paddies had defected from their sanctimonious principles. Kelly went wild as he felt highly betrayed.

Kelly started plotting a conspiracy against Munsey and his family. Unfortunately for Kelly, the conspiracy backfired as his own wife had started reading books to research the act of warfare and confrontation. Kelly was faced with disappointment everywhere. Every one of Kelly's friends had joined forces with Munsey to help deliver the young boy from hallucinations of the night. Everyone was sympathetic with the young boy. Everyone tried to play some form of role to assist Munsey to restore his son to normal. Kelly was seen as selfish and inhuman as he held on to his moralistic principles instead of seeking true salvation from the Holy Scriptures.

Kelly tried to persuade their pastor to expel Munsey and his family from the church, but the conspiracy triggered a unique revival. Instead, the pastor called for a fast and a prayer night vigil to support Munsey's family. The response was great. Everyone showed interest and supported the family with the fast. Kelly's wife played a major role at the night vigil. It was time for warfare and confrontation against the enemy. Though the major reason for the night vigil was to support Munsey's family, the Lord used the occasion to bless the whole church. People's eyes were opened as they saw and shared visions of how the enemy had been attacking many of the congregation members in their homes and private lives. Everyone had kept their challenges and difficulties secretly to avoid fear of rejection.

Kelly's conspiracy was in shambles. His money could no longer intimidate the pastor's decision to release freedom of worship to the church. The Sunday after the Friday night vigil orchestrated a fire-stormed worship service. Those who were not present at the Friday session were astonished. Those who had been praying for Holy Ghost revival termed the move as the result of answered prayers.

No matter what the case may be, the fact is that Esther's Progressive Prayer Fast that was recommended to solve one's family predicament finally uprooted a generational curse that had tormented a village of people in a denominational setting. A series of fasting treated each situation as doors were opened for other hindrances to be removed; long-awaited hopes were lifted while expectations were fulfilled. The plan of the enemy was crushed as the veil of ignorance was removed from the eyes of the people. At last, knowledge is power for freedom. A song of emancipation rent the air of a church as songs of revival broke the chains of ignorance, and the curse of religious bondage was destroyed.

Application

In order to achieve effective results in fasting, it is important that you identify the particular problems that need solution. Use the reflective questions provided to map out strategic solutions to the problems that affect your family members, environment, or anyone whom you intend to help besides yourself.

1. **List 3-5 lesson points that you have learned from today's reading.**

   _____
   _____
   _____
   _____
   _____

2. **Identify how the lesson affects you positively in 3-5 points.**

   _____
   _____
   _____
   _____
   _____

3. **Identify how you intend to use the lesson from today's passage to resolve your problem in 3-5 points.**

   _____
   _____
   _____
   _____
   _____

CHAPTER TWO

The Realms of Fasting

The realm of fasting is a realm of abstention and solitude. It is a realm of seeking solutions to problems. It is a realm of asking questions to seek answers. It is a realm of knocking on closed doors for entrance.

Fasting is a process of transformation, whereby one subdues the natural body in order to connect with the spirit realm. The ability to subdue the natural realm gives one the power to overcome the physical realm, so that you are able to detach yourself from the forces that rule the environment of our existence. Whenever we subdue our natural bodies and environment, we are able to gain entrance into the supernatural realm. Then we are able to listen attentively to the voice of the living God, to hear instructions and directions that affect our destiny and the purpose of the fast at hand.

The purpose of fasting is as follows:

- Fasting is a quicker procedure to push our prayers through the iron gates of difficulty.
- Fasting is an instrument that expedites our prayers from the stage of stagnancy to a progressive mode.

- Fasting is the weapon that pulls out the obstacles that hold ones destiny in bondage.
- Fasting is a faster lane of activity, wherever there has been a delay or denial.
- Fasting ignites the power that turns a case of denial into sudden approval.
- Fasting ignites the power that creates possibilities in the midst of impossibilities.
- Fasting causes the Almighty God to hear our petition.
- Fasting causes the Holy Spirit to remind Jehovah God about his promises concerning us.
- Fasting causes the Lord Jesus Christ to appeal our case before the Judge of the whole earth.

Different Types of Fasting:

There are different types of fasting. Each type of fasting provides certain realms of solutions that distinguish one type from the other. Some types of fasting require a series of observations, depending on the need and expectation that is involved. For instance, a problem that has besieged a family or a person for a hundred years or more requires a series of fasting that would be observed in sequence. Thus,

- The first segment of the fast would have to focus on self-investigation to find out where you were involved or connected to the situation.
- The second segment of the fast would focus on the root cause of the problem.
- The third segment of the fast would focus on seeking wisdom and direction to solve the matter at hand.

- The final segment of the fast would now focus on deleting the problems from the family and from one's personal life.

Fasting is effective when you abstain from public activities and stay in solitude. For effective connection to the spiritual realm, you must choose a time when you are not at work or active in the public. If you have to work during the process of your fasting, then you must stay away from unnecessary contact with colleagues. As soon as you have some break time, reconnect with your Bible and spend some time in the presence of the Lord.

(See more discussion on fasting in my book: *Strategic Deliverance Solutions: Discover and Destroy Ancestral Curses*.)

The Purpose of Fasting

The purpose of a fast is to separate yourself from all activities to stay in the presence of the Lord for divine communion with the Almighty Father. The separation demands dedication of your life and time for divine connection. You cannot share your fasting time with other activities that are not related.

In order to achieve effective results, choose a time when you can stay in His presence without interference.

Time of Fast: Options

- **Day Fast**: 6.00 a.m. to 6.00 p.m.
- **Night Fast**: 6.00 p.m. to 6.00 a.m.
- **Morning Fast**: 6.00 a.m. to 1.00 p.m.

- **Afternoon Fast:** 12.00 noon to 6.00 p.m.
- **Evening Fast:** 6.00 p.m. 12.00 midnight
- **Midnight Fast:** 12:00 a.m. to 6 a.m.

The purpose of the time option is to enable you to concentrate on praying with Scripture in order to experience the presence of the Lord. Also, each region or territory or nation operates in different time zones. For instance, the Eastern Time zone in the United States is a direct opposite of the time zone in East Asia. 9.00 a.m. in New York is 9.00 p.m. in the Philippines and other parts of Asia. Therefore, if we declare a fast in New York, for all our partners and supporters throughout the nations, we should expect each nation to respond to the fast, according to their time zone under which they operate.

More so, job schedules and assignments may not allow people to participate effectively in the fast if they are not given time options. The time option is necessary to allow everyone to participate in the fast at the time that they might be off duty, so that they can concentrate on praying with Scriptures. It will also enable participants to stay in silence and meditate on the Word of God.

Length of Days

If you are not used to fasting or you are not able to fast for too long because of medical reasons or the type of employment that you do, there is always a gracious option to adopt. Try to do one segment of the fast at a time. Thus, you may choose to fast three days at a time. You may choose to fast on a weekend for seven weeks or a within a period of three months until the matter is concluded. You do not need to rush the fast but you need to make it effective.

How to Observe a Fast

Bible Reading: Scripture declares in **Hebrews 4:12** that, **"For the Word of God is living and powerful, and sharper than any two-edged sword, piercing even to the division of soul and spirit, and of joints and marrow, and is a discerner of the thoughts and intents of the heart."** Therefore, prayer must be based on Scripture reading.

Whenever we spend our fasting season on reading and studying the Scripture, the Word of God becomes alive in our minds, souls, and bodies. We are able to distinguish between the voice of the Lord and the voice of our souls and minds. Whenever our natural souls and minds are saturated with Scripture, our spirits become alive against the voice of the stranger, and we are able to differentiate the voice of the Holy Spirit from that of the enemy of our destiny.

Prayer

Prayer is communication between you and your Father God. In order for your communication to be effective, you need to speak the kind of language that would attract the Father's attention. In order to be able to speak in your Father's tongue, you need to learn His language. The only way to learn how to speak in your Father's tongue is to study the Bible.

As you study the Bible, your language and your spirit will connect with that of your Father God. *As soon as you connect with the Holy Spirit, your eyes of understanding will open to truth.* Then, the spirit of truth will take over your heart, mind, and soul, and affect your thinking faculties. Once your reasoning is arrested, your language will start to change. In the process, you will begin to speak the Biblical language that flows from the lines of Scriptural verses.

It is important for you to study the Bible in order to gain the Scriptural language, because your personal prayer language is powerless without Scriptural support. Scriptural verses provide you with knowledge on how others have gained the Lord's attention in time of need. It also grants you wisdom to approach the Father from the perspective of His legal operations and promises.

Spiritual Protocol

Spiritual Protocol is the legal grounds for approaching the throne of heaven. In the Old Testament the priests were instructed to cleanse and purify themselves before entering into the temple of the living God. They were also supposed to observe special cleansing rituals before they performed certain special sacrifices and their routine duties in the Holy of Holies.

In the New Testament, Christ Jesus stated that he did not come to destroy the law but to affirm and establish it. Hence, we are admonished to confess our sins and forgive those who sin against us. Hear what these Scriptures say:

Leviticus 5:5 – "And it shall be, when he shall be guilty in one of these things, that he shall confess that he hath sinned in that thing."

Leviticus 16:21 – "And Aaron shall lay both his hands upon the head of the live goat, and confess over him all the iniquities of the children of Israel, and all their transgressions in all their

sins, putting them upon the head of the goat, and shall send him away by the hand of a fit man into the wilderness."

Leviticus 26:40 – "If they shall confess their iniquity, and the iniquity of their fathers, with their trespass which they trespassed against me, and that also they have walked contrary unto me."

Numbers 5:7 – "Then they shall confess their sin which they have done: and he shall recompense his trespass with the principal thereof, and add unto it the fifth part thereof, and give it unto him against whom he hath trespassed."

1 Kings 8:33 – "When thy people Israel be smitten down before the enemy, because they have sinned against thee, and shall turn again to thee, and confess thy name, and pray, and make supplication unto thee in this house."

1 Kings 8:35 – "When heaven is shut up, and there is no rain, because they have sinned against thee; if they pray toward this place, and confess thy name, and turn from their sin, when thou afflictest them."

2 Chronicles 6:24 – "And if thy people Israel be put to the worse before the enemy, because they have sinned against thee; and shall return and confess thy name, and pray and make supplication before thee in this house."

2 Chronicles 6:26 – "When the heaven is shut up, and there is no rain, because they have sinned against thee; yet if they pray

toward this place, and confess thy name, and turn from their sin, when thou dost afflict them."

Nehemiah 1:6 – "Let thine ear now be attentive, and thine eyes open, that thou mayest hear the prayer of thy servant, which I pray before thee now, day and night, for the children of Israel thy servants, and confess the sins of the children of Israel, which we have sinned against thee: both I and my father's house have sinned."

Psalms 32:5 – "I acknowledged my sin unto thee, and mine iniquity have I not hid. I said, I will confess my transgressions unto the LORD; and thou forgavest the iniquity of my sin. Selah."

James 5:16 – "Confess your faults one to another, and pray one for another, that ye may be healed. The effectual fervent prayer of a righteous man availeth much."

1 John 1:9 – "If we confess our sins, he is faithful and just to forgive us our sins, and to cleanse us from all unrighteousness."

Revelation 3:5 – "He that overcometh, the same shall be clothed in white raiment; and I will not blot out his name out of the book of life, but I will confess his name before my Father, and before his angels."

Prayer of Cleansing and Purification includes:

- Prayer of Confession
- Prayer of Repentance

- Prayer of Forgiveness
- Prayer of Restoration

Prayer of Confession: Even as no one talks to another person with his or her teeth unbrushed or with an unpleasant odor in one's mouth, so is it very crucial that we confess our sins and clean up our souls' mess before we approach our Father in heaven. God is holy and we must reverence his holiness.

Cleanliness is next to holiness, therefore we need to take a spiritual bath by recognizing the importance of the presence of God in our prayers.

One of the main reasons for fasting is to gain the attention of God against the wiles of the enemy. Therefore, release yourself from the nasty odor of sin and wear a sweet fragrance of purity to attract favor and attention during the fast. Unconfessed sin is like a filthy rag before the Lord. When you are going on a diplomatic mission or a job interview, you do not appear in rags, but in the best of outfit and appearance, so treat yourself with honor that your prayers might be answered.

Application

In order to achieve effective results in fasting, it is important that you identify the particular problems that need solution. Use the reflective questions provided to map out strategic solutions to the problems that affect your family members, environment, or anyone whom you intend to help besides yourself.

1. **List 3-5 lesson points that you have learned from today's reading.**

   _____
   _____
   _____
   _____

2. **Identify how the lesson affects you positively in 3-5 points.**

   _____
   _____
   _____
   _____

3. **Identify how you intend to use the lesson from today's passage to resolve your problem in 3-5 points.**

   _____
   _____
   _____
   _____

CHAPTER THREE

Strategies for Fasting

Whenever you sense a need to support your prayer with a fast, endeavor to plan the mode of the fast. It is important that you also prepare your mind and natural body for the fast, along with your spirit. The reason being that fasting is a weapon of war against the enemy of your destiny. Fasting attracts divine attention and causes the Holy Spirit to help us. If well prepared and all spiritual protocols are observed, the Holy Spirit makes intercession for us during fasting, as he prays with groanings which cannot be uttered with human understanding. Therefore, the kind of approach you adopt toward the fast could either be effective or wearing and exhausting.

In order to ensure that your fast is quickened, you should consider including the following points in your planning:

- **Purpose of the Fast**: *What is the purpose for your fasting?* State your need in simple terms that will enable you to focus in prayer. Itemize your problems in numerical order. Do not becloud your fast with too many needs so that the enemy will not frustrate your mind or weary your thoughts. Treat each need or problem differently. Make it one at a time.

Focus on one point persistently and consistently, so that you would be able to identify with the result that follows.

If you are on two or more days of fasting, then spread your needs by time slot, or allocate a certain amount of time to pray for specific issues. By so doing, you will be able to utilize your days and times effectively without feeling bored. It is easy to feel bored and tired during fasting, especially if you do not know what to say or pray. It is easy to become tired of repetition, while you feel as though you have been going round in circles without penetrating the realms for solutions. In order to break through the realms of difficulty during fasting, you need to make up a schedule with time slots.

- **Expectations:** *What do you need to achieve during and after a fast?* You must state your goal and expectation for a fast. Even if you are expecting a miracle that your mind cannot fathom, you still need to write down your kind of expectation.

    Stating your expectation does not mean that you are placing a limitation on what the Lord must do for you. Stating your expectation indicates your trust and belief in the power of God. The reason you are supporting your prayer with a fast is because you are expecting the Lord to do something regarding a situation—confronting someone, some place, or yourself.

    Stating your expectation could simply be that you are expecting a change in a situation that is devastating. However, you are praying and fasting for the perfect will of the Almighty God in the matter. Although you do not know how the matter would be resolved, you trust the Lord for divine intervention.

Experiences: *What are your encounters during this fast?* Compare this fast with other ones you have had in order to note your experiences and achievements. If the purpose of the fast is based on challenges or difficulties that are confronting some members of your family or yourself, then you may experience flashbacks relating to the root of the problem. Similarly, if the fast is in relation to an expectation, then your flashbacks will be a reconnection with a divine promise or a blessing that needs to be removed from the doldrums.

Your experiences may include:

- Frequent flashbacks
- Flashes of past dreams and visions
- Flashes of childhood experiences
- Flashes of family background
- Flashes of mishaps, disasters, and different types of accidents and incidents that might have affected you at one point or the other.
- Flashes of offences, hurts, pains, failures, disappointments, hindrances, and interferences.
- Flashes of matters that caused stagnancy and retrogression in your environment and life.

Take note of all occurrences during fasting and deal with each one of them accordingly by asking questions on how to deal with the situation at hand.

Revelations: *What kind of revelation have you been receiving and how?* One of the major purposes of fasting is to connect with the realm of the spirit so that you can receive divine encounters. Revelation plays a major role in fasting. Revelation comes when you connect with the realm of the spirit. When connected, you are able to see the things of the Spirit and hear the voice of the Spirit. Connection with the spirit realm will open your sensitivity to different types of revelations that include:

- Visions
- Dreams
- Intuitions
- Hearing
- Feelings
- Utterances

- **Instructions**: *Did you receive any kind of instruction?* What are the specific things that you have been told to do? Are you willing to follow this kind of instruction? The purpose of revelation during fasting is to receive divine instruction from the Lord. When you fast for divine encounter or intervention, you must be ready to receive divine instruction, because divine encounter comes with instruction. The Lord will give you instruction on how to open and handle the package so that the purpose will be effectively fulfilled.

- **Directions**: *How are you to carry out the instructions received? What are the specific steps that you are to follow in order to achieve the purpose of this fast?* Jehovah God is the Lord of direction. He guides and leads us in the path of righteousness. His Word is a lamp to our feet and a light to our path. Part of the instructions that he usually gives us include guidance for achievement and fulfillment. It is crucial for you to be attentive to His voice when fasting. His voice may come to us through different kinds of revelations as mentioned above.

- **Interference:** *Did you suffer any kind of interferences or obstacles during the period of this fast?* Your explanation would enable you to monitor the kind of spiritual battle that confronts you during fasting.

Fasting Attracts Spiritual Entities

The state of your mind, body, soul, and spirit usually determines the kind of spirit that you will attract into your life and environment. More often than not, the mercy of the Living God protects and delivers us from the fiery darts of the enemy. The grace of God shields us from demonic interferences when we do stuff ignorantly or innocently. Sooner or later, the Lord will bring us to the knowledge of the truth, to enable correction for effective prayer and fasting time in the future. **The Word of God also declares that,**

> **My people are destroyed for lack of knowledge.**
> **Because you have rejected knowledge,**
> **I also will reject you from being priest for Me;**
> **Because you have forgotten the law of your God,**
> **I also will forget your children. (Hosea 4:6)**

Scripture also states that **"What shall we say then? Shall we continue in sin that grace may abound?" (Romans 6:1).**

A period of fasting is a season to observe purity and holiness in all our lives and environment. Light and darkness cannot dwell together; likewise, righteousness and wickedness can never reside in the same temple. A desire to fast is a decision to purge yourself of uncleanness so that you can gain access into the presence of the Almighty Father.

Embarking on a fast without cleansing opens you up to demonic entities and different types of evil spirits. When you are not cleansed or purified, your soul will attract the spirit of its like. A dirty environment will attract flies, rodents, and pests. Similarly, a dirty soul that has not been cleansed from the stain of sin will attract spiritual pests and rodents (demons and evil spirits).

For details on the process of fasting see my book titled *Strategic Deliverance Solutions: Discover and Destroy Ancestral Curses.*

Breaking the Fast

- **Choice of Meals**: Stay away from meat or poultry during a period of fasting. Fasting could make the walls of your intestine tender. In order to avoid abrasion and soreness of the intestine, drink a lot of liquid to lubricate the walls of your stomach.

It is wise to end your fast with the following:

- Eat fruits and green vegetables.
- You may eat your salad with fish, nuts, and/or salad dressing.
- Drink a lot of water and fruit juice
- Avoid soda and artificial drinks

Application

In order to achieve effective results in fasting, it is important that you identify the particular problems that need solution. Use the reflective questions provided to map out strategic solutions to the problems that affect your family members, environment, or anyone whom you intend to help besides yourself.

1. **List 3-5 lesson points that you have learned from today's reading.**

   _____
   _____
   _____
   _____

2. **Identify how the lesson affects you positively in 3-5 points.**

   _____
   _____
   _____
   _____

3. **Identify how you intend to use the lesson from today's passage to resolve your problem in 3-5 points.**

   _____
   _____
   _____
   _____

CHAPTER FOUR

Purpose of Progressive Prayer Fast

Fast for Relief and Deliverance

Although chapter 4 verse14 has been earmarked as the heart of the book of Esther, the contents are much deeper and revealing in the realms of deliverance ministration and generational curse.

- **Relief:** The book of Esther speaks about liberation from oppression and suppression. It reveals the power of fasting as a yoke breaker. It provides an antidote for curbing the evil of conspiracies.
- **Deliverance: Rescue and freedom from satanic captivity.** The book of Esther focuses on deliverance from generational curses looming from the time of King Saul and his relationship with King Agag. It revealed how Haman manifested the curse of his great grandparent King Agag and attempted to revisit the situation with the family of Kish. Hence, the need for divine intervention.
- **Providence: Divine Intervention.** The need for divine intervention often sent people into a series of fasting and

different types of fasting. The need for divine intervention motivated Esther and the Jews to fast and cry out unto the Lord. Before Esther declared the three-day fast, most of the Jewish people living in various parts of the Persian kingdom had already embarked on some form of fasting.

Wherever the news of the annihilation of the Jews was heard, the people cried and wailed in mourning as they called upon Jehovah God to deliver them from the Hamanic devilish decree that had been promulgated against them. Esther 4:3 states that **"in every province, whithersoever the king's commandment and his decree came, there was great mourning among the Jews, and fasting, and weeping, and wailing; and many lay in sackcloth and ashes."**

- **Reason for the Progressive Prayer Fast**: More often than not we are confronted with different types of situations that demand divine intervention. Matters that need God's intervention would require prayer and fasting. Prayer is a spiritual communication between man and God. How else can we present our case to the Lord but through prayer. Prayer is the legal procedure through which we communicate with our Father God, the Creator of humankind.

Fasting is an enhancement that makes our prayer effective. It is a humble approach to the presence of the Righteous God. God is holy and everyone that comes into His presence must be holy. Scripture states that the effectual fervent prayer of a righteous man avails much. **"Confess your faults one to another, and pray one for another, that ye may be healed. The effectual fervent prayer of a righteous man availeth much (James 5:16)."** Therefore, righteousness is required if our fasting is effective.

In view of the different kinds of situations that confront us daily and periodically, we are poised to initiate different types of fasting to resist the enemy of our souls. We are encouraged to keep our environment void of demonic invasion and harassment. Satanic cohorts are terrorists who torment innocent and ignorant people unwittingly. In order to disperse demonic activities from our lives and environment, we need to observe fasting frequently as a part of spiritual maintenance.

Following the conquest of the Hamanic plot against the Jews, both Mordecai and Esther enacted a decree to establish the continuing observance of the fast that gave them victory, as well as celebration of the occasion. **Esther 9:20-23** states,

And Mordecai wrote these things, and sent letters unto all the Jews that were in all the provinces of the king Ahasuerus, both nigh and far, to stablish this among them, that they should keep the fourteenth day of the month Adar, and the fifteenth day of the same, yearly, As the days wherein the Jews rested from their enemies, and the month which was turned unto them from sorrow to joy, and from mourning into a good day: that they should make them days of feasting and joy, and of sending portions one to another, and gifts to the poor.

And the Jews undertook to do as they had begun, and as Mordecai had written unto them.

About Esther

Esther was an orphaned teenager who was raised and mentored by her uncle Mordecai after the death of her parents. Her original birth name was *Hadassah* which means "myrtle." Myrtle is an evergreen tree with a sweet fragrance. The name Hadassah represents a sweet aroma, aromatic flower, and beauty.

When Esther was taken into the Persian palace as one of the virgins that could qualify to be married to King Ahasuerus, Hadassah was divinely chosen. Her name was then changed to Esther. *Esther* is a royal name that means "star" and "happiness."

In retrospect, the transformation of her name from Hadassah to Esther reveals a combination of a royal destiny that must be fulfilled.

Originally, Esther was a descendant of King Saul of Israel. The combination of her names reflected in her character as an evergreen myrtle tree that is able to conquer the harsh desert weather conditions, to retain her beautiful flowering nature that produced a sweet fragrance.

Esther's integrity paved the way for her to be crowned queen earlier than the time of royal coronation. One night with the king plugged her into her destiny in the Persian kingdom. The sweetness of her fragrance arrested the heart of the king. The king had no choice but to crown her unceremoniously in order to resist the temptation of losing her. What about the happiness of personality? The combination of Esther's names spoke volumes of victory ahead of time. Hence, she won the victory over Haman's conspiracy to destroy her people. Finally, Esther became an influence in the Persian Kingdom and a force to be reckoned with, in the realms of fasting.

Prayer Points

- Pray that God will raise you to become a star.
- Pray that your image and personality will be that of a star.
- Pray that you will be an example for emulation.
- Pray that you will be a point of contact for hope.
- Pray that your name will be like a sweet fragrance.
- Pray that you will be like a tree planted by the rivers of living water.

Application

In order to achieve effective results in fasting, it is important that you identify the particular problems that need solution. Use the reflective questions provided to map out strategic solutions to the problems that affect your family members, environment, or anyone whom you intend to help besides yourself.

1. **List 3-5 lesson points that you have learned from today's reading.**

   _____
   _____
   _____
   _____

2. **Identify how the lesson affects you positively in 3-5 points.**

   _____
   _____
   _____
   _____

3. **Identify how you intend to use the lesson from today's passage to resolve your problem in 3-5 points.**

   _____
   _____
   _____
   _____

CHAPTER FIVE

Overview on Understanding Curses

(Except from the book, *Strategic Deliverance Solution: Discover and Destroy Ancestral Curses*)

- **What is a curse?** A curse is a problem, a plight or a nuisance that defies solutions.
- **What is an ancestral curse?** An ancestral curse is a problem that originated from one's foreparents (forefather and foremothers) which has afflicted many generations since then.
- **What is a generational curse?** Generational curse is a trouble or difficulty that emerged during the era of an ancestor. The affliction has become a curse that revisits generations of the family concerned, irrespective of all manner of solution that is devised.
- **What is breaking a curse?** Breaking a curse is a process of putting out of order or damaging a thing to provide temporary relief to a situation. In reality, breaking a curse is like trimming or cutting off the branch of a tree. If a branch

is cut off, the tree will grow another branch because the trunk of the tree is still alive, and its root is still very actively holding strong to the ground. A tree is a type of stronghold. If is not uprooted, it will flourish again.

- **What is uprooting a curse?** To uproot a tree is to remove the stump with its root from the ground. Uprooting a curse is a process of dealing with the root cause of a curse to ensure that the links to survival are removed and the legal path of sustenance is destroyed.
- **What is defeating a curse?** To defeat a curse is to overcome or overthrow a problem to declare supremacy over its existence. When a curse is defeated or subdued, the curse may distance itself from the victim for fear of being destroyed.
- **What is destroying a curse?** To destroy a curse is to wipe out or terminate the existence of a problem. Destroying a curse is a process of uprooting the root cause of existence, and destroying the pattern of reoccurrence so that the predicament will not have access to revive itself from generation to generation.

Application

In order to achieve effective results in fasting, it is important that you identify the particular problems that need solution. Use the reflective questions provided to map out strategic solutions to the problems that affect your family members, environment, or anyone whom you intend to help besides yourself.

1. List 3-5 lesson points that you have learned from today's reading.

   _____
   _____
   _____
   _____

2. Identify how the lesson affects you positively in 3-5 points.

   _____
   _____
   _____
   _____

3. Identify how you intend to use the lesson from today's passage to resolve your problem in 3-5 points.

   _____
   _____
   _____
   _____

Prayer Observations and Experiences

You may remember your dreams and some past occurrences while saying this prayer. You may also receive a revelation. It's important that you make notes for future reference.

Experiences

_____
_____
_____
_____
_____

Observations

_____
_____
_____
_____
_____

Revelations

_____
_____
_____
_____
_____

CHAPTER SIX

First Chapter of Esther

Esther 1:1-22

Now it came to pass in the days of Ahasuerus, (this is Ahasuerus which reigned, from India even unto Ethiopia, over an hundred and seven and twenty provinces:) that in those days, when the king Ahasuerus sat on the throne of his kingdom, which was in Shushan the palace, in the third year of his reign, he made a feast unto all his princes and his servants; the power of Persia and Media, the nobles and princes of the provinces, being before him: when he shewed the riches of his glorious kingdom and the honour of his excellent majesty many days, even an hundred and fourscore days. And when these days were expired, the king made a feast unto all the people that were present in Shushan the palace, both unto great and small, seven days, in the court of the garden of the king's palace; where were white, green, and blue, hangings, fastened with cords of fine linen and purple to silver rings and pillars of marble: the beds were of gold and silver, upon a pavement of red, and blue, and white, and black, marble. And they gave them drink in vessels of gold, (the vessels being diverse one from another,) and royal wine in abundance, according to the state of the king. And the drinking was according to the law; none did compel: for so the king had appointed to all the officers of his house, that they should do according to every man's pleasure. Also Vashti the queen made a feast for the women in the royal house which belonged to king Ahasuerus.

On the seventh day, when the heart of the king was merry with wine, he commanded Mehuman, Biztha, Harbona, Bigtha, and Abagtha, Zethar, and Carcas, the seven chamberlains that served in the presence of Ahasuerus the king, to bring Vashti the queen before the king with the crown royal, to shew the people and the princes her beauty: for she was fair to look on. But the queen Vashti refused to come at the king's commandment by his chamberlains: therefore was the king very wroth, and his anger burned in him. Then the king said to the wise men, which knew the times, (for so was the king's manner toward all that knew law and judgment: and the next unto him was Carshena, Shethar, Admatha, Tarshish, Meres, Marsena, and Memucan, the seven princes of Persia and Media, which saw the king's face, and which sat the first in the kingdom;) what shall we do unto the queen Vashti according to law, because she hath not performed the commandment of the king Ahasuerus by the chamberlains? And Memucan answered before the king and the princes, Vashti the queen hath not done wrong to the king only, but also to all the princes, and to all the people that are in all the provinces of the king Ahasuerus. For this deed of the queen shall come abroad unto all women, so that they shall despise their husbands in their eyes, when it shall be reported, The king Ahasuerus commanded Vashti the queen to be brought in before him, but she came not. Likewise shall the ladies of Persia and Media say this day unto all the king's princes, which have heard of the deed of the queen. Thus shall there arise too much contempt and wrath. If it please the king, let there go a royal commandment from him, and let it be written among the laws of the Persians and the Medes, that it be not altered, That Vashti come no more before king Ahasuerus; and let the king give her royal estate unto another that is better than she. And when the king's decree which he shall make shall be published throughout all his empire, (for it is great,) all the wives shall give to their husbands honour, both to great and small. And the saying pleased the king and the princes; and the king did according to the word of Memucan: for he sent letters into all the king's provinces, into every province according to the writing thereof, and to every people after their language, that every man should bear rule in his own house, and that it should be published according to the language of every people.

Day One:
Desire for Destiny Deliverance

Diabolical Concoction Dismayed a Family Business Greed

Tabisha comes from a lineage of an affluent family both on her paternal and maternal sides. The father's side being the Nichols, and the mother's side being the Matthews. (*Actual names withheld*). The Nichols family was once upon a time plagued with mental disorders. Every first male child suffered from schizophrenia that resulted in double personality. Although they were academically successful and financially powerful in all their endeavors, their mental challenge became a stigma of rejection. The people in their town who were familiar with Tabisha's family predicament would not encourage marital relationships with them. More often than not, the Nicholses were married to foreigners, or to people who had no knowledge of their family background.

Tabisha was the seventh born of nine children. Her parents had seven girls and two boys. The first-born son, Sonny Jr., who was named after his father and was bound by the spirit of schizophrenia. He married a foreigner and had one child. Unfortunately, his only son was also schizophrenic. Three of her sisters married foreigners, but the problem of mental disorders persisted in the family. While the other three sisters feared that marriage to both natives and foreigners had not eradicated the strange demon from their family, they decided to seek help before marriage. In the process, Tabisha and her three sisters dedicated their lives to Christ and sought deliverance ministration to break the curse of schizophrenia.

Prescription of Esther Fast

During the first counseling session with Tabisha and her sisters, they refused to answer questions and would not cooperate with counseling procedures. Tabisha later on persuaded her sisters to yield so that the problem could be solved. One of the sisters rudely said, *"We don't need so much interrogation to receive prayer. God already knows what is happening in our family. So you may as well just pray and let it be over."*

However, I led them in a prayer of salvation and prescribed the Esther fast as a measure to start the process of eradicating the root of the plague from their family. After a brief persuasion, they agreed to do the fast, but not exactly as recommended. They prefered a softer approach since they had never been involved in any kind of fasting. Herewith, we then agreed on water and fruits fasting.

Result of the First Fast

During the day, they were busy with other stuff and took the fast very lightly without persistent prayer. However, they were able to involve some of the men in their family in the prayer, as they met to pray together at the end of each day of the fast. After the fast, they continued in prayer nightly and on weekends seeking divine intervention to uproot the curse of mental ailment from the family.

Suddenly, they all began to have dreams about their foreparents and some of the shrewd business dealings that were practiced in the family. Papa Sidney's shylockness was prominent in everyone's revelation. It then became obvious to the whole family that their problems were connected to their business endeavors.

The Root of the Matter

While interceding for Tabisha and her family, I discovered that the root of their problem originally emerged from financial greed and insecurity. One of their forefathers whom I will refer to as Papa Sidney Nichols was a shrewd businessman. He was also a shylock who stole from the poor. He extorted money from his neighbors and employees with no intention to pay back whatever he owed. He even used his position to steal from all the denominational churches in his neighborhood. He was a chronic liar who told stories that were inconsistent to hold back other people's pennies.

Papa Sidney was a merchant who traded in different kinds of hardware. He was also a building contractor who distributed household goods. He was the head of the financial committee in the local church that he attended. Some of his employees were members of that church. Papa Sidney told his workers that it was mandatory for everyone to pay their tithe and offering to the church, alongside their taxes to the government. So, he would deduct ten percent from their salaries and pay it to the church directly. Although he took out the money, he never remitted a dime to the churches. Some of the workers knew he was dishonest, so they decided not to bother with him.

However, one particular man, who was nicknamed "Judas Iscariot" for his boldness, decided to confront the matter. Judas Iscariot did not fear anyone, and openly spoke his mind at any time. This person decided to fight for his money, as he insisted that he didn't need the assistance of anyone to remit his tithe to a church. More so, he was not a member of any church. Instead, Papa Sidney cursed Judas and threatened to order his arrest.

Eventually, Judas was arrested and held in custody for a while. After his release, Judas returned to work with diabolical substances to charm Papa Sidney and his family members. He decided to play a role of a fake submissive servant who was ready to serve Papa Sidney and his family at home and in the office. Judas trailed Papa Sidney and his family in these activities. He collected dust from their footprints. He collected remnants of food from the plates from which they ate. He managed to siphon some personal items from Papa Sidney's home and office. All the items collected were used as a point of contact to concoct diabolical curses upon Papa Sidney and his family.

In the process of administering his diabolical concoctions, Judas walked around the office early in the morning and sprayed some satanic incense around the business environment. Also, Judas waited by the parking lot very early in the morning to give Papa Sidney the first handshake and offer to carry his briefcase into the office.

In view of the voodoo incantations and enchantments released against the Nichols family, soon after Papa Sidney began to behave oddly. He started exhibiting double personalities. He began to dress weirdly and suffered from hallucinations. He was in and out of the hospital without any positive results. Thereafter, every male child born to the family of the Nichols began to exhibit similar behavior.

Solution

Discovering the root of the matter helped the Nichols to find solutions to the ancestral curse that had bedeviled their sons for many generations. Thus the series of Esther fasts prescribed to support the prayer of deliverance for the Nichols paid off. The fast motivated the Nichols to pray effectively. The fast kept every one of them focused and dedicated to the course of the action. Hence, they were able to discover the heart of the matter. They were able to investigate their personal lifestyles and some shrewd business practices.

A Competitive Desire

Now back to Esther's story. The king seemed to be competing with the existence of the whole earth, as the pride of his heart made him look forward to possessing everybody and everything on earth. Hence, he celebrated one of the most extravagant feasts to show off the riches of his glorious kingdom, and the honor of his excellent majesty.

While the king feasted with 127 princes (*from India to Ethiopia*) to show the honor of his majesty in the court of the garden for 180 days, his wife, Queen Vashti, and her ladies showed the honor of her modesty and entertained the women in the royal house.

Esther 1:1
Now it came to pass in the days of Ahasuerus, (this is Ahasuerus which reigned, from India even unto Ethiopia, over an hundred and seven and twenty provinces).

Comment

The book of Esther opens with the presentation of King Ahasuerus's celebration of his dominion.

- The great feast of the third year of the reign of Xerxes (also called Ahasuerus)
- The reign and dominion of King Ahasuerus from India to Ethiopia

Prayer Points

- *That the Lord will expand my coast (Jabez's Prayer)*
- *That my blessing will not be limited*
- *That I will experience fruitfulness, increase and multiplication*

Esther 1:2
That in those days, when the king Ahasuerus sat on the throne of his kingdom, which was in Shushan the palace.

Comment

Kings do not always sit on the throne. There were special seasons and occasions that required kings to mount the throne, such as:

- The season of great celebration
- The season of decision making
- The season of judgment
- The season of preparation for war
- The season of royal presentation
- The season of enthronement is when the king wears his royal apparel and crown.
- It is also the period when the queen and the princes are arrayed and elevated in royal apparel around the throne.

Prayer Points

- *I pray for my season of celebration.*

- *I pray that I will have my turn on the stage of life.*
- *I pray that I will be recognized.*
- *I pray that the world will gather for my sake in life and not in death.*
- *I pray that I will be honored in my season.*

Esther 1:3
"In the third year of his reign, he made a feast unto all his princes and his servants; the power of Persia and Media, the nobles and princes of the provinces, being before him."

Comment

The celebration of the feast was a great attraction. Very important persons (VIPs) were gathered from all over the world.

Prayer Points

- *I pray that my name will attract goodness.*
- *I pray that I will be surrounded with love and passion.*
- *I pray that I will be surrounded by people of wisdom and honor.*
- *I pray that I will be surrounded by people who exhibit the fear of God.*

Esther 1:4
When he shewed the riches of his glorious kingdom and the honour of his excellent majesty many days, even an hundred and fourscore days.

Comment

- It was a season of displaying his power, dominion, and authority.
- It was a season of displaying his wealth and treasure.
- For 180 days (about 6 months) the king exhibited the wealth of his kingdom.

Prayer Points

- *I pray that I will be accepted in my season.*
- *I pray that I will exhibit honor respectfully.*
- *I pray that I will not be rejected in my season.*
- *I pray that my gifts and abilities will be respected and promoted.*

Esther 1:5
And when these days were expired, the king made a feast unto all the people that were present in Shushan the palace, both unto *great and small, seven days*, in the court of the garden of the king's palace.

Prayer Points

- *I pray that both great and small will recognize and honor me.*
- *I pray that both great and small will promote me.*

Esther 1:6-7

Where were white, green, and blue, hangings, fastened with cords of fine linen and purple to silver rings and pillars of marble: the beds were of gold and silver, upon a pavement of red, and blue, and white, and black, marble. And they gave them drink in *vessels of gold*, (the vessels being *diverse* one from another,) and *royal wine in abundance, according to the state of the king.*

Prayer Points

- *I pray for abundance of wealth.*
- *I pray that God will prosper me with progressive supply for increase and multiplication.*
- *I pray that God will bless me with quality and the best.*

Esther 1:8

And the *drinking was according to the law*; none did compel: for so the king had appointed to all the officers of his house, that they should do *according to every man's pleasure.*

Prayer Points

- *I pray for wisdom and fear of God to guard my heart.*
- *I pray that I will not make foolish decisions in times of abundance.*
- *I pray that I will not curse God in time of plenty.*

- *I pray that I will not forget the days of small beginnings.*
- *I pray that my celebration of wealth will not destroy my destiny.*

Place and Position

Esther 1:9
Also *Vashti the queen made a feast for the women* in the royal house which belonged to king Ahasuerus.

Comment

- Queen Vashti did not realize that celebrating her season included managing her season against failure.
- She did not realize the importance of managing the activities that would help to stabilize her place as a wife and position as the queen.
- She forgot that the house and throne of celebration belonged to the king.
- She only had access to the house and throne as long as she was married to the king.

Prayer Points:

- *I pray that I will be given my place and position.*
- *I pray that I will not despise Your own blessings.*
- *I pray that I will recognize Your own honor.*

- *I pray that God will bless and teach me to manage my place and position.*

Esther 1:10

On the seventh day, when the *heart of the king* was *merry with wine*, he *commanded* Mehuman, Biztha, Harbona, Bigtha, and Abagtha, Zethar, and Carcas, *the seven chamberlains* that served in the presence of Ahasuerus the king,– To bring Vashti the queen before the king with the crown royal, to shew the people and the princes her beauty: for she was fair to look on.

Comment

Vashti disobeyed the seven honorable messengers who served in the presence of the king. She despised her own honor when she was supposed to be displaying her modesty to the women of the kingdom.

Prayer Points

- *I pray that I will understand authority.*
- *I pray that I will not despise authority.*
- *I pray that I will be able to respond to authority.*

Esther 1:12

But the queen *Vashti refused* to come at *the king's commandment* by his chamberlains:

therefore was the king *very wroth*, and *his anger burned in him.*

Comment

Vashti's Marital Affair

Although Vashti might have had a genuine reason for refusing to obey the king's command, her approach was wrong. Research reveals that Vashti refused the king's request because she was pregnant with a son, and did not feel good about doing the exhibit requested of her.

She could have obeyed the king before complaining.

It was time to present and recognize her, but she refused the honor.

Instead, she (Vashti) despised the blessings of his authority.

She traded her blessings with pride.

She allowed anger to smear and stain her beauty.

She messed up her glory.

She lacked wisdom of presentation.

Her approach to royalty was weak.

She did not understand the importance of sitting on the throne.

King Ahasuerus's Marital Affair

The king displayed his weaknesses in public.

The king could have covered up for the queen.

The king could have made a joke out of the embarrassment and say something like "she is shy" to appear before such a huge crowd of men.

Prayer Point

- I pray that I will not trade my blessings for pride.
- I pray that I will not stain the fragrance of my beauty.
- I pray that I will understand authority and royalty
- I pray that I will have wisdom to manage my stardom and beauty.
- I pray for wisdom to cover up in situations that could bring embarrassment or disgrace to my marital relationship.
- I pray that my marriage will be respected no matter what happens.
- I pray that I will not be seen as a bad influence in times of difficulty when I do not have the opportunity to explain my condition.
- I pray that no one will broadcast my marital failure.
- I pray that our marital issues will be treated with privacy so as to avoid exposing my family weakness.

Esther 1:13-14

Then the king said to *the wise men*, which *knew the times*, (for so was the king's manner toward *all that knew law and judgment*: …And the next unto him was Carshena, Shethar, Admatha, Tarshish, Meres, Marsena, and Memucan, *the seven princes* of Persia and Media, which *saw the king's face*, and which *sat the first in the kingdom*).

Comment

Liquor as a Weapon of Destruction

- The king opened the door for the public (the legislators and judiciary) to interfere with his marriage when he presented the matter for public discussion and also asked questions.
- Hence, the king was embarrassed that Vashti's attitude brought shame, disgrace, and embarrassment to the throne.
- The king had to seek wisdom from his counselors since he opened up the matter for public interference.
- The king had to seek for the interpretations of the seasons and times to avoid reoccurrence of a curse (ancestral curse).
- Vashti should have sought counsel when her appearance was not convenient but she decided to act on her own. Therefore, she suffered the repercussion of her foolishness.

Prayer Point

- *I pray against shame and disgrace when I mount my stardom.*
- *I pray against embarrassment in the midst of elevation and celebration.*

Public Interference

The Team of Lawmakers consists of the Legislature and Judiciary. Whenever the team of law makers intervenes in any matter, it becomes a public affair. Marriage is a family matter which should sometimes be treated as private. However, where the personalities involved are public figures, it is very likely that the public would also interfere, especially in the case where the incident took place before the cynosure of very important personalities in the Persian kingdom during a high powered celebration.

In the case of Vashti, she was a public figure because she was married to the king of the land. Unfortunately, the incident happened in the presence of the law makers. Hence, the law makers stepped in to caution the consequences of the matter on the whole kingdom.

Esther 1:15-16

What *shall we do unto the queen Vashti according to law,* **because** *she hath not performed the commandment of the king* **Ahasuerus by the chamberlains? And Memucan answered before the king and the princes,** *Vashti the queen hath not done wrong to the king only, but also to all the princes, and to all the people that are in all the provinces of the king Ahasuerus.*

Comment

- Do not start a war you cannot finish.
- Sometimes our actions open up the door to a war in which we cannot determine its vastness or the end.
- Sometimes, offending one person may affect thousands of people and a disagreement with one person may affect an existing relationship with an innocent person.
- The reason is that one person often represents a multitude of people directly or indirectly.

Esther 1:17-18

For *this deed of the queen shall come abroad unto all women*, so that *they shall despise their husbands* in their eyes, when *it shall be reported, The king Ahasuerus commanded Vashti the queen to be brought in before him, but she came not*. Likewise *shall the ladies* of Persia and Media *say* this day unto all the king's princes, which have heard of the deed of the queen. *Thus shall there arise too much contempt and wrath.*

Comment

Familiarity Brings Contempt

- Consequences of a measure of correction taken against Vashti (a royal decree or governmental decision)
- Consequences of sweeping a public matter under the carpet
- Call to repentance could avert a royal decree against the queen
- She persisted to please herself despite consistent pleas.
- Hence, it was decreed that she would no longer come into the king's presence.
- Do not take people for granted because of familiarity, because you will mess up your destiny, and your divine connections may be disrupted.

Prayer Points

- *I pray that I will honor the authority over me, especially in public.*
- *I pray that I will crucify my pride to submit to authority where my marriage is concerned.*

Esther 1:19

If it please the king, let there go a royal commandment from him, and let it be written among the laws of the Persians and the Medes, that it be not altered, *that Vashti come no m*ore *before king Ahasuerus; and let the king give her royal estate unto another that is better than she.*

Prayer Points

- *I pray that no one will take my place, in Jesus's name.*
- *I pray that anyone occupying my position shall be removed, in Jesus's name.*
- *I evict all trespassers from interfering with my destiny, prosperity, and blessing, in Jesus's name.*
- *I release a quit order against destiny destroyers, in Jesus's name.*

Esther 1:20-22

And when the king's decree which he shall make shall be *published* throughout all his empire, (for it is great,) *all the wives shall give to their husbands honour, both to great and small.* And the saying pleased the king and the princes; and the king did according to the word of Memucan: for *he sent letters into all the king's provinces,* into every province according to the writing thereof, and *to every people after their language,* that *every man should bear rule in his own house,* and that it should be *published according to the language of every people.*

This was part of the reason for women's subjection in the Middle East, especially among the Indians and the nations that are connected with the Persian and Medes. More so, Vashti was believed to be pregnant and could not do the type of display that the king expected of her. Since the king was tipsy with wine, he was acting out of the influence of alcohol, yet his counselors and the wise men did not take the situation at hand into consideration.

Prayer Point

- I pray against inheriting the punishment due to the behavior of others, in Jesus' name.
- I pray that no negative or evil message will be published against me, in Jesus' name.
- I pray that my marriage will not be a bad example to the younger ones and our environment, in Jesus' name.
- I pray that we will not be a scarecrow in the eyes and mind of the public, in Jesus's name.

Application

In order to achieve effective results in fasting, it is important that you identify the particular problems that need solution. Use the reflective questions provided to map out strategic solutions to the problems that affect your family members, environment, or anyone whom you intend to help besides yourself.

1. **List 3-5 lesson points that you have learned from today's reading.**
   _____
   _____
   _____
   _____

2. **Identify how the lesson affects you positively in 3-5 points.**
   _____
   _____
   _____
   _____

3. **Identify how you intend to use the lesson from today's passage to resolve your problem in 3-5 points.**
   _____
   _____
   _____
   _____

Prayer Observations and Experiences

You may remember your dreams and some past occurrences while doing this prayer. You may also receive a revelation. It's important that you make notes for future reference.

Experiences
_____
_____
_____
_____
_____
_____

Observations
_____
_____
_____
_____
_____
_____

Revelations
_____
_____
_____
_____
_____
_____

Day Two:
The Nemesis of Generational Curses

Analysis

Queen Vashti's father Belshazzar was probably not yet conceived when Nebuchadnezzar went warring, capturing nations, and destroying humans and properties. Princess Vashti was not yet born when Nebuchadnezzar was dehumanizing people, casting them into the lion's den to be mauled by beasts and throwing his offenders into the burning fiery furnace to be consumed by fire.

- Belshazzar was probably a youth when his father the king Nebuchadnezzar erected the gold image and demanded everyone bow down and worship it.
- Belshazzar was probably naïve when his father Nebuchadnezzar was driven out of his palace to dwell among beasts in the field.
- Yet, Belshazzar inherited the traits of Nebuchadnezzar and did more evil that provoked Jehovah God's finger to write on the wall of his palace.

The third generation of Nebuchadnezzar, Princess Vashti, who became a Persian queen far away from home in another land, also practiced the wickedness of her fathers. Nemesis caught up with Queen Vashti as the curses of her fathers affected her destiny. In similar traits, as her fathers were disgraced at the peak of ovation, Queen Vashti also fell into shameful rejection, as she was driven out of her royal throne and marital home at the peak of a great celebration.

- Vashti's grandfather, King Nebuchadnezzar, was driven out of his palace to dwell with beasts in the field at the height of his reign, when the whole earth worshipped and adored him as the most powerful ruler on earth.
- Vashti's father, King Belshazzar, was stripped of his power and struck with mental confusion amidst a feast of celebration, while he was still seated on his throne.
- Vashti herself was dethroned and banished from the Persian palace at the peak of celebration.
- Vashti was holding a great feast for all the very important women in the Persian Empire from India to Ethiopia, when her pride suddenly halted the celebration and dismissed the great gathering.
- Vashti's insolence opened up the carnage of curses that had once attacked her fathers in the Babylonian empire.
- Vashti was as powerful as her fathers Nebuchadnezzar and Belshazzar, as she ruled over the women from all the nations that had been captured and subdued by the Persian Empire.

Queen Vashti's Insolence

Despite all the glorious celebration held for 180 days, King Ahasuerus ended up heartbroken and depressed as his own wife embarrassed him at the peak of the celebration. An embarrassing situation ended the feast abruptly and sent the guests away shamefully.

At the peak of the celebration when his heart was merry with wine, the king wanted satisfaction from the glamorous appearance of the queen. He had requested the queen appear with the royal crown on her head, that the whole world might see that even the beauty of his wife matched the wealth of his kingdom. Unfortunately, that turned out to be a sad request.

Queen Vashti's Defense

Several reasons were given for Vashti's refusal to obey the king's command:

- It was assumed that women were not permitted to appear in that manner of gathering at the time.
- It was assumed that the princes, the nobles, the servants, and the visiting guests from the Persian provinces practiced high-class prostitution during that season as the king granted them permission to drink and celebrate freely.
- It was assumed that the king wanted Vashti to appear in the beauty of her nakedness, *with just the crown on her head*.
- It was assumed that the king should have courted the queen to such a gathering, rather than commanding her, as it revealed the weakness in his home.
- It was assumed that Vashti refused to do the royal dance because she had a cogent reason, which she was not allowed to explain.
- It was assumed that Vashti was pregnant at the time and would not be able to do the dance as expected of her.

The king could have made a passionate excuse for the queen, but because he was drunk with wine, he openly displayed an anger that brought the lawmakers into the matter to decide what to do with Vashti.

Who Is King Ahasuerus?

The name Ahasuerus is equivalent to the Greek name Xerxes as translated into English. The translation was created as the name moved across each of the language groups from Persia until it entered the translation of the Bible into English Language. The name *Ahasuerus* means "prince, head, and chief."

Ahasuerus is one of the kings of Persia in the Book of Esther. He was the king who crowned Esther queen instead of Vashti who was disposed for her insolent attitude.

Who Is Queen Vashti?

Queen Vashti's name originates from Persian words for "beautiful woman." She was one of the most beautiful princesses in her day. She was the daughter of Belshazzar, and the granddaughter of King Nebuchadnezzar who destroyed Solomon's temple in Jerusalem, and drove the Jewish people into exile. Vashti's father, King Belshazzar, was the last king of Babylon before the invasion of the Medes and Persians. Before the Babylonian captivity, the Davidic lineage reigned over the Jewish nation for almost 350 years, until the kingdom fell to the Babylonian Empire. The incident led to the destruction of the first temple of Jerusalem that was built by King Solomon.

Vashti's father, King Belshazzar, was murdered on the night when the Medes and the Persians invaded his palace. Before his death, Belshazzar had a feast during which he desecrated the golden vessels that his father removed from the temple of Jerusalem. Belshazzar's mockery behavior provoked Jehovah God of Israel to meet judgment of condemnation upon the Babylonian kingdom, the repercussion of which led to the handwriting on the wall (Daniel 5:1-31). That night, the Babylon kingdom was attacked. The invasion led to killing and looting of the Babylonian palace, including the murder of Belshazzar. In the midst of the pandemonium, Princess Vashti was captured by Darius who took pity on her, and betrothed her to his son Ahasuerus for marriage.

According to investigative reports from various sources, Queen Vashti was an insolent woman who arrogated herself beyond the royal position that she occupied. Report from Midrash Panim Aherim stated that when the king summoned Vashti for a dance, she sent the messenger with the following response "You were Father's steward. My Father Belshazzar would drink wine in the measure of one thousand men and would not be inebrieted, while you act the fool from the wine of a single man! She thereby hinted that she was the daughter of royalty, while he was a simple person who had reached his exalted status (BT Megillah)"

Some reports stated that:

- She was cruel and inhuman to Jewish women as her father was to the Israelites.
- She was wicked and vain.
- She worshipped the gods of Babylon.
- She was a Jew-hater and wanton adulteress.
- She stripped the Jewish women naked and ordered them to perform work at odd times.
- She enslaved the Jewish women and forced them to work on the Sabbath.

- She hosted the women's banquet for licentious activities in the royal palace.
- She was a disobedient woman who ridiculed and controlled her husband in public before the incident of the dance.
- She was like Jezebel and Athaliah, who practiced idolatry and killed the prophets and princes of Israel.
- She resisted the rebuilding of the temple that her grandfather Nebuchadnezzar had destroyed.

Some reports also stated that "her plans were upset when leprosy erupted over her entire body, so that she could not make an appearance before all the guests. According to another tradition, the angel Gabriel cam and fixed a tail to her (BT Megillah)." It was believed that Vashti punishment was as a result of how she treated Jewish women. "The wicked Vashti would bring Jewish women, strip them naked and order them to perform work on the Sabbath."

Generational Curse Haunts Queen Vashti

Manifestation of curses has no limit. The omen of curses can penetrate any regional or territorial hemisphere where the name of Jehovah God has not been adored, and blood of Jesus has not been sprinkled or recognized. The only power that can place a limitation to a curse is the worship of Jehovah El Shaddai and the exaltation of the name of Jesus Christ our Redeemer.

A curse is the opposite of blessing. A person that is blessed carries the unction of blessing with him/her everywhere he/she goes to and fro on the earth. Similarly, an accursed person lives under the manipulation and control of the spell that has been set up to interfere with one.

Whatever behavior Vashti exhibited as a princess who transited into a wife and a queen can be related to the manifestation of a generational curse that emanated from her grandfather, King Nebuchadnezzar, to her father, King Belshazzar, and then to herself as a queen in a foreign land.

Queen Vashti's grandfather, King Nebuchadnezzar of Babylon, incurred a curse when he took all the wealth of vessels from the first Jerusalem temple built by Solomon, and then destroyed it. During his reign, King Nebuchadnezzar elevated himself to the level of an immortal god, and he erected a golden image to be worshipped by all.

The Deeds of King Nebuchadnezzar

Nebuchadnezzar was the king of Babylon, the modern day Iraq. He built one of the most powerful nations in the world by ruthlessly attacking nations and annexing neighboring countries into the Babylonian empire.

- He wreaked havoc and mayhem on nations in the Middle East.
- He conquered Jerusalem.
- He destroyed the city of Jerusalem.
- He slaughtered 100,000 Jews and sent the rest of them into exile.
- He took the Jewish people as prisoners, servants, and slaves.
- He took vessels from the temple of Jerusalem.
- He set the first Jerusalem temple on fire.
- He stole the wealth of the nations that he besieged and conquered.

- He used the wealth of nations to build monuments to his own glory.
- He built the legendary Hanging Gardens of Babylon and each brick was inscribed with his name.
- He was overbearing and abusive.
- He howls for his wise men—magicians, sorcerers and astrologers.
- When dissatisfied with his expectation, he cut his wise men into pieces and turned their houses into dunghill.
- He threatened to destroy all the wise men of Babylon for their inability to reveal and interpret his dreams.
- He posed as a supreme human power on earth.
- He arrogates himself to the level of the Almighty God, as he dreamed of becoming a golden god.
- He erected a golden image that the whole world might worship him as a god.
- He enacted a decree that compelled all his officials to pay homage to his statue.
- He demanded that when the music started to play, all attendants must immediately fall down and worship the golden images that Nebuchadnezzar the king had set up.
- He was full of pride and arrogance as a multitude of people bowed low to the ground to worship him.
- He punished his offenders by death.
- He cast humans into the lion's den for destruction.
- He cast humans into the burning fiery furnace for destruction.

Daniel 3:16-28

Shadrach, Meshach, and Abed-Nego answered and said to the king, "O Nebuchadnezzar, we

have no need to answer you in this matter. If that is the case, our God whom we serve is able to deliver us from the burning fiery furnace, and He will deliver us from your hand, O king. But if not, let it be known to you, O king, that we do not serve your gods, nor will we worship the gold image which you have set up."

Then Nebuchadnezzar was full of fury, and the expression on his face changed toward Shadrach, Meshach, and Abed-Nego. He spoke and commanded that they heat the furnace seven times more than it was usually heated. And he commanded certain mighty men of valor who were in his army to bind Shadrach, Meshach, and Abed-Nego, and cast them into the burning fiery furnace. Then these men were bound in their coats, their trousers, their turbans, and their other garments, and were cast into the midst of the burning fiery furnace. Therefore, because the king's command was urgent, and the furnace exceedingly hot, the flame of the fire killed those men who took up Shadrach, Meshach, and Abed-Nego. And these three men, Shadrach, Meshach, and Abed-Nego, fell down bound into the midst of the burning fiery furnace.

Then King Nebuchadnezzar was astonished; and he rose in haste and spoke, saying to his counselors, "Did we not cast three men bound into the midst of the fire?" They answered and said to the king, "True, O king." "Look!" he answered, "I see four men loose, walking in the midst of the fire; and they are not hurt, and the form of the fourth is like the Son of God."

Then Nebuchadnezzar went near the mouth of the burning fiery furnace and spoke, saying, "Shadrach, Meshach, and Abed-Nego, servants of the Most High God, come out, and come here." Then Shadrach, Meshach, and Abed-Nego came from the midst of the fire. And the satraps, administrators, governors, and the king's counselors gathered together, and they saw these men on whose bodies the fire had no power; the hair of their head was not singed nor were their garments affected, and the smell of fire was not on them.

Nebuchadnezzar spoke, saying, "Blessed be the God of Shadrach, Meshach, and Abed-Nego, who sent His Angel and delivered His servants who trusted in Him, and they have frustrated the king's word, and yielded their bodies, that they should not serve nor worship any god except their own God!

The Plagues and Curses of Nebuchadnezzar

- He was driven out of the midst of mankind.
- He dwelt with the beasts of the field.
- He ate grass like oxen.
- His body was washed by the dew of heaven.
- His hair grew like an eagle's feathers.
- His nails were like birds' claws.

Daniel 4:28-33

All this came upon King Nebuchadnezzar. At the end of the twelve months he was walking about the royal palace of Babylon. The king spoke, saying, "Is not this great Babylon, that I have built for a royal dwelling by my mighty power and for the honor of my majesty?"

While the word was still in the king's mouth, a voice fell from heaven: "King Nebuchadnezzar, to you it is spoken: the kingdom has departed from you! And they shall drive you from men, and your dwelling shall be with the beasts of the field. They shall make you eat grass like oxen; and seven times shall pass over you, until you know that the Most High rules in the kingdom of men, and gives it to whomever He chooses."

That very hour the word was fulfilled concerning Nebuchadnezzar; he was driven from men and ate grass like oxen; his body was wet with the dew of heaven till his hair had grown like eagles' feathers and his nails like birds' claws.

Belshazzar Inherits King Nebuchadnezzar's Curses

Queen Vashti's father, King Belshazzar, inherited the Babylonian throne with all the curses therein from his father King Nebuchadnezzar. Belshazzar's evil ways plummeted into some form of atrocities, where the Jews were enslaved and dehumanized incessantly. Belshazzar also desecrated the holy vessels that his father Nebuchadnezzar took from the temple of Jerusalem. The repercussion of which led to his death and the capture of his daughter, PrincessVashti.

The Deeds of Belshazzar

- He was a tyrannous oppressor.
- He oppressed his Jewish subjects and the nation of Israel.
- He was impious.
- He put the sacred vessels of the temple of Jerusalem to sacrilegious use.
- He made mockery of Jehovah God as they mingled the sound of revelry with hymns to the heathen gods.
- He allowed his nobles, wives, and concubines to drink from the sacred vessels.
- They drank from the vessels to honor their idols made of gold, silver, bronze, iron, wood, and stone.

Belshazzar Inherited a Series of Curses from His Ancestors

- He inherited and manifested the curse of drinking liquor.
- The curse of alcohol caused him to act foolishly until he blasphemed against Jehovah God of Israel.
- The curse of alcohol brought down the Babylonian empire.
- He inherited and manifested the curse of idolatry.
- He inherited and manifested the curse of immorality.
- He inherited and manifested the curse of pride and arrogance.

Belshazzar Manifested Nebuchadnezzar's Plagues

- He saw the finger of God, and the writing on the wall.
- His countenance changed and his thoughts troubled him.
- The joints of his hips were loosed and his knees knocked against each other.
- He called for the astrologers, the Chaldeans, and the soothsayers.
- His lords were astonished and the wise men could not read the writing.
- His wise men could not interpret the handwriting.
- That same night the king was slain.

Daniel 5:1-31

Belshazzar the king made a great feast for a thousand of his lords, and drank wine in the presence of the thousand. While he tasted the wine, Belshazzar gave the command to bring the gold and silver vessels which his father Nebuchadnezzar had taken from the temple which had been in Jerusalem, that the king and his lords, his wives, and his concubines might drink from them. Then they brought the gold vessels that had been taken from the temple of the house of God which had been in Jerusalem; and the king and his lords, his wives, and his concubines drank from them. They drank wine, and praised the gods of gold and silver, bronze and iron, wood and stone.

In the same hour the fingers of a man's hand appeared and wrote opposite the lampstand on

the plaster of the wall of the king's palace; and the king saw the part of the hand that wrote. Then the king's countenance changed, and his thoughts troubled him, so that the joints of his hips were loosened and his knees knocked against each other.

The king cried aloud to bring in the astrologers, the Chaldeans, and the soothsayers. The king spoke, saying to the wise men of Babylon, "Whoever reads this writing, and tells me its interpretation, shall be clothed with purple and have a chain of gold around his neck; and he shall be the third ruler in the kingdom." Now all the king's wise men came, but they could not read the writing, or make known to the king its interpretation. Then King Belshazzar was greatly troubled, his countenance was changed, and his lords were astonished.

The queen, because of the words of the king and his lords, came to the banquet hall. The queen spoke, saying, "O king, live forever! Do not let your thoughts trouble you, nor let your countenance change. There is a man in your kingdom in whom is the Spirit of the Holy God. And in the days of your father, light and understanding and wisdom, like the wisdom of the gods, were found in him; and King Nebuchadnezzar your father—your father the king—made him chief of the magicians, astrologers, Chaldeans, and soothsayers.

Inasmuch as an excellent spirit, knowledge, understanding, interpreting dreams, solving riddles, and explaining enigmas were found in this Daniel, whom the king named Belteshazzar, now let Daniel be called, and he will give the interpretation." Then Daniel was brought in before the king. The king spoke, and said to Daniel, "Are you that Daniel who is one of the captives from Judah, whom my father the king brought from Judah?

I have heard of you, that the Spirit of God is in you, and that light and understanding and excellent wisdom are found in you. Now the wise men, the astrologers, have been brought in before me, that they should read this writing and make known to me its interpretation, but they could not give the interpretation of the thing. And I have heard of you, that you can give interpretations and explain enigmas. Now if you can read the writing and make known to me its interpretation, you shall be clothed with purple and have a chain of gold around your neck, and shall be the third ruler in the kingdom."

Then Daniel answered, and said before the king, "Let your gifts be for yourself, and give your rewards to another; yet I will read the writing to the king, and make known to him the interpretation. O king, the Most High God gave Nebuchadnezzar your father a kingdom and majesty, glory and honor.

And because of the majesty that He gave him, all peoples, nations, and languages trembled and feared before him. Whomever he wished, he executed; whomever he wished, he kept alive; whomever he wished, he set up; and whomever he wished, he put down. But when his heart was lifted up, and his spirit was hardened in pride, he was deposed from his kingly throne, and they took his glory from him. Then he was driven from the sons of men, his heart was made like the beasts, and his dwelling was with the wild donkeys. They fed him with grass like oxen, and his body was wet with the dew of heaven, till he knew that the Most High God rules in the kingdom of men, and appoints over it whomever He chooses. "But you his son, Belshazzar, have not humbled your heart, although you knew all this.

And you have lifted yourself up against the Lord of heaven. They have brought the vessels of His house before you, and you and your lords, your wives and your concubines, have drunk wine from them. And you have praised the gods of silver and gold, bronze and iron, wood and stone, which do not see or hear or know; and the God who holds your breath in His hand and owns all your ways, you have not glorified.

Then the fingers of the hand were sent from Him, and this writing was written. "And this is the inscription that was written: MENE, MENE, TEKEL, UPHARSIN. This is the interpretation of each word. MENE: God has numbered your kingdom, and finished it; TEKEL: You have been weighed in the balances, and found wanting; PERES: Your kingdom has been divided, and given to the Medes and Persians."

Then Belshazzar gave the command, and they clothed Daniel with purple and put a chain of gold around his neck, and made a proclamation concerning him that he should be the third ruler in the kingdom.

That very night Belshazzar, king of the Chaldeans, was slain. And Darius the Mede received the kingdom, being about sixty-two years old.

Prayer Points

- I pray that my celebration will not be greeted with shame and disgrace.
- I pray that my joy will not be turned into sorrow or embarrassment.
- I pray that strangers will not interfere with my marital home.
- I pray that strangers will not make decisions for my family.
- I pray that lawmakers (the judiciary or court of law and the legislature or senate) will not steal away our passionate affection for marriage in times of challenges and difficulties, or kill and destroy our homes with ungodly decisions.

Songs of Inspiration
God, give us Christian homes!

Author and Composer: B. B. McKinney (1949)
Philippians 2:15

God, give us Christian homes!
Homes where the Bible is loved and taught,
Homes where the Master's will is sought,
Homes crowned with beauty Your love has wrought;
God, give us Christian homes;
God, give us Christian homes!

God, give us Christian homes!
Homes where the father is true and strong,
Homes that are free from the blight of wrong,
Homes that are joyous with love and song;
God, give us Christian homes,
God, give us Christian homes!

God, give us Christian homes!
Homes where the mother, in caring quest,
Strives to show others Your way is best,
Homes where the Lord is an honored guest;
God, give us Christian homes,
God, give us Christian homes!

God, give us Christian homes!
Homes where the children are led to know
Christ in His beauty who loves them so,
Homes where the altar fires burn and glow;
God, give us Christian homes,
God, give us Christian homes!

Application

In order to achieve effective results in fasting, it is important that you identify the particular problems that need solution. Use the reflective questions provided to map out strategic solutions to the problems that affect your family members, environment, or anyone whom you intend to help besides yourself.

1. **List 3-5 lesson points that you have learned from today's reading.**

    _____
    _____
    _____
    _____

2. **Identify how the lesson affects you positively in 3-5 points.**

    _____
    _____
    _____
    _____

3. **Identify how you intend to use the lesson from today's passage to resolve your problem in 3-5 points.**

    _____
    _____
    _____
    _____

Strategic Deliverance Prayer

The Problem

That our marital challenges will not become public issues that will attract the attention of law makers

The Situation

That our spouses will learn to cover up for us and make a joke out of a situation that seems to carry an element of embarrassment
That we will endeavor to apply wisdom when we lack self-control in matters that regard our families
That we will not lose our inheritance, blessings, and honor at the peak of our promotion
That the Lord will deliver us from the evil of marital separation and divorce whenever we fall short of wisdom and knowledge
That the legislators and judiciary of our territory will not despise our passion and affection in times of challenges

Goal:

That my spouse will exercise self-control in matters that concern the public
That the public will not make decisions for our marriage

Authority of Scripture

Esther 1:10-18

On the seventh day, when the *heart of the king was merry with wine*, he *commanded* Mehuman, Biztha, Harbona, Bigtha, and Abagtha, Zethar, and Carcas, *the seven chamberlains* that *served in the presence* of Ahasuerus the king, to bring Vashti the queen before the king with the crown royal, to shew the people and the princes her beauty: for she was fair to look on ... What shall we do unto the queen Vashti according to law, because she hath not performed the commandment of the king Ahasuerus by the chamberlains? And Memucan answered before the king and the princes, Vashti the queen hath not done wrong to the king only, but also to all the princes, and to all the people that are in all the provinces of the king Ahasuerus. For this deed of the queen shall come abroad unto all women, so that they shall despise their husbands in their eyes, when it shall be reported, The king Ahasuerus commanded Vashti the queen to be brought in before him, but she came not. Likewise shall the ladies of Persia and Media say this day unto all the king's princes, which have heard of the deed of the queen. Thus shall there arise too much contempt and wrath.

Prayer in Action

O Lord and my God, forgive me for dishonoring
my spouse and me in public.
I am sorry for displaying lack of self-control and
disrespect for my spouse and official authority.
I am sorry for allowing the public to see our family's shortcomings.
I am sorry for allowing the public to intervene in
matters that should have been solved in privacy.
Please, Lord, forgive me for every negative influence that my
weaknesses might have caused the Christian community.
O Lord, forgive me and my spouse and enable us to
make our peace in the secret place of our marriage.
O Lord, help us to love and submit to each other.
Help us to respect and honor our marriage
irrespective of our environment.
Help us to establish ourselves as a good influence in our territory,
That Your name will be glorified in our
marriage and lifestyle. Amen!

Deliverance Warfare

In the name of Jesus and with the authority in the
blood of Jesus Christ our Lord and Savior,
I uproot and cast out any spirit of drunkenness
from my spouse and marital home.
In the name of Jesus, I uproot and cast out any evil
spirit that will influence my spouse to disrespect
or dishonor our marital relationship.
In the name of Jesus, I evict and banish the spirit of
separation and divorce out of my married life.
In the name of Jesus, I release my marriage
from satanic control and manipulations.
In the name of Jesus, I uproot and cast out the
spirit of depression and oppression,
Therefore I shall not perish, but shall have long
life and prosperity in Jesus's name.
In the name of Jesus, I cover my life and destiny with the
blood that was shed for me on the cross of Calvary.
In the name of Jesus, I build a hedge of protection
over my life with the fire of the Holy Ghost.
The arrows that fly by day and the terror by night
shall not come after me nor interfere with me.
There shall be no enchantment or divination against me,
in the name of Jesus Christ my Lord and Savior. Amen!

Breaking and Uprooting Curses— Curses Affecting My Marriage

In the name of Jesus, and with the authority in the blood of Jesus, I bind and uproot the tree of curses planted against my life.
I speak to the tree of **curses affecting my marriage** that affects my life, You shall not prosper against my destiny.
I command you, tree of **curses affecting my marriage** to be uprooted out of my destiny right now.
In the name of Jesus, you tree of **curses affecting my marriage** shall not prosper in my life.
Be uprooted out of my life and destiny right now, in the name of Jesus.
Be cast out into the sea of destruction right now, in the name of Jesus.
I shall not see you, tree of **curses affecting my marriage** again, and you shall not come by me, in Jesus's name.
I shall not invite you, tree of **curses affecting my marriage** again, and you shall not harass me, in Jesus's name
I shall not entertain you, tree of **curses affecting my marriage** again, and you shall not terrorize my life, in Jesus's name.
Let the blood of Jesus separate me from the tree of **curses affecting my marriage** that steals the joy of my salvation.
Let the fire of the Holy Ghost destroy the root of **curses affecting my marriage** that afflicts me.
The tree of **curses affecting my marriage** shall no longer have access to me, in Jesus's name.
The tree of **curses affecting my marriage** shall no longer manifest within and around me again, in Jesus's name.
I am washed and cleansed by the blood of Jesus Christ my Lord and Savior.
I am covered and sealed in the name of Jesus.
I am protected and guarded by the fire of the Holy Ghost. Amen!

Declarations

In the name of Jesus and with the authority in the blood of Jesus, I declare that there shall be wisdom and understanding in my marital relationship.
I declare that there shall be an application of love, passion, and affection in our marital decisions, in Jesus's name.
I declare that our mistakes will not ridicule our relationship in public, in Jesus's name.
I declare that we shall settle our disagreement without external influence or interference, in Jesus's name. Amen!

Prayer Observations and Experiences

You may remember your dreams and some past occurrences while doing this prayer. You may also receive a revelation. It's important that you make notes for future reference.

Experiences

_____
_____
_____
_____
_____
_____

Observations

_____
_____
_____
_____
_____
_____

Revelations

_____
_____
_____
_____
_____
_____

CHAPTER SEVEN

Second Chapter of Esther

Esther 2:1-23

After these things, when the wrath of King Ahasuerus subsided, he remembered Vashti, what she had done, and what had been decreed against her. Then the king's servants who attended him said: "Let beautiful young virgins be sought for the king; and let the king appoint officers in all the provinces of his kingdom, that they may gather all the beautiful young virgins to Shushan the citadel, into the women's quarters, under the custody of Hegai the king's eunuch, custodian of the women. And let beauty preparations be given them. Then let the young woman who pleases the king be queen instead of Vashti." This thing pleased the king, and he did so.

In Shushan the citadel there was a certain Jew whose name was Mordecai the son of Jair, the son of Shimei, the son of Kish, a Benjamite. Kish had been carried away from Jerusalem with the captives who had been captured with Jeconiah king of Judah, whom Nebuchadnezzar the king of Babylon had carried away. And Mordecai had brought up Hadassah, that is, Esther, his uncle's daughter, for she had neither father nor mother. The young woman was lovely and beautiful. When her father and mother died, Mordecai took her as his own daughter.

So it was, when the king's command and decree were heard, and when many young women were gathered at Shushan the citadel, under the custody of Hegai, that Esther also was taken to the king's palace, into the care of Hegai the custodian of the women. Now the young woman pleased him, and she obtained his favor; so he readily gave beauty preparations to her, besides her allowance. Then seven choice maidservants were provided for her from the king's palace, and he moved her and her maidservants to the best place in the house of the women. Esther had not revealed her people or family, for Mordecai had charged her not to reveal it. And every day Mordecai paced in front of the court of the women's quarters, to learn of Esther's welfare and what was happening to her. Each young woman's turn came to go in to King Ahasuerus after she had completed twelve months' preparation, according to the regulations for the women, for thus were the days of their preparation apportioned: six months with oil of myrrh, and six months with perfumes and preparations for beautifying women. Thus prepared, each young woman went to the king, and she was given whatever she desired to take with her from the women's quarters to the king's palace. In the evening she went, and in the morning she returned to the second house of the women, to the custody of Shaashgaz, the king's eunuch who kept the concubines. She would not go in to the king again unless the king delighted in her and called for her by name.

Now when the turn came for Esther the daughter of Abihail the uncle of Mordecai, who had taken her as his daughter, to go in to the king, she requested nothing but what Hegai the king's eunuch, the custodian of the women, advised. And Esther obtained favor in the sight of all who saw her. So Esther was taken to King Ahasuerus, into his royal palace, in the tenth month, which is the month of Tebeth, in the seventh year of his reign. The king loved Esther more than all the other women, and she obtained grace and favor in his sight more than all the virgins; so he set the royal crown upon her head and made her queen instead of Vashti. Then the king made a great feast, the Feast of Esther, for all his officials and servants; and he proclaimed a holiday in the provinces and gave gifts according to the generosity of a king.

When virgins were gathered together a second time, Mordecai sat within the king's gate. Now Esther had not revealed her family and her people, just as Mordecai had charged her, for Esther obeyed the command of Mordecai as when she was brought up by him.

In those days, while Mordecai sat within the king's gate, two of the king's eunuchs, Bigthan and Teresh, doorkeepers, became furious and sought to lay hands on King Ahasuerus. So the matter became known to Mordecai, who told Queen Esther, and Esther informed the king in Mordecai's name. And when an inquiry was made into the matter, it was confirmed, and both were hanged on a gallows; and it was written in the book of the chronicles in the presence of the king.

Switching Positions and Blessings

Genesis 48:10-19 (NKJV)
Now the eyes of Israel were dim for age, so that he could not see. And he brought them near unto him; and he kissed them, and embraced them. And Israel said unto Joseph, I had not thought to see thy face: and, lo, God hath shewed me also thy seed. And Joseph brought them out from between his knees, and he bowed himself with his face to the earth. And Joseph took them both, Ephraim in his right hand toward Israel's left hand, and Manasseh in his left hand toward Israel's right hand, and brought them near unto him. And Israel stretched out his right hand, and laid it upon Ephraim's head, who was the younger, and his left hand upon Manasseh's head, guiding his hands wittingly; for Manasseh was the firstborn. And he blessed Joseph, and said, God, before whom

my fathers Abraham and Isaac did walk, the God which fed me all my life long unto this day, The Angel which redeemed me from all evil, bless the lads; and let my name be named on them, and the name of my fathers Abraham and Isaac; and let them grow into a multitude in the midst of the earth. And when Joseph saw that his father laid his right hand upon the head of Ephraim, it displeased him: and he held up his father's hand, to remove it from Ephraim's head unto Manasseh's head. And Joseph said unto his father, Not so, my father: for this is the firstborn; put thy right hand upon his head. And his father refused, and said, I know it, my son, I know it: he also shall become a people, and he also shall be great: but truly his younger brother shall be greater than he, and his seed shall become a multitude of nations.

1 Chronicles 5:1-2

Now the sons of Reuben the firstborn of Israel, (for he was the firstborn; but, forasmuch as he defiled his father's bed, his birthright was given unto the sons of Joseph the son of Israel: and the genealogy is not to be reckoned after the birthright. For Judah prevailed above his brethren, and of him came the chief ruler; but the birthright was Joseph's).

Psalm 51:11

Cast me not away from thy presence; and take not thy holy spirit from me.

Day Three:
The Discovery of a Royal Destiny

The book of Esther chapter two contains two segments of the prayer fast for days three and four. The first part is the third day fast that focuses on the repercussions of Vashti's accursed inheritance of evil behavior, while the second part of the chapter concentrates on how Jehovah God can use anybody and anything to perform His will and plans. It reveals how a common servant or a non-entity could be used to influence a move that could effect changes in the corridors of power in order to create a shift in destiny allocation.

Your case may not be exactly like that of Esther, yet you have the opportunity to liaise with Esther's situation in this fast, in order for Jehovah God to use anybody and anything to get you connected to your destiny. Let no one despise your youth, and do not despise anyone's position at any time, as Paul said in **1 Timothy 4:12, "Let no man despise thy youth; but be thou an example of the believers, in word, in conversation, in charity, in spirit, in faith, in purity."**

Focus: Fast against Accursed Hereditary and Contaminated Inheritance

Vashti's royal inheritance could have been one of the best, yet it was contaminated with human blood and atrocities.

The focus of this fast is to eliminate any form of atrocities committed by members of our families which contaminated our inheritance. The story of Vashti is an example of what can be related to our own family history or marital background.

Tragedy Comedy of Royal Leadership

The rise to leadership may either bring pain to your family, or generate an everlasting honor that no situation can destroy. The memory of a leader or a king may either bring joy to the heart of his or her subjects, or sorrow to the lives of the people.

Vashti's Tragedy

This chapter exposes the tragedy of Queen Vashti's royal inheritance from her ancestry to the day she was banished from the Persian palace. Her day of tragedy started when her father was murdered in the Babylonian palace, and she was captured amidst confusion and pandemonium. Her comedy began when her captor gave her to his son in marriage.

Although Vashti rose from the status of a princess in Babylon to a queen in the foreign land of Persia, the comedy of her glamorous ascension to the Persian throne turned into another sad tragedy. The torment from a curse that emerged from the various evils that her fathers had incurred haunted her destiny. Babylon was the greatest empire in the days of Nebuchadnezzar and Belshazzar, her grandfather and father. The Persian Empire took over from Babylon, and became the greatest kingdom, with Ahasuerus as the king and Vashti as the queen. It was as though the empires of Babylon merged with that of Persia through marital union.

Esther's Comedy

This chapter also reveals the comedy of how a rejected dynasty of a forgotten king was restored in a foreign land. Whereby, the Jewish orphan girl Hadassah had no thought of any link-up with her royal ancestry, even if she ever knew the history of her background. One day, Hadassah found herself at the pinnacle of restoration, as she was chosen to be groomed as a wife and queen, and later, a commander-in-chief to lead a war that would forever be in the annals of Jewish history, and celebrated as an important festival. In totality, the chapter exposes how the act of a leader usually attracts blessings or formulates generational curses that could torment a host of descendants unknown.

In paradox, both a nation and a people living within an environment can suffer the repercussions of a misbehavior demonstrated by one person who misuses his leadership position and authority.

Uprooting Generational Curse of Royal Rejection

Many years after Saul was rejected as king of Israel because of disobedience and rebellion to divine authority, Esther's obedience and fear of God brought restoration of the royal lineage to the tribe of Benjamin, and to the entire Jewish race living in foreign lands. Although Saul's family lost the legacy of inheriting the royal throne of Israel, Mordecai unconsciously raised Esther to regain that legacy in a foreign land.

The restoration of royal destiny was established when Esther obeyed her uncle Mordecai to conceal her identity. Mordecai had instructed her to remain simple and comply with all rules and regulations required of her in the Persian Empire.

Hence, the search for a virgin led to the discovery of a virgin seed in the family of the Benjamites living in the Persian Empire. The discovery of the virgin seed in Hadassah also led to the planting of a new beginning where the curses of the forefathers had to be uprooted, in order to preserve the land for planting the blessings of fruitfulness and harvesting of the fruits of restoration.

Hadassah's enthronement in a foreign land was a restoration of royal dynasty and destiny fulfillment. Her enthronement reinforced her identity from the status of an "evergreen" princess with a sweet fragrance, to a unique "star." Hadassah's aromatic fragrance elevated her to the position of the most powerful queen, whose sweet smell turned the heart of wickedness into a passionate and affectionate one. Hence, she won the king's heart and was chosen as a wife and the queen in her season. She also became the fruitful land on which the Jewish race poured out their tears as they cried out to Jehovah God for deliverance from evil.

A Search for a Virgin Meant

- The search for a virgin land
- Discovery of a virgin land
- Preparing the land for planting
- Preserving the land for fruitfulness
- Tending the land for fulfillment

Summary

- Vashti was dethroned from royalty for being a symbol of pride, arrogance, disobedience, insubordination, and rudeness.
- Vashti was an insolent woman.
- Esther was enthroned into royalty as she emerged as a symbol of humility, simplicity, obedience, submissiveness, and God-fearing faith.
- Esther was a respectful woman.
- Therefore, the search and discovery of Esther as a young virgin was connected to preservation of a fruitful people for fulfillment in a foreign land.

Release from the Impact of Liquor

The act of anger and drunkenness can cause you to behave foolishly and spew out destructive words that could dehumanize your loved ones.

- Both anger and drunkenness are destroyers of destiny.
- It is not good to utter a word when you are angry or drunk.
- It is better to walk away from the face of anger and seek fresh air than to stay in the presence of frustration.
- It is better to go to your bed and lie down to sleep when you are intoxicated with liquor or anger—the reason being that both anger and liquor may cause you to lose control of your actions and utterances. A matter that should be resolved between a husband and wife may become a public matter, requiring a public decision.

- Anger that burst out of drunkenness destroyed the relationship between the king and his queen.
- In his state of drunkenness, the king could not exhibit patience and respect for his marriage. Intoxication influenced the king to make demands that gave birth to the exhibition of anger. Hence, the king forgot that Vashti was pregnant and could not have done the belly dance.
- Furthermore, those who made the decision on behalf of the king did not know that Vashti was pregnant with a baby boy who was to be an heir to the throne.

Esther 2:1
After these things, *when the wrath of king Ahasuerus was appeased, he remembered Vashti,* and *what she had done,* and *what was decreed against her.*

Prayer Points

- *Pray that your (my) spouse, the authority, or the king over your (my) life will not forget but remember you (me).*
- *Pray that your (my) spouse, the authority, or king over your (my) life will not put you (me) down in public but respect you (me).*
- *Pray that your (my) spouse, authority, or the king over your (my) life will protect you (me) from the eyes of the public and will not disgrace you (me).*
- *Pray that your (my) spouse, the authority, or the king over your (my) life will not exhibit excessive anger against you (me) in public, but will exercise wisdom.*

- *Pray that your (my) spouse, the authority, or the king will exercise patience in all matters that concern you (me).*
- *Pray that you (I) will find favor in the relationship with your (my) spouse or the king that is over your (my) life.*

A Moment of Regret: The Search for Restoration

Aftermath of His Action

- When the drunkenness cleared out of the king's system, and his temper calmed down, the king remembered where he had gone wrong.
- The king began to long for Vashti and wanted to have her.
- He needed the passion and affection of a spouse and not a concubine.
- Unfortunately, it was too late to reverse the decree made against Vashti.
- At this point, the king was full of regret and was troubled at heart.
- Unfortunately, the concubines could not fill up Vashti's space in the heart of the king.
- The vacuum was deep because Vashti (his wife) was missing.
- Of course there is a big difference between a spouse and a concubine. A concubine is a shadow, while a spouse offers a committed and trusted relationship.
- The king's attendant noticed the disposition of the king and his longing for Vashti his wife.
- The absence of Vashti affected him so much so that he was no longer himself.
- Genuine love is powerful and can be intoxicating.

- Hence, according to royal custom, the king's attendant suggested that virgins be sought for in all the provinces, so that the king could make a choice as the custom demanded.
- In royal customs around the world, kings were not permitted to marry non-virgins. Kings deserved the best. Young virgins were considered the best choices for kings.

Summary

No matter what, nemesis had caught up with Vashti. Her cup was full. The curse from evil behavior was ripe. It was time to pay back what her fathers and she owed the Jewish race. Jehovah God of Yahweh had begun to vindicate His people. The battle is the Lord's. **Zechariah 4:6** says, **"Then he answered and spake unto me, saying, This is the word of the LORD unto Zerubbabel, saying, Not by might, nor by power, but by my spirit, saith the LORD of hosts."**

The Bill Was Overdue

The Babylonians had committed grievous atrocities in the land of Israel and among the Jewish people. They owed the Jews both the lives of thousands of people whose blood was shed and financial restoration of a nation rendered useless and hopeless. This was classic terrorism displayed through the act of power and invasion of kingdoms and territories. Hence, the bill was overdue for payment. The list on the invoice was unlimited.

The Babylonians were indebted to the Jewish people. They owed them trillions of dollars or more than what was needed to rebuild a nation and restore the people to their original state of life and daily endeavors.

In view of the classic terrorism and invasion, the Babylonians also incurred a series of curses that became a debt of problems, challenges, and difficulties for which Vashti was held accountable. As an heir to the throne of Babylon and a descendant of Nebuchadnezzar, Vashti had trod the path of her ancestors and practiced a similar cruelty against the Jews in her days.

The seemingly unlimited list of items on the invoice included:

1. The destruction of Solomon's temple
2. The destruction of many lives—both young and old
3. The destruction of the nation of Israel
4. The destruction of cities and towns
5. The destruction of capital resources
6. The destruction of a nation's posterity
7. The capture of intelligent youths
8. The capture of a nation's posterity
9. The disarmament of a nation's wisdom
10. The disarmament of a nation's existence
11. The eradication of a nation's destiny
12. The eradication of a people with a mission

Repercussion

As a result of the overdue bill, Vashti was bearing the consequences of the evil atrocities committed against the Jewish people and their nation. An action of repercussion was looming against Vashti and her people. Even if she had developed a tail, it was considered a trait of the kind of punishment that Nebuchadnezzar suffered for his pride and self-arrogated proclamation as a god that deserved to be reverenced and worshipped daily at the sound of a symphony.

As part of the payment, a Jewish virgin took over Vashti's position as a replacement in the realm of royalty and displaced authority. There was a sort of exchange in the realms of the spirit that affected the natural. This was a switch of position and a shift in the realms of authority. Hence, Vashti was banished from the Persian kingdom in order for Esther to take over the throne. It was an involuntary bargain by barter. Vashti had no choice but to yield, because Yahweh God was the commander-in-chief, and he was in charge of the action. Every knee must bow and every tongue must confess that He is Lord of all.

Application

In order to achieve effective results in fasting, it is important that you identify the particular problems that need solution. Use the reflective questions provided to map out strategic solutions to the problems that affect your family members, environment, or anyone whom you intend to help besides yourself.

1. **List 3-5 lesson points that you have learned from today's reading.**

   _____
   _____
   _____
   _____
   _____

2. **Identify how the lesson affects you positively in 3-5 points.**

   _____
   _____
   _____
   _____
   _____

3. **Identify how you intend to use the lesson from today's passage to resolve your problem in 3-5 points.**

   _____
   _____
   _____
   _____
   _____

Prayer Observations and Experiences

You may remember your dreams and some past occurrences while doing this prayer. You may also receive a revelation. It's important that you make notes for future reference.

Experiences

_____
_____
_____
_____
_____
_____

Observations

_____
_____
_____
_____
_____
_____

Revelations

_____
_____
_____
_____
_____
_____

Day Four:
Fasting for Destiny Connections

The Lord uses anyone and anything to connect you to your destiny. He uses anything available to influence the people responsible to fix your stage for performance.

In this segment of the fast, the situation that led to Esther's discovery could be your case today. You may not be an orphan or a virgin, but if you repent and ask forgiveness of your sins, the blood of Jesus will wash and cleanse you from all unrighteousness, and then make you a useful vessel in the hands of the Lord.

Destiny Switch

Jehovah God works in mysterious ways. He used the king's servant to bring forth his divine plans and purpose for the deliverance of the Jewish race. God can use anything at any time to accomplish His purpose. The king's servants may be considered powerless or little people. Yet, they could be influential as the king trusts them with his food and drink as well as daily survival and security. They witnessed the king's weakness and frustration.

It was the turn of the palace servants to advise the king—a promotion in disguise.

- The voice of the common people suddenly became important.
- God was using the voice of the common man (insignificant persons) to turn the Persian kingdom around.

- God was using the palace servants and cleaners to shift the realms of authority from the hands of the wicked to the righteous.
- God was using the insignificant people to judge the case of the righteous.
- God was using the palace servants and cleaners (insignificant people) to influence the exchange of authority in the corridors of power.

Esther 2:2-4
Then said the king's servants that ministered unto him, *Let there be fair young virgins sought for the king***: And let the king** *appoint officers in all the provinces of his kingdom,* **that they may gather together all the fair young virgins** **unto Shushan the palace, to** *the house of the women,* **unto the** *custody of Hege the king's chamberlain, keeper of the women***; and** *let their things for purification be given them:* **And let the maiden which pleaseth the king be queen instead of Vashti. And the thing pleased the king; and he did so.**

Mordecai the Descendant of Saul the Son of Kish

Saul was the first king of Israel. He was the son of *Kish* from *the tribe of Benjamin*. While serving as king of Israel, Saul the son of Kish was given the command to utterly destroy the Amalekites **1 Samuel 15:2-3** says, **"Thus saith the LORD of hosts, I remember that which Amalek did to Israel, how he laid wait for him in the**

way, when he came up from Egypt. **Now go and smite Amalek, and utterly destroy all that they have, and spare them not; but slay both man and woman, infant and suckling, ox and sheep, camel and ass."**

Saul succeeded in capturing the king of the Amalekites, Agag, but he did not execute him as commanded. Samuel finally terminated the life of King Agag (1 Samuel 15:8-33).

In view of Saul's disobedience to eliminate the Amalekites as divinely commanded, Saul was rejected and David was appointed to replace him over the kingdom. Hence, when Saul died, no member of his family inherited from him. As David became king, the members of Saul's family were unhappy about losing the throne. As a result, Shimei mocked and cursed when David was temporarily overthrown by his son, Absalom. Shimei felt that David's predicament was some sort of vengeance for Saul's family.

Shimei was a member of Saul's family. David was confronted by Shimei while he was on his way to exile (2 Samuel 16: 5-13).

Mordecai was the grandson of Shimei, a relation of King Saul from the tribe of Benjamin.

Esther was the daughter of Mordecai's uncle. Mordecai adopted Esther when her parents died.

> **Esther 2:5-7**
>
> *Now* **in Shushan the palace there was a certain Jew, whose name was** *Mordecai, the son of Jair, the son of Shimei, the son of Kish, a Benjamite*; **Who had been carried away from Jerusalem with the captivity which had been carried away with Jeconiah king of Judah,** *whom Nebuchadnezzar the king of Babylon had carried away.* **And he brought up Hadassah, that is, Esther, his uncle's**

daughter: for *she had neither father nor mother,* and *the maid was fair and beautiful*; whom Mordecai, when her father and mother were dead, *took for his own daughter.*

Mordecai is the descendant from the lineage of King Saul. Kish was the father of King Saul. Shimei was one of the brothers of King Saul. Shimei was the man who rained curses on King David when he was dethroned by his son, and was on his way to exile. Instead of inheriting the repercussion from the misbehavior of King Saul, Mordecai was inheriting the blessings of Abraham.

Prayer Points

Disobedience: The spirit of Saul was a spirit of pride that resisted the voice of the Lord—the command of supreme authority.

Elimination: Obey the voice of divine authority and eliminate the entities of evil from your environment.

Accursed Stuff: Do not keep the accursed stuff among your blessings.

Contamination: The accursed stuff will contaminate your blessings and inheritance if you hide it away.

Prayer

- *In the name of Jesus, I break and reverse the curses of the forefathers that affect my destiny.*
- *In the name of Jesus, I break and reverse the curses of disobedience and pride.*

- *In the name of Jesus, I break and reverse the curses of rejection, shame, and disgrace.*
- *In the name of Jesus, I break and reverse the curses of hatred, envy, and strife.*
- *In the name of Jesus, I break and reverse the curses of unending battles.*
- *In the name of Jesus, I reverse the repercussion of curses that you might have inherited from my family lineage.*

Application

In order to achieve effective results in fasting, it is important that you identify the particular problems that need solution. Use the reflective questions provided to map out strategic solutions to the problems that affect your family members, environment, or anyone whom you intend to help besides yourself.

1. **List 3-5 lesson points that you have learned from today's reading.**

   _____
   _____
   _____
   _____
   _____

2. **Identify how the lesson affects you positively in 3-5 points.**

   _____
   _____
   _____
   _____
   _____

3. **Identify how you intend to use the lesson from today's passage to resolve your problem in 3-5 points.**

   _____
   _____
   _____
   _____
   _____

Day Five:
The Power and Impact of Obedience

Obedience: Obedience is the ability to yield to explicit instructions or orders from an authority figure without struggle and resistance. Obedience attracts favor.

Obedience to the Word of God is compliance to the precepts and statues that constitute the laws and commandments of the Almighty God. Obedience is the act of following instructions.

- It is the act of submission to authority.
- It is the practice of complying with rules and regulations
- It is the act of conformity.
- It is the act of abiding by laws.
- Obedience means docility.
- Obedience means meekness.
- Obedience means respect.

Disobedience: Disobedience is an act of rebellion and insubordination.

- Disobedience is the practice of breaking rules and regulations.
- It is an act of disrespect for authority.

Favor: Favor is to be surrounded with unconditional preference and kindness that meets every need and want with little or no effort. It is an unmerited validation or approval that one receives from familiar persons and strangers in one's life and endeavors.

- Favor is to have God's undeserved blessings.
- Favor is an act of kindness.
- It is an act of good will.
- It is an unconditional support and assistance.
- It is an act of love and acceptance.

Disfavor: While favor is to give support or approval to someone or something, disfavor is an act of rejection.

- Disfavor is an act of refusal, denial, decline, elimination.

King Saul: When King Saul disobeyed divine authority, he lost a series of blessings:

- He lost his divine appointment with Jehovah God.
- He lost favor before the priests and prophets of God.
- He lost the peace and joy of his life.
- He lost his royal destiny.
- He lost every blessing that he had received.
- He lost the legacy of inheritance that should have been passed on to his descendants.

1 Samuel 15:22-23
And Samuel said, Hath the LORD as great delight in burnt offerings and sacrifices, as in obeying the voice of the LORD? Behold, to obey is better than sacrifice, and to hearken than the fat of rams. For rebellion is as the sin of witchcraft, and stubbornness is as iniquity and idolatry. Because thou hast rejected the word

of the LORD, he hath also rejected thee from being king.

Obedience Is Better than Sacrifice: Simple obedience became a strong attraction for favor in the realms of Esther's life and destiny. Her obedience to parental instruction paid off from beginning to end. Obedience is an attribute which brings down the glory of God upon our life endeavors. **Esther 2:8-9** says:

> So it came to pass, when the king's commandment and his decree was heard, and when many maidens were gathered together unto Shushan the palace, to the custody of Hegai, *that Esther was brought also unto the king's house, to the custody of Hegai, keeper of the women.* And *the maiden pleased him*, and *she obtained kindness of him*; and he *speedily gave her her things for purification*, with such things as belonged to her, and *seven maidens, which were meet to be given her*, out of the king's house: and *he preferred her and her maids unto the best place of the house of the women.*

Prayer Points

- *I pray for restoration of favor upon my life.*
- *I pray that I would be favored among all friends and enemies.*
- *I pray that I would be preferred wherever I go.*

Concealment of Identity

> Esther had not shewed her people nor her kindred: for Mordecai had charged her that she should not shew it. And Mordecai walked every day before the court of the women's house, to know how Esther did, and what should become of her. (Esther 2:10-11)

Reasons Mordecai Walked the Court of the Women

- He was prepared to rescue Esther from evil in case her identity was revealed
- He was prepared to save her from the repercussion of being a Jew.

Prayer Points

- *I pray that I will not lack divine protection.*
- *I pray that the Lord will continually watch over me.*

Bridal Preparation

The manner of preparation to become a wife of a king was a rigorous process. The procedure demanded time for purity, smell, and beauty. Every good thing takes time to formulate. It is easier to destroy than to build.

Similarly, it is easier to curse than to bless. While it takes seconds to destroy out of intoxication and expression of anger, it is difficult to restore what has been destroyed in the same space of time.

Whilst it probably took a day or two to dethrone and banish Vashti from her royal position and from her family home, it took over two years to find a new wife for the king. The procedure of choosing a woman who could qualify as potential wife and queen was a long process.

The qualification of a woman to occupy such a position would include:

- Character and behavior
- Respect and reverence
- Personality and integrity

Preparation for Destiny

Consider your desire to be a bride to our Lord and Savior Jesus Christ, how much preparation would you need?

- If an earthly king demanded such a high level of preparation to choose a bride, why would the Savior not deserve a better preparation?
- Our entire lives on earth are invested in the preparation of our marriage to Jesus Christ our Lord and groom.
- From the day we confess Jesus Christ as our Lord and Savior, we enter into a dating relationship with him.
- From the moment we yield to the will of Jesus Christ our Lord, we advance into a courtship relationship with him.
- The wedding ceremony is the funeral procession to heaven.

- The marriage is when we are joined with Him after we have gone before the judgment throne, where we will be crowned as bride if we have been washed in the blood of the Lamb.

Anyone who has not been washed in the blood will not be accepted into the kingdom. Such a one will be thrown into the lake of fire as one will not be qualified to even stand before the judgment throne.

> **Esther 2:12-14**
>
> **Now when every maid's turn was come to go in to king Ahasuerus, after that she had been twelve months, according to the manner of the women, (for so were the days of their purifications accomplished, to wit, *six months with oil of myrrh*, and *six months with sweet odors*, and *with other things for the purifying of the women;*) then thus came every maiden unto the king; whatsoever she desired was given her to go with her out of the house of the women unto the king's house. In the evening she went, and on the morrow she returned into the second house of the women, to the custody of Shaashgaz, the king's chamberlain, which kept the concubines: she came in unto the king no more, except the king delighted in her, and that she were called by name.**

Contentment Attracts Favor

With simplicity and obedience to authority, Esther captured the various destinations leading into her destiny. She was peaceful and respectful. She was content with whatever she was given. She focused her ambition on managing the materials that were originally designed for her upkeep, instead of seeking what she did not need. Hence, her simplicity opened greater doors of favor within and around her.

> **Esther 2:15-16**
> Now when *the turn of Esther, the daughter of Abihail the uncle of Mordecai,* who had taken her for his daughter, was come to go in unto the king, *she required nothing but what Hegai the king's chamberlain, the keeper of the women, appointed.* And Esther obtained favour in the sight of all them that looked upon her. So *Esther was taken unto king Ahasuerus into his house royal in the tenth month, which is the month Tebeth, in the seventh year of his reign.*

Application

In order to achieve effective results in fasting, it is important that you identify the particular problems that need solution. Use the reflective questions provided to map out strategic solutions to the problems that affect your family members, environment, or anyone whom you intend to help besides yourself.

1. **List 3-5 lesson points that you have learned from today's reading.**

   _____
   _____
   _____
   _____
   _____

2. **Identify how the lesson affects you positively in 3-5 points.**

   _____
   _____
   _____
   _____
   _____

3. **Identify how you intend to use the lesson from today's passage to resolve your problem in 3-5 points.**

   _____
   _____
   _____
   _____
   _____

Day Six:
A Step into Royal Destiny

Favor Opens the Door to a Destiny

- The very first step into the presence of the king won her the royal inheritance that she had lost in King Saul.
- Lack of obedience caused King Saul to lose his divine favor and legacy to the royal blessings that the Lord had bestowed upon the Benjamites.
- Obedience later became the instrument that was needed for Esther to gain favor for the restoration of royalty to the tribe of Benjamin in a foreign land.
- Even in a foreign land, one can repossess what has been lost or misplaced.
- Royalty was flowing in Esther's DNA. She did not struggle for her position.

Esther 2:17-18

And *the king loved Esther above all the women,* **and** *she obtained grace and favour in his sight more than all the virgins; so that he set the royal crown upon her head, and made her queen instead of Vashti.* Then the king made a great feast unto all his princes and his servants, *even Esther's feast;* and he *made a release to the provinces, and gave gifts, according to the state of the king.*

Prayer Points

- *I pray that no matter the offence committed by a member of our family, we will not lose our divine blessings.*
- *I pray that no situation will reverse the blessing that the Lord bestows on our lives.*
- *I pray that we shall be restored even when we are not conscious of our legacy.*

Obedience Opens Door of Favor

Esther 2:19-20
And when the virgins were gathered together the second time, then Mordecai sat in the king's gate. Esther had not yet shewed her kindred nor her people; as Mordecai had charged her: *for Esther did the commandment of Mordecai, like as when she was brought up with him.*

Prayer Points

- *I pray that I shall be able to recognize our destiny propellers.*
- *I pray that I shall listen to and obey our destiny motivators.*
- *I pray that we shall be able to tolerate and endure our destiny supervisors.*

Esther 2:21-23
In those days, while Mordecai sat in the king's gate, two of the king's chamberlains,

Bigthan and Teresh, of those which kept the door, were wroth, and sought to lay hand on the king Ahasuerus. And the thing was known to Mordecai, who told it unto Esther the queen; and Esther certified the king thereof in Mordecai's name. And when inquisition was made of the matter, it was found out; therefore they were both hanged on a tree: and it was written in the book of the chronicles before the king.

Analysis: Reversing the Curse of Destiny Interference

King Ahasuerus was destined to marry women who emerged from royal descent. Both Vashti and Esther were descendants from royal ancestries. While Vashti was from King Nebuchadnezzar of Babylon's lineage, Esther was from King Saul of Israel's pedigree. Each of these women had lost their royal heritage before they found themselves in the palace of King Ahasuerus.

While Vashti was tragically captured in the midst of the pandemonium that ensued in the Babylonian palace following the assassination of her father King Belshazzar, the orphan girl Esther was honorably chosen among other young virgins who qualified to be a wife and a queen to the king.

While Vashti was an insolent woman who disrespected the Jewish people and enslaved them in the king's palace, as she caused them to work on the Sabbath, Esther was a humble woman who called for a fast to deliver the Jewish race from evil.

Interestingly, Nebuchadnezzar who destroyed the royal monarchy of Israel and sent the foreparents of Esther into exile in Persia, was the grandfather of Queen Vashti. Like her foreparents,

Queen Vashti dehumanized the Jews in Persia, until the curse of torment was reversed, and Esther took over her position.

In retrospect, a war that Nebuchadnezzar started as a powerful king who captured the kingdom of Israel and destroyed the temple of Jerusalem, was suddenly overturned in a manner that caused Vashti, his granddaughter, to suffer the consequences in a foreign land. The fact is that Jehovah God had promised Abraham and his descendants that thus, "**I will bless them that bless thee, and curse him that curseth thee: and in thee shall all families of the earth be blessed**" (Genesis 12:3).

Application

In order to achieve effective results in fasting, it is important that you identify the particular problems that need solution. Use the reflective questions provided to map out strategic solutions to the problems that affect your family members, environment, or anyone whom you intend to help besides yourself.

1. **List 3-5 lesson points that you have learned from today's reading.**

   _____
   _____
   _____
   _____
   _____

2. **Identify how the lesson affects you positively in 3-5 points.**

   _____
   _____
   _____
   _____
   _____

3. **Identify how you intend to use the lesson from today's passage to resolve your problem in 3-5 points.**

   _____
   _____
   _____
   _____
   _____

Strategic Prayer Solutions

The Problem

That the Lord will restore the legacy of our destiny.

The Situation

My family was cursed because of lack of obedience.
The sin of rebellion caused my family to lose
our divine blessing and identity.

The Goal

That my divine blessing will be restored to me
That my inheritance will be restored to me
That every curse will be reversed so that I can enjoy my destiny
That the favor of the Lord will surround me
so that there will be no struggle over
the restoration of my prosperity.
That I will be loved, accepted, honored, and celebrated.

Authority of Scripture

Esther 2:15, 17-18

Now when the *turn of Esther, the daughter of Abihail the uncle of Mordecai,* who had taken her for his daughter, was come to go in unto the king, *she required nothing but what Hegai the king's chamberlain, the keeper of the women, appointed.* And *Esther obtained favour in the sight of all them that looked upon her.*

And the king loved Esther above all the women, and she obtained grace and favour in his sight more than all the virgins; so that he set the royal crown upon her head, and made her queen instead of Vashti. Then the king made a great feast unto all his princes and his servants, *even Esther's feast*; and he *made a release to the provinces, and gave gifts, according to the state of the king.*

Prayer in Action:

Dear Lord and my God,
You are the Creator of the world and the knower of all things.
Blessings and honor be unto you.
You are worthy to be praised and adored.
You deserve all the glory, honor, and adoration.
Lord, I ask this day that you will forgive the sins of my forefathers.
O Lord, forgive that my divine blessing will be restored to me,
And that my inheritance will be restored to me.
O Lord, You have the power to make and unmake;
Therefore destroy the yoke of curses that is terrorizing my family,
That every curse will be reversed so that I can enjoy my destiny;
Father God, grant me your grace and mercy,
That the favor of the Lord will surround me so that there
will be no struggle over the restoration of my prosperity.
O Lord, let your blessings bring me unconditional favor
That I will be loved, accepted, honored, and celebrated.

Deliverance Warfare

In the name of Jesus Christ my Lord and Savior,
And with the authority in the blood of Jesus,
I uproot and cast out the spirit of rebellion and disobedience out of my life and family.
I uproot and cast out the spirit of rejection and dejection out of my life and family.
Let the fire of the Holy Spirit consume the tree of rebellion and disobedience from around my life, in Jesus's name
Let the blood of Jesus wash and cleanse every facet of my life endeavors.
Let the blood of Jesus release me from the curses that have been uprooted and cast out into the consuming fire.
In the name of Jesus, I uproot and cast out the spirit of depression and oppression;
Therefore I shall not perish, but shall have long life and prosperity, in Jesus's name.
In the name of Jesus, I cover my life and destiny with the blood of Jesus that was shed for me on the cross of Calvary.
In the name of Jesus I build a hedge of protection around my life with the fire of the Holy Ghost.
The arrows that fly by day and the terror by night shall not come after me nor interfere with me.
There shall be no enchantment or divination against me, in the name of Jesus Christ my Lord and Savior. Amen!

Breaking and Uprooting Curses: Curses Affecting My Destiny

In the name of Jesus, and with the authority in the blood of Jesus,
I bind and uproot the tree of curses planted against my life.
I speak to the tree of **curses affecting my destiny**
That affects my life.
You shall not prosper against my destiny.
I command you, tree of **curses affecting my destiny**
to be uprooted out of my destiny right now.
In the name of Jesus, you tree of **curses affecting my destiny** shall not prosper in my life.
Be uprooted out of my life and destiny right now, in the name of Jesus
Be cast out into the sea of destruction right now, in the name of Jesus
I shall not see you, tree of **curses affecting my destiny**
again, and you shall not come by me, in Jesus's name.
I shall not invite you, tree of **curses affecting my destiny**
again and you shall not harass me, in Jesus's name
I shall not entertain you, tree of **curses affecting my destiny**
again and you shall not terrorize my life, in Jesus's name.
Let the blood of Jesus separate me from the tree of **curses affecting my destiny** that steals the joy of my salvation.
Let the fire of the Holy Ghost destroy the root of
curses affecting my destiny that afflicts me.
The tree of **curses affecting my destiny** shall no
longer have access to me, in Jesus's name.
The tree of **curses affecting my destiny** shall no longer manifest within and around me again, in Jesus's name.
I am washed and cleansed by the blood of
Jesus Christ my Lord and Savior.
I am covered and sealed in the name of Jesus.
I am protected and guarded by the fire of the Holy Ghost. Amen!

Declaration and Thanksgiving

In the name of Jesus, I declare the repossession of my inheritance,
That I shall repossess any legacy that
belongs to me, in Jesus's name;
In the name of Jesus, I declare the restoration of my destiny,
That I shall be restored into my prosperity and
the place of honor, in Jesus's name;
In the name of Jesus, I declare favor and honor into my life,
That I shall be loved, accepted, honored,
and celebrated, in Jesus's name.
In the name of the Jesus, I declare that the faults of
my foreparent shall not hinder my blessings,
That I shall no longer bear the sins of
my parents and grandparents.
In the name of Jesus, I declare a total freedom into my life,
For the spirit of the dead and the grave shall not hunt the living,
Even as the Lord forgives and remembers my sins no more.
Therefore, I declare my life freed and released
from the past, in Jesus's name. Amen!

Thanksgiving:

Jehovah God, I thank You for the restoration of my royal destiny.
Thank You, Lord, that you have forgiven
the sins of my foreparents.
Thank you for releasing my family from the curse of rebellion
and disobedience that affected us through the past generations.
Thank you for uprooting the curse of
rejection from our family lineage.
Thank you for showing me your favor so that the
authorities of this world would honor me.
Thank you for promoting me from nobody to somebody.
Thank you for granting me total freedom and release
from the curse and bondage of the dead. Amen!

Declare and Decree

I decree favor upon my life,
Therefore, I call you, spirit of favor.
Come unto me.
Come into my life.

Prayer Observations and Experiences

You may remember your dreams and some past occurrences while doing this prayer. You may also receive a revelation. It's important that you make notes for future reference.

Experiences

_____
_____
_____
_____
_____
_____

Observations

_____
_____
_____
_____
_____
_____

Revelations

_____
_____
_____
_____
_____
_____

CHAPTER EIGHT

Third Chapter of Esther

Esther 3:1-15

After these things did king Ahasuerus promote Haman the son of Hammedatha the Agagite, and advanced him, and set his seat above all the princes that were with him. And all the king's servants, that were in the king's gate, bowed, and reverenced Haman: for the king had so commanded concerning him. But Mordecai bowed not, nor did him reverence. Then the king's servants, which were in the king's gate, said unto Mordecai, Why transgressest thou the king's commandment? Now it came to pass, when they spake daily unto him, and he hearkened not unto them, that they told Haman, to see whether Mordecai's matters would stand: for he had told them that he was a Jew. And when Haman saw that Mordecai bowed not, nor did him reverence, then was Haman full of wrath. And he thought scorn to lay hands on Mordecai alone; for they had shewed him the people of Mordecai: wherefore Haman sought to destroy all the Jews that were throughout the whole kingdom of Ahasuerus, even the people of Mordecai.

In the first month, that is, the month Nisan, in the twelfth year of king Ahasuerus, they cast Pur, that is, the lot, before Haman from day to day, and from month to month, to the twelfth month, that is, the month Adar. And Haman said unto king Ahasuerus, There is a certain people scattered abroad and dispersed among the people in all the provinces of thy kingdom; and their laws are diverse from all people; neither keep they the king's laws: therefore it is not for the king's profit to suffer them. If it please the king, let it be written that they may be destroyed: and I will pay ten thousand talents of silver to the hands of those that have the charge of the business, to bring it into the king's treasuries. And the king took his ring from his hand, and gave it unto Haman the son of Hammedatha the Agagite, the Jews' enemy. And the king said unto Haman, The silver is given to thee, the people also, to do with them as it seemeth good to thee. Then were the king's scribes called on the thirteenth day of the first month, and there was written according to all that Haman had commanded unto the king's lieutenants, and to the governors that were over every province, and to the rulers of every people of every province according to the writing thereof, and to every people after their language; in the name of king Ahasuerus was it written, and sealed with the king's ring. And the letters were sent by posts into all the king's provinces, to destroy, to kill, and to cause to perish, all Jews, both young and old, little children and women, in one day, even upon the thirteenth day of the twelfth month, which is the month Adar, and to take the spoil of them for a prey. The copy of the writing for a commandment to be given in every province was published unto all people, that they should be ready against that day. The posts went out, being hastened by the king's commandment, and the decree was given in Shushan the palace. And the king and Haman sat down to drink; but the city Shushan was perplexed.

Day Seven:
The Repercussion of Disobedience

Ancestral War Emerges as Generational Curse Looms

The book of Esther chapter 3 focuses on the emergence of ancestral war. It reveals how a curse starts to manifest when our prayer reaches up to heaven, and into the presence of Jehovah God. As soon as our prayer enters the presence of God, the realm of the spirit quakes and the problem escalates as though there is no help from above. The reason is that the problem trembles at the presence of the Lord as our prayer receives the breath of God. The breath of the Lord shakes the foundation of the problem, and causes pandemonium in the kingdom of darkness. The strongholds of satanic entities and workers of iniquity are thrown into mayhem. The impact of the chaos would seem as though there is increase in evil activities, but rather, the time of demonic atrocities is coming to an end. Each time you pray for a problem to be removed, the response from the Lord usually shakes the foundation of the problem and the camp of evil entities in charge is shaken. Like the impact of an earthquake or volcanic eruption, the situation is shaken to be uprooted from existence. Therefore, whenever you pray for an evil to be removed from your life and environment, expect a kind of shaking or an earthquake that will uproot the problem from interfering with you again. We read in **2 Samuel 22:14-18:**

> **The LORD thundered from heaven, and the most High uttered his voice. And he sent out arrows, and scattered them; lightning, and discomfited**

them. And the channels of the sea appeared, the foundations of the world were discovered, at the rebuking of the LORD, at the blast of the breath of his nostrils. He sent from above, he took me; he drew me out of many waters; he delivered me from my strong enemy, and from them that hated me: for they were too strong for me.

The Genesis of Esther's War

The origination of Esther's war can be traced down to a family dispute that emerged between a set of twin brothers—Esau and Jacob. The disagreement created a perpetual enmity between the descendants of the twin brothers of Esau **and Jacob.**

There might not be the same problem in your family, yet this information can empower you to help someone someday. In retrospect, you may use the wisdom gathered from this situation to examine similar situations in your environment. More often than not, we are surrounded by certain individuals who are petty and touchy. Such persons are unnecessarily sensitive and insecure. They exhibit strife and keep malice consciously and unconsciously. Their weaknesses rub off on us and we are somehow affected by their behavior and attitude.

Traditional Robbery

A war of robbery started when the twin brothers were conceived in the womb. Human tradition usually bestows family inheritance on the firstborn of a family, especially where males are concerned. The tradition of bequeathing a family's blessings on the first male son of a family oftentimes became a contention that divided family members and created perpetual enmity.

So it was that the predestination of two brothers was switched around by divine mandate. Even at their embryonic stage, the bane of tradition erupted a war in the womb, as the twin brothers fought over the legacy of their destiny. The older brother insisted on traditional protocol, while the younger one held on to divine order. The divine order of their destiny led to a struggle in the womb.

In view of the intensity of the war, Rebecca inquired of the Lord about her challenges with the pregnancy. The struggle over the agendas of the destiny of the unborn twins affected her physical and natural disposition. Initially, she had no idea that she was pregnant with twins.

During her enquiry, it was then revealed that Rebecca was pregnant with twins. The twins were not identical. They were two separate people with different agendas. Each of them was a nation. It was clearly stated that the older brother shall serve the younger one.

Genesis 25:21-26 states:

> **And Isaac intreated the LORD for his wife, because she was barren: and the LORD was intreated of him, and Rebekah his wife conceived. And the children struggled together within her; and she said, If it be so, why am I thus? And she went to enquire of the LORD. And the LORD said unto her, Two nations are in thy womb, and two manner of people shall be separated from thy bowels; and the one people shall be stronger than the other people; and the elder shall serve the younger. And when her days**

to be delivered were fulfilled, behold, there were twins in her womb. And the first came out red, all over like an hairy garment; and they called his name Esau. And after that came his brother out, and his hand took hold on Esau's heel; and his name was called Jacob: and Isaac was threescore years old when she bare them.

Traditional Interference

Whilst Rebecca kept the word of the Lord in her heart, Isaac held on to the tradition of birthright. He planned to transfer the Abrahamic covenant blessing to his first son Esau according to traditional procedure. He probably did not understand or remember what the Lord had said to him concerning the predestination of his children

The Value of a Plate of Dinner:

By divine order, Esau started to release his traditional birthright to Jacob unconsciously. He had despised his birthright and sold it to Jacob for a red pottage. Esau did not understand the consequences of selling his birthright. He did not realize that selling his birthright meant switching his blessings, and giving up his inheritance for a bowl of pottage. When Esau sold his birthright:

- He established the legal grounds for Jacob to take over his traditional position.
- He also gave Jacob the legal authority to inherit whatever belonged to him as the firstborn of the family.

- He unconsciously agreed with divine order on predestination.
- He legally relinquished his position and authority as the firstborn of the family.

The Exchange of Destiny:

Soon after, Jacob would take the blessing and inherit the Abrahamic covenant promise that his father Isaac inherited on behalf of Abraham's descendants.

When the season was ripe to transfer the Abrahamic blessings, Isaac resorted to traditional protocol, while Rebecca connected with divine order and predestination. As tradition demanded, Isaac ordered Esau to prepare a sumptuous dinner meal for him to eat, so that he would bless him. Rebecca responded by switching Isaac's traditional plan to transferring the blessing wrongfully. Already, Esau was walking in disobedience. He had married a wife from among a people whose way of life did not conform to the new belief system that Father Abraham had adopted for his family. Jacob escaped for his life, and the matter was kept in the doldrums.

The Emergence of a Lifetime Furor

The Amalekites were the descendants of Esau. Esau was the twin brother of Jacob. Esau was angry with Jacob and hated him. He purposed in his heart to kill Jacob for taking his supposed blessings.

Esau's attempted murder is not the first case. Cain killed Abel, his junior brother, in an indirect argument that resulted from envy and anger. Cain hated his junior brother Abel for offering an honorable sacrifice unto Jehovah God, while he offered unpleasant produce as sacrifice.

God accepted Abel's offering because it was healthy and beautiful. It came out of the best of his flock. Cain offering was rejected because it was the unwanted farm produce that was meant for the garbage. Cain's offering was without honor and fragrance. His offering was a mixture of rotten produce and thrash.

Like many of us, Cain did not realize that offerings should be a sacrifice from the best part of your firstfruit. God deserves the best and the firstfruit of our strength and effort. Instead, to make adjustment and correction, he decided to eliminate his brother Abel from existence.

The Quest for Vengeance

Over four hundred years later, when the descendants of Jacob were on their way from the land of slavery to inherit the Abrahamic Covenant promise, the descendants of Esau (the Amalekites) came out to attack Jacob's descendants (the Israelites) at a time when they were thirsty for water and weary in the wilderness.

The Israelites were forced to go to war against the Amalekites. Moses's hands were lifted up throughout the period of the war, until Israel prevailed. In view of that attack, the Lord God swore to wipe out the Amalekites from the face of the earth for attacking Israel to avenge the hatred of Esau against Jacob.

Esther's Involvement

Esther arrived about 550 years after the death of King Agag the Amalekite. Despite the length of time, both Haman the descendant of King Agag and Mordecai the descendant of King Saul were at war with each other as a result of a generational curse.

When a generational curse is looming, the victims would be compelled to tilt toward the impact of the curse. So when Haman became pompous in his self-important attitude, Mordecai refused to bow down to him. Hence, Haman became vicious and wanted to exterminate Mordecai and his people—King Saul's people and Jacob's descendants. Meanwhile in defence of the Abrahamic Covenant promise to the Israelites, Jehovah God promised to preserve and protect the Jews (Genesis 17: 1-8) but swore to extinguish the Amalekites (Genesis 17:14, Deuteronomy 25: 17-19).

> **Deuteronomy 25:17-19**
> **Remember what Amalek did unto thee by the way, when ye were come forth out of Egypt; how he met thee by the way, and smote the hindmost of thee, even all that were feeble behind thee, when thou wast faint and weary; and he feared not God. Therefore it shall be, when the LORD thy God hath given thee rest from all thine enemies round about, in the land which the LORD thy God giveth thee for an inheritance to possess it, that thou shalt blot out the remembrance of Amalek from under heaven; thou shalt not forget it.**

So, as a generational curse was threatening, God was preparing Esther for marriage with the king. God's strategy was meant to equip and empower Esther to uproot the ominous generational curse that was interfering with the peace of the Jewish race.

Application

In order to achieve effective results in fasting, it is important that you identify the particular problems that need solution. Use the reflective questions provided to map out strategic solutions to the problems that affect your family members, environment, or anyone whom you intend to help besides yourself.

1. **List 3-5 lesson points that you have learned from today's reading.**

   _____
   _____
   _____
   _____
   _____

2. **Identify how the lesson affects you positively in 3-5 points.**

   _____
   _____
   _____
   _____
   _____

3. **Identify how you intend to use the lesson from today's passage to resolve your problem in 3-5 points.**

   _____
   _____
   _____
   _____
   _____

Day Eight:
The Discovery of Generational Curses

A curse is a war. Every war has a cause and a beginning. Many people have an idea of the existence of curses, but some do not know that there are different types of curses. Similarly, many people do not know how to discover a particular curse that affects them, and how it started. Many of the problems that affect us in recent times are the result of unfinished wars that started many generations before some of us were born. Since we do not know how and when the plague started, we try to ignore it or live with it. In this discussion, you will learn how to discover the cause of the spiritual wars in your life and how to put an end to the problems that have plagued many generations in your family.

Generational Wars

The war that started between Esau and Jacob in the womb continued even unto the generation of Esther in a foreign land. While Esau and Jacob were in conception in the womb as twins, the pregnancy was terrorized with wars that affected their expectant mother, Rebecca.

> **Genesis 25:19-26**
> **And these are the generations of Isaac, Abraham's son: Abraham begat Isaac: And Isaac was forty years old when he took Rebekah to wife, the daughter of Bethuel the Syrian of Padanaram, the sister to Laban the Syrian.** *And*

Isaac intreated the LORD for his wife, because she was barren: and the LORD was intreated of him, *and Rebekah his wife conceived.* And *the children struggled together within her*; and she said, If it be so, why am I thus? *And she went to enquire of the LORD.* And the LORD said unto her, *Two nations are in thy womb, and two manner of people shall be separated from thy bowels; and the one people shall be stronger than the other people; and the elder shall serve the younger.* And when her days to be delivered were fulfilled, behold, *there were twins in her womb.* And *the first came out red*, all over like an hairy garment; and *they called his name Esau.* And *after that came his brother out*, and *his hand took hold on Esau's heel*; and *his name was called Jacob*: and Isaac was threescore years old when she bare them.

Prayer Points

- *That we will not take the word of the Lord for granted*
- *That we will watch over the prophetic word prayerfully*
- *That our pregnancy will not be conceived in confusion*
- *That our pregnancy will not attract curses*

Triggering the Manifestation of a Curse

Following their birth, as the twin brothers grew older, the war that emerged from the womb developed into a curse that would ardently affect their descendants and many generations after them. Soon, there will be an incident that would trigger the manifestation of the war that had started in the womb. One day, hunger for bread and red stew caused Esau to despise his birthright and sell it to Jacob his junior twin brother.

> **Genesis 25:29-34**
> And Jacob sod pottage: and Esau came from the field, and he was faint: And *Esau said to Jacob, Feed me, I pray thee, with that same red pottage; for I am faint:* therefore was his name called Edom. And Jacob said, *Sell me this day thy birthright.* And *Esau said, Behold, I am at the point to die: and what profit shall this birthright do to me?* And Jacob said, *Swear to me this day; and he sware unto him: and he sold his birthright unto Jacob.*

Prayer Points

- *That a need will not cause us to betray or despise our destiny*
- *That our weakness will not cause us to sell our birthright*
- *That we will think before we act or make an utterance*

Suffering the Curse

Once again, the quest for food would instigate the prenatal struggles that have been in the doldrums to resurface. This time, their parents would galvanize the trigger. Isaac their father requested Esau to give him food to eat so that he would switch the Abrahamic Covenant blessing around for Esau's benefit. Then Rebecca their mother intercepted the request and empowered Jacob to provide the meal so that the blessings would not be switched around as it happened at their birth. Hence, Jacob received the Abrahamic Covenant blessing before Esau returned from the field. By receiving the Abrahamic blessing from Isaac, Jacob also gained the advantage of the birthright that Esau had sold out to him as a payment for eating the red porridge.

The action of both parents stirred up a riot in the family between the twin brothers Esau and Jacob. Without considering the fact that they were twins from the same womb, Esau became angry and hated Jacob. Then Esau vowed to kill Jacob. *Esau's anger and hatred for Jacob continued to loom from generation to generation through the Amalekites until the days of Haman the Agagite.* Haman was seeking revenge from the curses that emanated from the struggles that ensued during the conception of Esau and Jacob. The struggle went through the days of King Agag, until the two descendants from many generations of Jacob and Esau met again in a foreign land.

> **Genesis 27:41-46**
> **And Esau hated Jacob because of the blessing wherewith his father blessed him: and Esau said in his heart, the days of mourning for my father are at hand; then will I slay my brother Jacob. And these words of Esau her elder son were told**

to Rebekah: and she sent and called Jacob her younger son, and said unto him, Behold, thy brother Esau, as touching thee, doth comfort himself, purposing to kill thee. Now therefore, my son, obey my voice; and arise, flee thou to Laban my brother to Haran; And tarry with him a few days, until thy brother's fury turn away; Until thy brother's anger turn away from thee, and he forget that which thou hast done to him: then I will send, and fetch thee from thence: why should I be deprived also of you both in one day? And Rebekah said to Isaac, I am weary of my life because of the daughters of Heth: if Jacob take a wife of the daughters of Heth, such as these which are of the daughters of the land, what good shall my life do me?

Prayer Points

- *That I will not hate or be hated to the point of destruction of life*
- *That I will not purpose in my heart to kill anyone*

Identifying Generational Curses Esau's Anger Manifested in His Descendants, the Amalekites

It is very easy for anger and strife to become the root of a generational curse. It is important to identify the curse and deal with it before it germinates into one's personal life and becomes a tree that bears fruit from one generation to another. Esau's anger and hatred for Jacob turned into a generational curse and a war that lingered between their descendants after several hundred years.

Over four hundred years had passed since Esau and Jacob parted ways following the fiasco that resulted from the exchange of blessings and payment of the birthright. Although Jacob had made a vivid attempt to establish peace between Esau and himself, Esau's children would not let go. Esau's descendants were still seeking vengeance against Jacob and his descendants.

Out of anger, Esau hated Jacob and vowed to kill him. Over four hundred years later when the descendants of Jacob were coming out of slavery, and on their way to inherit the Abrahamic Covenant blessings, the anger and hatred that Esau had planted against Jacob suddenly emerged in the Amalekites who attacked Israel at the point of thirst and weariness.

The Amalekites recognized the fact that the Israelites were on their way to inherit their blessings and to possess the Promised Land. Hence, they tried to hinder them from doing so.

The Amalekites Are Descendants of Esau

> **Genesis 36:12, 16**
> **And Timna was concubine to Eliphaz Esau's son; and she bare to Eliphaz Amalek: these were the sons of Adah Esau's wife.**
>
> **Duke Korah, duke Gatam, and duke Amalek: these are the dukes that came of Eliphaz in the land of Edom; these were the sons of Adah.**

We pick up the story of the generations affected by this curse at **Exodus 17:1-16:**

And all the congregation of the children of Israel journeyed from the wilderness of Sin, after their journeys, according to the commandment of the LORD, and pitched in Rephidim: and *there was no water for the people to drink.* Wherefore the people did chide with Moses, and said, Give us water that we may drink. And Moses said unto them, Why chide ye with me? wherefore do ye tempt the LORD? *And the people thirsted there for water*; and the people murmured against Moses, and said, Wherefore is this that thou hast brought us up out of Egypt, to kill us and our children and our cattle with thirst? And *Moses cried unto the LORD, saying, What shall I do unto this people?* they be almost ready to stone me. And the *LORD said unto Moses, Go on before the people, and take with thee of the elders of Israel; and thy rod, wherewith thou smotest the river, take in thine hand, and go. Behold, I will stand before thee there upon the rock in Horeb; and thou shalt smite the rock, and there shall come water out of it, that the people may drink. And Moses did so in the sight of the elders of Israel.* And he called the name of the place Massah, and Meribah, because of the chiding of the children of Israel, and because they tempted the LORD, saying, Is the LORD among us, or not?

Then came Amalek, and fought with Israel in Rephidim. And Moses said unto Joshua, Choose us out men, and go out, fight with Amalek: to morrow I will stand on the top of the hill with the rod of God in mine hand. So Joshua did as Moses had said to him, *and fought with Amalek*: and Moses, Aaron, and Hur went up to the top of the hill. And it came to pass, *when Moses held up his hand, that Israel prevailed: and when he let down his hand,* Amalek prevailed. But *Moses' hands were heavy*; and *they took a stone, and put it under him, and he sat thereon; and Aaron and Hur stayed up his hands, the one on the one side, and the other on the other side; and his hands were steady until the going down of the sun. And Joshua discomfited Amalek and his people with the edge of the sword.* And the LORD said unto Moses, *Write this for a memorial in a book, and rehearse it in the ears of Joshua: for I will utterly put out the remembrance of Amalek from under heaven.* And Moses built an altar, and called the name of it *Jehovahnissi*: for he said, *Because the LORD hath sworn that the LORD will have war with Amalek from generation to generation.*

Deuteronomy 25:19:

Therefore it shall be, when the LORD thy God hath given thee rest from all thine enemies round about, *in the land which the LORD thy God giveth thee for an inheritance to possess it, that thou shalt blot out the remembrance of Amalek from under heaven; thou shalt not forget it.*

1 Chronicles 4:42:

And some of them, even of the sons of Simeon, five hundred men, went to mount Seir, having for their captains Pelatiah, and Neariah, and Rephaiah, and Uzziel, the sons of Ishi.

1 Chronicles 4:43:

And they smote the rest of the Amalekites that were escaped, and dwelt there unto this day.

Application:

In order to achieve effective results in fasting, it is important that you identify the particular problems that need solution. Use the reflective questions provided to map out strategic solutions to the problems that affect your family members, environment, or anyone whom you intend to help besides yourself.

1. **List 3-5 lesson points that you have learned from today's reading.**

   _____
   _____
   _____
   _____
   _____

2. **Identify how the lesson affects you positively in 3-5 points.**

   _____
   _____
   _____
   _____
   _____

3. **Identify how you intend to use the lesson from today's passage to resolve your problem in 3-5 points.**

   _____
   _____
   _____
   _____
   _____

Day Nine:
An Unpleasant Inheritance

Characteristic Trait

Haman the Agagite was an Amalekite and the descendant of Esau. His great grandfather was a chief of Edom—Chief Amalek. Esau was given the name Edom because of his love for *red* pottage (Genesis 25:30). Haman inherited the anger of his great ancestor Esau. As Esau was, so was Haman.

Haman was the king's favorite, as Esau his ancestor was Isaac's favorite son. He was promoted above all the captive princes. He was the king's confidant and prime minister. He was so influential that the king's servants were commanded to bow before him and give him reverence. Unknown to the king, Haman was deceitful, arrogant, and vengeful. Unfortunately, Mordecai would not condescend to Haman's boastful attitude. Rather, Mordecai adhered to his Jewish principles not to adore Haman, especially because of his insolence. As a Jew, Mordecai's religion forbade him to pay such an extravagant reverence to an Amalekite, a nation that God had sworn to wipe off the surface of the earth (Exodus 17:16). Mordecai would not share the glory of God with mankind—or with a wicked man in the person of Haman.

Haman's Plot for Revenge

While observers reported Mordecai's refusal to pay homage to Haman, Haman also took notice of Mordecai's attitude. Since Haman was an insolent person, Mordecai's action hurt the pride that grew deeply in him. Although everyone in the nation bowed but only one person refused, his anger burned so hot that his happiness disappeared from him. So Haman decided to yank off the head of Mordecai so that he could gain his pleasure. Therefore, out of a selfish heart, Haman decided that the head that refuses to bow to him (Haman) must be taken to the gallows.

As much as Saul the Benjamite spared Agag the Amalekite and as a result paid the price for sparing Agag with his royal destiny and life, Haman was not prepared to show any form of gratitude. Rather, he desired to wipe away the Jewish race from the surface of the earth. Since Israel was then a captive state that had become one of the provinces under King Ahasuerus's kingdom, Haman's plot was to eradicate all the Jews that lived within the empire.

Esther 3:1-6
After these things did king Ahasuerus promote Haman the son of Hammedatha the Agagite, and advanced him, and set his seat above all the princes that *were* with him. And all the king's servants, that *were* in the king's gate, bowed, and reverenced Haman: for the king had so commanded concerning him. *But Mordecai bowed not, nor did him reverence.* **Then the king's servants, which *were* in the king's gate, said unto Mordecai, Why transgressest thou the king's commandment? Now it came to**

> pass, when they spake daily unto him, and he hearkened not unto them, that *they told Haman, to see whether Mordecai's matters would stand: for he had told them that he was a Jew.* And when Haman saw that Mordecai bowed not, nor did him reverence, then was Haman full of wrath. And he thought scorn to lay hands on Mordecai alone; for they had shewed him the people of Mordecai: *wherefore Haman sought to destroy all the Jews that were throughout the whole kingdom of Ahasuerus, even the people of Mordecai.*

Haman Indulges in Divination

More often than not, people in authority indulge in some form of clairvoyance or divination to influence their operation in the human realm. Most of the people who operate in the corridors of power do seek spiritual assistance by either holding on to the Christian faith that believes Jesus Christ as our Lord and Savior, or affiliating themselves with some secret cults that practice magic and divination. Some dignitaries may declare themselves as belonging to the Christian faith, yet consult the services of clairvoyants and magicians to aid their public activities and maintain their status quo in the corridors of power. The desire to be influential makes some dignitaries gullible in the hands of the powers of darkness. Individuals who are power drunken can be diabolical and nefarious, as it was in the character of Haman.

Haman exhibited deceitfulness in every bit of his character and position as the second person in command in the Persian kingdom.

Despite his status quo in the kingdom, Haman relied on divination and the occult to gain superficial influence over the king and the kingdom.

Haman surrounded himself with soothsayers and diviners to empower himself to carry out the plot against Mordecai and the Jews. Without a divination, he would probably not be able to convince the king to support his wickedness. He also needed the soothsayers to select the lucky date that would favor his satanic plot. Haman performed the divination for about a year. He deliberately engaged the powers of darkness to execute diabolical activities against the Jews.

> **Esther 3:7**
> **In the first month, that is, the month Nisan, in the twelfth year of king Ahasuerus, they cast Pur, that is, the lot, before Haman from day to day, and from month to month, to the twelfth month, that is, the month Adar.**

Prayer Points

- *That there shall be no enchantment against the righteous*
- *That the divination of the wicked shall not prosper*
- *That any diabolical activity performed against us shall fail*
- *The wisdom of the wicked shall be turned into folly*
- *That any deliberate attempt made on our lives shall fail*

Haman the Destroyer of Destiny

Haman attempted to revenge the curse of destruction that was originally planted by Esau. In his original plan, Esau vowed to kill Jacob. Over four hundred years later, the Amalekites attacked Jacob's descendants in the wilderness when they were thirsty and weary from their journey. So the Lord gave the Israelites the command to eradicate them from the surface of the earth. Hence Saul was given the mandate to carry out that assignment but he disobeyed.

Many years later, Haman the Agagite, an Amalekite and descendant of Esau was plotting another war of destruction. Instead of dealing with the person who offended him, he wanted to deal with a whole human race—the Jewish race.

> **Esther 3:8-9**
> **And Haman said unto king Ahasuerus, There is a certain people scattered abroad and dispersed among the people in all the provinces of thy kingdom; and their laws are diverse from all people; neither keep they the king's laws: therefore it is not for the king's profit to suffer them.** *If it please the king, let it be written that they may be destroyed:* **and** *I will pay ten thousand talents of silver to the hands of those that have the charge of the business, to bring it into the king's treasuries.*

Haman gave a false impression about the Jews. He accused them falsely and lied against them. He was envious of them. He lusted for their wealth.

Since the Jews were very lucrative business people and paid high revenue to the king's treasury, their massacre would be a great loss of income to the Persian government, so Haman convinced the king that he would pay an equivalent of such losses to the king's treasury. Without a thought for tomorrow and continuity of the expansion of his kingdom, the king was foolishly convinced as he accepted Haman's offer of ten thousand talents, which would probably be a month's revenue.

Since Haman indulged in diabolical activities, it could be assumed that he had used divination to hypnotize the king, so that King Ahasuerus would consent to the satanic plot against such a great economic and financial venture in the empire.

Prayer Points

- *Uproot the spirit of envy and jealousy*
- *That no one will plot evil against me and I will also not do so*
- *Uproot the spirit of false accusation and deception from my environment and relationships*
- *That the authorities will thoroughly and fairly investigate all accusations against me instead of compromising with the destruction of souls*

Haman Influences Spiritual Wickedness in High Places

Haman was so persuasive that he was able to win the heart of the king to agree with his wicked and deceptive plot. Hence, the king gave him his signet ring as an open authority to use his signature and royal seal to carry out the destruction. *Esau hated Jacob and purposed* in his heart to kill him. Haman also hated Mordecai and plotted to eradicate him (Mordecai) and his people.

The king who was supposed to protect his people gave them up for destruction instead. If the people are destroyed, whom will the king rule over?

> **Esther 3:10-11**
> And *the king took his ring from his hand, and gave it unto Haman the son of Hammedatha the Agagite, the Jews' enemy.* **And the king said unto Haman, The silver is given to thee, the people also, to do with them as it seemeth good to thee.**

Prayer Points

- *That we will not destroy the people that we are supposed to care for*
- *That the enemy will not steal our minds and influence us to do evil*
- *That the love of money will not influence our decision making*
- *That our loved ones will not manipulate us to commit atrocities*

Haman Disintegrated King Ahasuerus with Liquor

Liquor is a weapon of destruction used by the powers of darkness to mobilize evil.

- Haman had a close relationship with the king.

- He knew how to manipulate the king to adhere to his decisions.
- Having lured the king with deception to empower Haman to annihilate the Jews, he was afraid that the king might change his mind when he sobered up from the intoxication of liquor.
- Haman realized the severity of the decree that had been published.
- Haman therefore engaged the king in drinking until his consciousness totally disappeared from him.
- Haman then cajoled the king to seal the decree in the state of stupor.

King Ahasuerus's Weakness

The king was known to lose control of himself whenever he was under the influence of alcohol. The king had lost his queen Vashti because of a decision made under the influence of alcohol. Once again, having manipulated him to agree to a wicked offer, Haman used alcoholic wine to disarm the thinking ability of the King Ahasuerus. While the city of Shushan was perplexed, Haman deliberately engaged the king in a drinking party, so that he would not be aware of what was happening in the kingdom.

> **Esther 3:12-15**
> **Then were the king's scribes called on the thirteenth day of the first month, and there was written according to all that Haman had commanded unto the king's lieutenants, and to the governors that were over every province, and**

to the rulers of every people of every province according to the writing thereof, and *to* every people after their language; *in the name of king Ahasuerus was it written, and sealed with the king's ring.* **And the letters were sent by posts into all the king's provinces, to destroy, to kill, and to cause to perish, all Jews, both young and old, little children and women, in one day, even upon the thirteenth day of the twelfth month, which is the month Adar, and to take the spoil of them for a prey. The copy of the writing for a commandment to be given in every province** *was published unto all people, that they should be ready against that day.* **The posts went out, being hastened by the king's commandment, and the decree was given in Shushan the palace.** *And the king and Haman sat down to drink; but the city Shushan was perplexed.*

Prayer Points

- *That the work of iniquity fashioned against me shall not prosper*
- *Uproot the handwriting of ordinances written against me*
- *Erase the publication of evil report planted and published against my destiny*
- *That the enemy will not have the opportunity to blindfold me and distract my attention in any situation*

Songs of Inspiration
Teach Me Thy Way O Lord

Words: Benjamin M. Ramsey, 1919.
Music*: **Camacha, Benjamin M. Ramsey**

Teach me Thy way, O Lord, teach me Thy way!
Thy guiding grace afford, teach me Thy way!
Help me to walk aright, more by faith, less by sight;
Lead me with heav'nly light, teach me Thy way!

When I am sad at heart, teach me Thy way!
When earthly joys depart, teach me Thy way!
In hours of loneliness, in times of dire distress,
In failure or success, teach me Thy way!

When doubts and fears arise, teach me Thy way!
When storms o'erspread the skies, teach me Thy way!
Shine through the cloud and rain, through sorrow, toil and pain;
Make Thou my pathway plain, teach me Thy way!

Long as my life shall last, teach me Thy way!
Where'er my lot be cast, teach me Thy way!
Until the race is run, until the journey's done,
Until the crown is won, teach me Thy way!

Application:

In order to achieve effective results in fasting, it is important that you identify the particular problems that need solution. Use the reflective questions provided to map out strategic solutions to the problems that affect your family members, environment, or anyone whom you intend to help besides yourself.

1. **List 3-5 lesson points that you have learned from today's reading.**

   _____
   _____
   _____
   _____
   _____

2. **Identify how the lesson affects you positively in 3-5 points.**

   _____
   _____
   _____
   _____
   _____

3. **Identify how you intend to use the lesson from today's passage to resolve your problem in 3-5 points.**

   _____
   _____
   _____
   _____
   _____

Strategic Deliverance Prayer

The Problem

That the enemy will not gain approval to
destroy me (or the righteous)

The Situation

False accusation is being raised against me.
Someone is attempting to influence an evil decision against me.
An evil report has been written against my promotion.
There is envy and jealousy around me
(or my colleagues and friends).

The Goal

That the enemy will not influence the authority over
my life to compromise with satanic verses
That the workers of iniquity will not be empowered to
make decisions in my environment and territory
That the enemy will not publish evil
against me (and my loved ones)

Authority of Scripture

Esther 3:15

The posts went out, being hastened by the king's commandment, and the decree was given in Shushan the palace. *And the king and Haman sat down to drink; but the city Shushan was perplexed.*

Esther 3:8-9

And Haman said unto king Ahasuerus, There is a certain people scattered abroad and dispersed among the people in all the provinces of thy kingdom; and their laws are diverse from all people; neither keep they the king's laws: therefore it is not for the king's profit to suffer them. *If it please the king, let it be written that they may be destroyed*: and *I will pay ten thousand talents of silver to the hands of those that have the charge of the business, to bring it into the king's treasuries*

Prayer in Action

Blessed be the name of our Lord God Almighty
Blessings and honor be unto You, O Lord.
Glory and adoration be onto Your holy name.
Your name is holy.
Your name is righteous.
Your name is glorious.
Your name is righteous.
Your name is beautiful.
At the mention of Your name,
Every knee shall bow and every tongue shall confess You as Lord.
Your name is healing.
Your name is deliverance.
Your name is signs and wonders.
Your name is miracle.
At the mention of Your name,
The floodgates of heavens are opened
And the powers of the earth are subdued.
Thanks You, Lord, for giving us the name that
is above every other name. Amen!

Deliverance Warfare

In the name of Jesus Christ my Lord and Savior,
I uproot and cast out the spirit of divination and manipulation
that influences decision making over my life and environment.
In the name of Jesus, I uproot and cast out the spirit of conspiracy
that publishes false accusation against me (or the righteous).
In the name of Jesus I uproot and cast out the spirit of mass
destruction that publishes satanic verses against me (or the righteous).
Let the blood of Jesus wash and cleanse me from the powers of darkness.
Let the blood of Jesus wash and cleanse me from the workers of iniquity.
Let the consuming fire of the Holy Ghost destroy the
handwriting of satanic verses written against me.
Let the fire of the Holy Ghost consume the arrows that
fly by day and the terror sent against me by night.
Let the power of the blood of Jesus Christ that was shed
on the cross set me free and release me from satanic
annihilation and destruction, in Jesus's name.
Let the atoning blood of Jesus Christ cover and protect
me and my loved one from evil, in Jesus's name.
In the name of Jesus I uproot and cast out the
spirit of depression and oppression,
Therefore I shall not perish, but shall have long
life and prosperity, in Jesus's name.
In the name of Jesus, I cover my life and destiny with the
blood of Jesus that was shed for me on the cross of Calvary.
In the name of Jesus I build a hedge of protection
around my life with the fire of the Holy Ghost.
The arrows that fly by day and the terror by night
shall not come after me nor interfere with me.
There shall be no enchantment or divination against me,
in the name of Jesus Christ my Lord and Savior. Amen!

Breaking and Uprooting Curses: Tree of Ancestral Enmity and Wars

In the name of Jesus, and with the authority in the blood of Jesus
I bind and uproot the tree of curses planted against my life.
I speak to the tree of **ancestral enmity and wars** that affects my life.
You shall not prosper in my destiny.
I command you, curse of **ancestral enmity and wars**
to be uprooted out of my destiny right now.
In the name of Jesus, you tree of **ancestral enmity and wars** shall not prosper in my life.
Be uprooted out of my life and destiny right now, in the name of Jesus.
Be cast out into the sea of destruction right now, in the name of Jesus.
I shall not see you, tree of **ancestral enmity and wars**
again and you shall not come by me, in Jesus's name.
I shall not invite you, tree of **ancestral enmity and wars**
again and you shall not harass me, in Jesus's name.
I shall not entertain you, tree of **ancestral enmity and wars**
again and you shall not terrorize my life, in Jesus's name.
Let the blood of Jesus separate me from the curse of **ancestral enmity and wars** that steals the joy of my salvation.
Let the fire of the Holy Ghost destroy the root of
ancestral enmity and wars that afflicts me.
The tree of **ancestral enmity and wars** shall no
longer have access to me, in Jesus's name.
The tree of **ancestral enmity and wars** shall no longer
manifest within and around me again, in Jesus's name.
I am washed and cleansed by the blood of
Jesus Christ my Lord and Savior.
I am covered and sealed in the name of Jesus.
I am protected and guarded by the fire of the Holy Ghost. Amen!

Declaration

In the name of Jesus and with the authority in the
blood of Jesus Christ my Lord and Savior,
I declare a divine protection over my life
and destiny, in Jesus's name.
In the name of Jesus, I declare that no weapon
fashioned against me shall prosper,
And every tongue that shall rise up against me shall fail.
In the name of Jesus, I declare that I shall not share
the glory of the Almighty God with anyone.
And the spirit of Haman shall not compel
me to worship a human authority
In the name of Jesus, I declare that no man shall
exhibit the spirit of Haman in my life,
And I shall not entertain any demonic
influence from Hamanic spirit.
In the name of Jesus, I surround my life with the fear of
God and the presence of the Most High God. Amen!

Prayer Observations and Experiences

You may remember your dreams and some past occurrences while doing this prayer. You may also receive a revelation. It's important that you make notes for future reference.

1. **List 3-5 lesson points that you have learned from today's reading.**

   _____
   _____
   _____
   _____
   _____

2. **Identify how the lesson affects you positively in 3-5 points.**

   _____
   _____
   _____
   _____
   _____

3. **Identify how you intend to use the lesson from today's passage to resolve your problem in 3-5 points.**

   _____
   _____
   _____
   _____
   _____

CHAPTER NINE

Fourth Chapter of Esther

Esther 4:1-17

When Mordecai perceived all that was done, Mordecai rent his clothes, and put on sackcloth with ashes, and went out into the midst of the city, and cried with a loud and a bitter cry; and came even before the king's gate: for none might enter into the king's gate clothed with sackcloth. And in every province, whithersoever the king's commandment and his decree came, there was great mourning among the Jews, and fasting, and weeping, and wailing; and many lay in sackcloth and ashes. So Esther's maids and her chamberlains came and told it her. Then was the queen exceedingly grieved; and she sent raiment to clothe Mordecai, and to take away his sackcloth from him: but he received it not.

Then called Esther for Hatach, one of the king's chamberlains, whom he had appointed to attend upon her, and gave him a commandment to Mordecai, to know what it was, and why it was. So Hatach went forth to Mordecai unto the street of the city, which was before the king's gate. And Mordecai told him of all that had happened unto him, and of the sum of the money that Haman had promised to pay to the king's treasuries for the Jews, to destroy them. Also he gave him the copy of the writing of the decree that was given at Shushan to destroy them, to shew it unto Esther, and to declare it unto her, and to charge her that she should go in unto the king, to make supplication unto him, and to make request before him for her people. And Hatach came and told Esther the words of Mordecai. Again Esther spake unto Hatach, and gave him commandment unto Mordecai; All the king's servants, and the people of the king's provinces, do know, that whosoever, whether man or woman, shall come unto the king into the inner court, who is not called, there is one law of his to put him to death, except such to whom the king shall hold out the golden sceptre, that he may live: but I have not been called to come in unto the king these thirty days. And they told to Mordecai Esther's words. Then Mordecai commanded to answer Esther, Think not with thyself that thou shalt escape in the king's house, more than all the Jews. For if thou altogether holdest thy peace at this time, then shall there enlargement and deliverance arise to the Jews from another place; but thou and thy father's house shall be destroyed: and who knoweth whether thou art come to the kingdom for such a time as this? Then Esther bade them return Mordecai this answer, Go, gather together all the Jews that are present in Shushan, and fast ye for me, and neither eat nor drink three days, night or day: I also and my maidens will fast likewise; and so will I go in unto the king, which is not according to the law: and if I perish, I perish. So Mordecai went his way, and did according to all that Esther had commanded him.

Day Ten:
The Cry for Deliverance

Practical Steps to Deliverance

Mordecai's approach to his deliverance may seem raw and uncultured, but he needed to get down to the root of his problem. The matter at hand demanded that he risk his life because of the situation that could be as dangerous as being slaughtered like a hopeless animal. Therefore, he decided to pace the front of the king's palace in mourning attire, which was not permitted. Appearance in the king's palace in a mournful apparel was an abomination that called for serious repercussion, yet Mordecai decided to risk his life for the deliverance of his people—the Jewish race.

The Revenge Mission

Unresolved anger creates bitterness. Unhealed bitterness is a breeding ground for the germination of a curse. Any hatred that is brewed from protracted anger will grow up into an outburst of wrath which usually results in destruction of life.

Imagine that the disagreement between Esau and Jacob traversed over thousands of years, so that their posterity remained enemies over Abrahamic Covenant promise. Esau's hatred for Jacob turned into a curse that would haunt nations of their posterity. Hence, thousands of years later, Haman the descendant of Esau and King Agag the Amalekite were still fighting the major war that was generated between a set of twin brothers. In retrospect,

Haman hated Mordecai as Esau hated Jacob. Haman plotted to kill Mordecai and the Jewish people as Esau purposed in his heart to kill Jacob.

Haman the Destiny Destroyer

Just like Esau and the Amalekites his descendants, Haman's thoughts and plans were wrought in anger. A mango tree does not bear apple's fruit. Haman thought the best way to satisfy his selfish ambition was to eliminate the descendants of Jacob. Every Jew represents Jacob and the Israelites just as every Amalekite represents Esau and King Agag.

Esther's Response

> **Esther 4:1-2**
> **When Mordecai** *perceived all that was done*, **Mordecai** *rent his clothes*, **and** *put on sackcloth with ashes*, **and** *went out into the midst of the city, and cried with a loud and a bitter cry*; **and** *came even before the king's gate*: **for** *none might enter into the king's gate clothed with sackcloth.*

Prayer Points

- *That the Lord will grant me wisdom to discover the root of my problems*

- *That I will take humble steps to uproot the chronic problems that affect generations of my foreparents to the present*

Esther 4:3-4

And in *every province,* **whithersoever the king's commandment and his decree came, *there was great mourning among the Jews, and fasting, and weeping, and wailing; and many lay in sackcloth and ashes.* So Esther's maids and her chamberlains came and told it her. Then was *the queen exceedingly grieved*; and *she sent raiment to clothe Mordecai,* and *to take away his sackcloth from him: but he received it not.***

Seeking Knowledge

Esther 4:5

Then called Esther for Hatach, **one of the king's chamberlains, whom he had appointed to attend upon her, and *gave him a commandment to Mordecai, to know what it was, and why it was.***

Prayer Points

- *That I will seek to know the truth of a matter with understanding*
- *That I will not make decisions without knowing the truth*

Steps to Uprooting Generational Curses

The procedure to uprooting generational curses demands a high level of trust and honesty. The victim of a curse must be sincere with the presentation of the matter. A curse cannot be uprooted if the truth of the matter is hidden. A person cannot uproot a tree that exists in the spirit realm or physical realm without first investigating the root cause. Do not assume that people know what you are thinking or expecting until you have stated the problem as it is.

Mordecai did not despise Esther or the errand man Hatach in the matter of presenting the core of the problem. As an errand man, Hatach was entrusted with the destiny of the problem that needed urgent attention. Hatach presented himself as a wise and submissive royal servant as he presented the messages entrusted into his hands with care and wisdom—as it was, so that there was no record of misinformation or misinterpretation.

It is very crucial that when we are chosen to mediate as royal servants in a matter of this nature, we should be credible and God-fearing because the repercussion of our failure or complacency may lead to destruction of destiny. When we need help, we must be able to say exactly what we need by presenting the details with sincerity.

> **Esther 4:6-9**
> So Hatach went forth to Mordecai unto the street of the city, which was before the king's gate. And *Mordecai told him of all that had happened unto him*, and of the *sum of the money that Haman had promised to pay to the king's treasuries for the Jews, to destroy them.* Also *he gave him the copy of the writing of the decree that was given at Shushan to destroy them, to shew it*

unto Esther, **and** to declare it unto her, **and** to charge her **that** she should go in unto the king, to make supplication unto him, **and** to make request before him for her people. **And Hatach came and told Esther the words of Mordecai.**

Prayer Points

- *That I will identify the problem that affects me*
- *That I will not despise the status of the people who are appointed to assist me*
- *That I will understand the kind of solution that is needed*
- *That I will utilize our position wisely*
- *That I will consider the destiny of others besides myself*
- *That the enemy will not sell my destiny for selfish gain*

The Risk involved in Uprooting Curses

Curses are dangerous and the process of breaking and uprooting the tree that bears a curse can also be perilous. All the parties involved in the process of demolishing a curse must be well equipped and prepared. The process of breaking and uprooting curses is a confrontation with the enemy. The whole procedure sets a battle array, and the warriors must be alert and up to the task to defeat and destroy the root of the curse in order to erase the matter from existence.

Hence, all the parties involved in the process of uprooting the Hamanic curse that was set against the descendants of Jacob had to risk their lives in the heart of the matter. Although the matter concerned the deliverance of the Jews from the Hamanic plot, Hatch the royal servant, together with the maidens who served the queen, joined forces with Esther to gamble their lives with the royal colony, as the Hamanic plot carried the king's seal. Mordecai's life was already in jeopardy. No matter the threat involved, Esther's marriage had to be used as instrument of deliverance in the heart of the matter.

Esther 4:10-12

Again Esther spake unto Hatach, and *gave him commandment* unto Mordecai; All the king's servants, and the people of the king's provinces, do know, that whosoever, whether man or woman, shall come unto the king into the inner court, who is not called, *there is one law of his to put him to death, except such to whom the king shall hold out the golden sceptre*, that he may live: but *I have not been called to come in unto the king these thirty days. And they told to Mordecai Esther's words.*

Prayer Points

- *That we will know the importance of risking our lives for our loved ones*
- *That we will trust the Lord to turn the law of the land around for our favor*
- *That we will seek knowledge in order to deal with the root of the matter*
- *That we will not be afraid to release the truth that makes free*

Application:

In order to achieve effective results in fasting, it is important that you identify the particular problems that need solution. Use the reflective questions provided to map out strategic solutions to the problems that affect your family members, environment, or anyone whom you intend to help besides yourself.

1. **List 3-5 lesson points that you have learned from today's reading.**

   _____
   _____
   _____
   _____
   _____

2. **Identify how the lesson affects you positively in 3-5 points.**

   _____
   _____
   _____
   _____
   _____

3. **Identify how you intend to use the lesson from today's passage to resolve your problem in 3-5 points.**

   _____
   _____
   _____
   _____
   _____

Day Eleven:
Marriage as an Instrument of Wisdom

Wisdom is a formulation of solutions that one devises in time of need. When there is no trouble, one may never know the importance of one's relationship or status in a place or situation. Usually, you do not know the ability that you possess until there arises a need for it. Likewise, where there is no problem, there is no need for solution. Therefore wisdom is the ability to devise solutions in the time of a problem or challenge that is beyond human comprehension.

Marriage can either be used as an instrument of godly wisdom or a weapon of abuse and destruction. The Philistines used marriage as a weapon of abuse and destruction against Samson and his ministry on earth. Thus the Philistines used Samson's wife to lure and subject him to suffer satanic assault. So, Samson ended up a blind man and perished with his enemies.

God ordained marriage as a blessing to advance his purpose on earth. No matter the situation that surrounds a marriage, God can always turn it into a blessing if we cry to him for deliverance.

When Vashti was thrown out of her royal status and relationship, little did anyone know that the situation was a divine providence to prepare a way for the deliverance of the Jewish race from Esauic captivity.

Every marriage has a purpose. Some marriages are divinely orchestrated, while some are satanically influenced. Sometimes a divinely predestinated marriage may not be in a pattern that seems morally correct, yet the Lord designed it to fulfill a mandate. Sometimes what the enemy planned for evil can also be turned around by the act of prayer and fasting to glorify the name of the Lord.

Esther's orphan status and adoption by an uncle were part of the preparations that the Lord had predestined for the deliverance of the Jewish race. No one imagined that a teenage orphan would ever be used as a mediator through marriage to deliver the Jewish race from an Esauic curse. Once upon a time, there was a young lady called Miriam. Miriam assisted the mother in the act of Moses's deliverance from Pharaohic destruction. Miriam's role was phenomenal as the love for her baby brother empowered her to walk the dangerous banks of the river Nile in a bid to deliver him (Moses) from the mouth of the crocodiles and the reptile-infested environment of the river.

God has always used both males and females to perform acts of deliverance beyond human comprehension. Women have always been part of God's gracious agenda for the salvation and deliverance of mankind. This time around, it was the turn of an orphan teenage girl named Hadassah. Just like little Miriam, Hadassah's transformation from an orphan to a queen registered her name and personality in the corridors of power beyond an ordinary dream and human ability. Her transformation was a great promotion that influenced her existence. As evergreen myrtle, she was a sweet fragrance that deserved to be a star and happiness for a people. Beyond ordinary marriage, the evergreen Hadassah mounted the royal throne of "stardom."

- Esther's marriage was divinely orchestrated.
- It was a marriage of purpose.
- It was a marriage of destiny fulfillment.
- It was a marriage of deliverance.
- It was a marriage of stardom.
- It was a marriage of great influence.

The statement "for such a time as this" reveals that Esther came into the royal marriage as an instrument of deliverance to rescue the Jewish race from perishing.

From the days of Esau's conflict with Jacob, marriage has been an instrument that has been to either devise a problem or a solution in destiny-oriented matters. Soon after Esau had lost his blessing of the Abrahamic Covenant promise, he married from among the women of Canaan, who displeased his parents, Isaac and Rebecca (Genesis 36:2). In view of that, Rebecca admonished Jacob not to marry from the same choice of people—the daughters of Canaan. Hence, Jacob was sent to Laban's house. When Esau realized that his choices displeased his parents and that Jacob was sent to Padan Aram to go marry from his mother's family house, he also decided to take a wife from Ishmael's family house (Ishmael was the son of Abraham from Haggai) in addition to the wives he had (Genesis 27:46; 28:6-9).

Now Mordecai used the royal marital status of Esther as an instrument of wisdom to devise deliverance for the Jews. So he reminds Esther of her royal status and charges her to utilize it for the benefit of her people in verse 14: "**and who knoweth whether thou art come to the kingdom for such a time as this?**" Until that very moment, no man, including the Jews, thought of the need to honor Esther's royal status in the Persian kingdom. Even if her marriage had been despised because of the pattern of the king's flirtations with so many women and concubines, God would use the foolishness of the governmental laws to establish his purpose in us and on earth.

Esther 4:13-17

Then Mordecai commanded to answer Esther, Think not with thyself that thou shalt escape in the king's house, more than all the

Jews. For if thou altogether holdest thy peace at this time, then shall there enlargement and deliverance arise to the Jews from another place; but thou and thy father's house shall be destroyed: and who knoweth whether thou art come to the kingdom for such a time as this? Then Esther bade *them* return Mordecai *this answer, Go, gather together all the Jews that are present in Shushan, and fast ye for me, and neither eat nor drink three days, night or day: I also and my maidens will fast likewise; and so will I go in unto the king, which is not according to the law: and if I perish, I perish.* So Mordecai went his way, and did according to all that Esther had commanded him.

Prayer Points

- That we will know and realize the importance of our marriage to certain individuals
- That our marriage will be an instrument to devise wisdom for solutions
- That our marital relationship will be established in the appropriate season when it will be a benefit to the purpose and plans of God
- That our marriage will be a benefit and blessing to our loved ones

Songs of Inspiration
It Is Well with My Soul

Words: Horatio G. Spafford, 1873.
Music: Ville du Havre, Philip P. Bliss, 1876 (MIDI, score). The tune is named after the ship on which Spafford's children perished, the S.S. *Ville de Havre*. Ironically, Bliss himself died in a tragic train wreck shortly after writing this music.

> When peace, like a river, attendeth my way,
> When sorrows like sea billows roll;
> Whatever my lot, Thou has taught me to say,
> It is well, it is well, with my soul.

Refrain

> *It is well, with my soul,*
> *It is well, with my soul,*
> *It is well, it is well, with my soul.*
> Though Satan should buffet, though trials should come,
> Let this blest assurance control,
> That Christ has regarded my helpless estate,
> And hath shed His own blood for my soul.

Refrain

> My sin, oh, the bliss of this glorious thought!
> My sin, not in part but the whole,
> Is nailed to the cross, and I bear it no more,

Praise the Lord, praise the Lord, O my soul!

Refrain

> For me, be it Christ, be it Christ hence to live:
> If Jordan above me shall roll,
> No pang shall be mine, for in death as in life
> Thou wilt whisper Thy peace to my soul.

Refrain

> But, Lord, 'tis for Thee, for Thy coming we wait,
> The sky, not the grave, is our goal;
> Oh trump of the angel! Oh voice of the Lord!
> Blessèd hope, blessèd rest of my soul!

Refrain

> And Lord, haste the day when my faith shall be sight,
> The clouds be rolled back as a scroll;
> The trump shall resound, and the Lord shall descend,
> Even so, it is well with my soul.

Refrain

This hymn was written after two major traumas in Spafford's life. The first was the great Chicago Fire of October 1871, which ruined him financially (he had been a wealthy businessman). Shortly after, while crossing the Atlantic, all four of Spafford's daughters died in a collision with another ship. Spafford's wife Anna survived and sent him the now famous telegram, "Saved alone." Several weeks later, as Spafford's own ship passed near the spot where his daughters died, the Holy Spirit inspired these words. They speak to the eternal hope that all believers have, no matter what pain and grief befall them on earth.

Application

In order to achieve effective results in fasting, it is important that you identify the particular problems that need solution. Use the reflective questions provided to map out strategic solutions to the problems that affect your family members, environment, or anyone whom you intend to help besides yourself.

1. **List 3-5 lesson points that you have learned from today's reading.**

   _____
   _____
   _____
   _____
   _____

2. **Identify how the lesson affects you positively in 3-5 points.**

   _____
   _____
   _____
   _____
   _____

3. **Identify how you intend to use the lesson from today's passage to resolve your problem in 3-5 points.**

   _____
   _____
   _____
   _____
   _____

Strategic Deliverance Prayer:

The Problem

Need to use my status to devise solutions
against generational curse

The Situation

Satanic verses have been concocted against me (the righteous)
Workers of iniquity want to annihilate me (the righteous)
Have limited time to devise solution to rescue me from perishing
Need boldness to confront my challenges and difficulties
That I will not be ashamed to cry out for my deliverance

The Goal

Need wisdom to approach the authority concerned
Need a faithful person to relate to in time of difficulties
That my voice will be heard in the corridors of power
That there will be no betrayal of trust during this season
That God will intervene and deliver us from evil
That the Lord will hold up peace from the people
concerned until the matter is resolved

Authority of Scripture

Esther 4:13-14

Then Mordecai commanded to answer Esther, *Think not with thyself that thou shalt escape in the king's house, more than all the Jews. For if thou altogether holdest thy peace at this time, then shall there enlargement and deliverance arise to the Jews from another place; but thou and thy father's house shall be destroyed: and who knoweth whether thou art come to the kingdom for such a time as this?*

Prayer in Action

Jehovah Boreh, the God of Creation,
The God who created and established marriage,
The God who gave us marriage for a blessing
and advancement of mankind,
The God who blessed marriage and commanded
fruitfulness and multiplication,
You are Jehovah Adon Olam, the Master of the World.
You have power and control over the rising of
the sun and the going down of the same.
You cause the heavens to open and pour out rain,
And you also cause the sky to shut up and hold back the waters.
You are Jehovah El ha-Gibbor, our Great Warrior
And the Conqueror of all battles.
Jehovah God, my battles belong to You,
For You are my Lord and Savior.
You are able to rescue me from perishing
in the hand of the wicked one.
O Lord, do not allow the iniquitous to gain advantage over me.
O Lord, set your eyes upon me and deliver
me from nefarious entities
Who have plotted atrocities with their handwriting against me.
O Lord, cause them to lose their peace and make them restless
Until the dread of the wickedness fails
and all atrocities are nullified.

Deliverance Warfare

In the name of Jesus and with the authority in the blood of Jesus,
I command the power of the Most High
God to come down on my behalf.
In the name of Jesus Christ, I decree the counsel of the Almighty God
That the blood of Jesus Christ that was shed for me
shall speak louder than the blood of Abel.
Therefore let every tree of curse that is planted against me be
uprooted and cast into the fire right now, in the name of Jesus.
Let the handwriting of atrocities that was written since
the days of my foreparents be uprooted and cast into
the fire of destruction right now, in Jesus's name.
Let the workers of iniquity that gather against me
be scattered right now, in the name of Jesus.
Let every satanic verse that is concocted be turned
into foolishness right now, in the name of Jesus.
Let my marriage be an instrument of wisdom that
crushes satanic weapons, in Jesus's name.
In the name of Jesus, I uproot and cast out the
spirit of depression and oppression;
Therefore I shall not perish, but shall have long
life and prosperity, in Jesus's name.
In the name of Jesus, I cover my life and destiny with the
blood that was shed for me on the cross of Calvary.
In the name of Jesus, I build a hedge of protection
around my life with the fire of the Holy Ghost.
The arrows that fly by day and the terror by night
shall not come after me nor interfere with me.
There shall be no enchantment or divination against me in
the name of Jesus Christ my Lord and Savior. Amen!

Breaking and Uprooting Curses: Satanic Verses Written Against My Destiny

In the name of Jesus, and with the authority in the blood of Jesus, I bind and uproot the tree of curses planted against my life.
I speak to the tree of **satanic verses written against my destiny** that affects my life.
You shall not prosper against my destiny.
I command you, curse of **satanic verses written against my destiny** to be uprooted out of my destiny right now
In the name of Jesus, you tree of **satanic verses written against my destiny** shall not prosper in my life.
Be uprooted out of my life and destiny right now, in the name of Jesus.
Be cast out into the sea of destruction right now, in the name of Jesus.
I shall not see you, tree of **satanic verses written against my destiny** again and you shall not come by me, in Jesus's name.
I shall not invite you, tree of **satanic verses written against my destiny** again and you shall not harass me, in Jesus's name.
I shall not entertain you, tree of **satanic verses written against my destiny** again and you shall not terrorize my life, in Jesus's name.
Let the blood of Jesus separate me from the curse of **satanic verses written against my destiny** that steals the joy of my salvation.
Let the fire of the Holy Ghost destroy the root of **satanic verses written against my destiny** that afflicts me.
The tree of **satanic verses written against my destiny** shall no longer have access to me, in Jesus's name.
The tree of **satanic verses written against my destiny** shall no longer manifest within and around me again, in Jesus's name.
I am washed and cleansed by the blood of Jesus Christ my Lord and Savior.
I am covered and sealed in the name of Jesus.
I am protected and guarded by the fire of the Holy Ghost. Amen!

Declaration

In the name of Jesus I decree and declare the
counsel of the Word of God upon my life,
That the Word and blessings of the most
High God shall be manifested in me.
In the name of Jesus, I declare and decree that whatever
I bind on earth shall be bound in heaven,
And whatever I loose and release on earth
shall be manifested in heaven.
In the name of Jesus I declare and decree that every satanic
verse concocted against me shall not prosper but fail.
I declare and decree that my voice for deliverance
shall be heard and respected, in Jesus's name.
I declare and decree that my cry for help shall not be
despised but shall be honored, in Jesus's name.
I declare and decree that my status and marriage shall be a well
of wisdom that devises solutions for destiny, in Jesus's name.
I declare and decree that I shall gain favor of my
spouse in time of trouble, in Jesus's name.
I declare and decree that I shall have access into the presence
of my Lord and king freely, in Jesus's name. Amen!

Prayer Observations and Experiences

You may remember your dreams and some past occurrences while doing this prayer. You may also receive a revelation. It's important that you make notes for future reference.

Experiences

_____
_____
_____
_____
_____
_____

Observations

_____
_____
_____
_____
_____
_____

Revelations

_____
_____
_____
_____
_____
_____

CHAPTER TEN

Fifth Chapter of Esther

Esther 5:1-14

Now it came to pass on the third day, that Esther put on her royal apparel, and stood in the inner court of the king's house, over against the king's house: and the king sat upon his royal throne in the royal house, over against the gate of the house. And it was so, when the king saw Esther the queen standing in the court, that she obtained favour in his sight: and the king held out to Esther the golden sceptre that was in his hand. So Esther drew near, and touched the top of the sceptre. Then said the king unto her, What wilt thou, queen Esther? and what is thy request? it shall be even given thee to the half of the kingdom. And Esther answered, If it seem good unto the king, let the king and Haman come this day unto the banquet that I have prepared for him. Then the king said, Cause Haman to make haste, that he may do as Esther hath said. So the king and Haman came to the banquet that Esther had prepared. And the king said unto Esther at the banquet of wine, What is thy petition? and it shall be granted thee: and what is thy request? even to the half of the kingdom it shall be performed. Then answered Esther, and said, My petition and my request is; If I have found favour in the sight of the king, and if it please the king to grant my petition, and to perform my request, let the king and Haman come to the banquet that I shall prepare for them, and I will do to morrow as the king hath said.

Then went Haman forth that day joyful and with a glad heart: but when Haman saw Mordecai in the king's gate, that he stood not up, nor moved for him, he was full of indignation against Mordecai. Nevertheless Haman refrained himself: and when he came home, he sent and called for his friends, and Zeresh his wife. And Haman told them of the glory of his riches, and the multitude of his children, and all the things wherein the king had promoted him, and how he had advanced him above the princes and servants of the king. Haman said moreover, Yea, Esther the queen did let no man come in with the king unto the banquet that she had prepared but myself; and to morrow am I invited unto her also with the king. Yet all this availeth me nothing, so long as I see Mordecai the Jew sitting at the king's gate. Then said Zeresh his wife and all his friends unto him, Let a gallows be made of

fifty cubits high, and to morrow speak thou unto the king that Mordecai may be hanged thereon: then go thou in merrily with the king unto the banquet. And the thing pleased Haman; and he caused the gallows to be made.

Day Twelve:
Marriage as an Instrument of Deliverance

Wisdom and Strategies to Uproot Generational Curses

Although God has a purpose for establishing marriage, people marry for different reasons. Every race and culture handles marriage differently. While some cultural settings see marriage as an expansion of family ties, some see it as opportunity to break away from their traditional families. In certain cultures marriage is seen as advancement in family possession of wealth, while in certain cultures it is a minus in their financial wealth or pubic status. In certain environments, the choice of a spouse is a great and careful decision that demands investigation and involvement of a group of family members because of the personality involved and the expectations.

Once upon a time in certain Christian communities, intending partners were compelled to seek the divine counsel before a proposal was made, in order to ensure that one was married into divine connection and fulfillment. This could be said of the choice that Abraham desired for his son Isaac. Abraham refused for Isaac to marry from a people that he did not trust to accept his faith in Jehovah God. Rebecca also passed on the same message to Jacob in order to maintain the Abrahamic Covenant.

Mordecai could be referred to as a prophet in the case of Esther. Mordecai saw through the eyes of a prophet as he had mentored and groomed Hadassah to become an instrument of deliverance. Hence, marriage became the vehicle on which to ride on to the palace where her assignment would be carried out. Some of the instructions that

Mordecai gave to Hadassah were very peculiar, especially the need to conceal her identity.

Hadassah's obedience and submission earned her a great honor. In the process, her beloved uncle Mordecai was promoted and her people, the Jewish race, were delivered. Her marriage became a great instrument for deliverance from destruction. Although the deliverance did not come easy as it was full of dangerous moves, the perfect will of God prevailed because of the principle of divine intervention.

Esther assumed some dangerous but perfect strategies toward deliverance:

1. Esther targeted the third day of the fast. Third day represents resurrection power, as when Jesus rose from the dead and the grave.
2. Esther wore her royal apparel to attract the king's attention. The king delighted in his royalty and yearned to be pleased with matters that promoted his royal majesty. Esther's appearance in her royal apparel was likely to stir up a desire for her majesty.
3. Esther took a strategic position that would likely capture the king's attention and tantalize him to grant her favor.
4. While the king sat upon the throne—*over against* the gate of the house, Queen Esther also stood—*over against* the king's house. Esther applied wisdom in a manner that conformed to the emotional disposition of the king at that very moment.
5. Esther did not only fast for divine intervention, but also for wisdom to capture the king's attention and attract favor of love and acceptance. It's one thing to be loved, but it's another dimension to be accepted. Esther also fasted and prayed for strategic moves and presentation that would

arouse an excitement for tolerance and endurance until her petition was granted and established in the king's heart.
6. Before Esther asked, the king felt the heart of the queen and positioned himself to satisfy her.

Esther 5:1-2

Now it came to pass on the third day, that *Esther put on her royal apparel,* and *stood in the inner court of the king's house,* *over against* the king's house: and the king sat upon his royal throne in the royal house, *over against* **the gate of the house. And it was so, when the king saw Esther the queen standing in the court,** *that she obtained favour in his sight*: **and the** *king held out to Esther the golden sceptre* **that was in his hand. So Esther drew near, and** *touched the top of the sceptre.*

Prayer Points

- *That I will know how to position myself to attract the king's attention*
- *That my personal appearance and countenance will attract favor of love and acceptance*

Wisdom to Make Petitions

In every situation, we need the application of either common sense or wisdom. Some situations require the use of common sense, while some require more than common sense. However, common sense usually motivates the application of wisdom. Common sense opens the door for one to take initiative. Common sense often calls for help or assistance whenever it is needed. Pride has no respect for common sense, therefore arrogance opens the door for foolishness and stupidity to take over a simple matter and turn it into a big issue. Lack of common sense often leads to embarrassment.

Mordecai respected common sense by asking for help from an adopted daughter who had become a royal queen and the wife to King Ahasuerus. By asking for assistance, Mordecai humbled himself and opened the door for wisdom which also attracted favor to resolve the matter at hand.

> **Esther 5:3-5**
> **Then said the king unto her, *What wilt thou, queen Esther? And what is thy request? it shall be even given thee to the half of the kingdom.* And Esther answered, If *it seem* good unto the king, *let the king and Haman come this day unto the banquet that I have prepared for him.* Then the king said, *Cause Haman to make haste, that he may do as Esther hath said.* So the king and Haman came to the banquet that Esther had prepared.**

Prayer Points

- *That the Lord will hear my cry even before my petition is presented*

- *That my petition will be respected and honored with a sense of urgency*

The King's Heart Falls into Esther's Bosom

Esther had succeeded in arousing favor from the depth of the king's heart. Esther had been able to tantalize the king's heart to the point that the king could not wait for Esther to make her request. He kept urging Esther with an open assurance for fulfillment. This was the point where Esther probably experienced a divine intervention with the King.

For the second time, the king would pull out Esther's heart with the same question as indicated thus in **Esther 5:6: "And the king said unto Esther at the banquet of wine,** *What is thy petition?* **And** *it shall be granted thee***: and** *what is thy request? even to the half of the kingdom it shall be performed."*

Esther Tested the Sincerity of the King's Heart

Despite the fact that the king urged Esther with the same words and also encouraged her with the same language over and over again to make her petition, Esther applied so much wisdom in testing the water. She needed to build a strong foundation of success and victory. The matter was so dangerous and delicate because the victim (Haman) might turn around to be the judge of the case.

Esther did not take the king's words for granted. Despite the king's promises, Esther acted carefully, because Haman was a vicious person and he was very close to the king. The relationship between Haman and the king was too strong for Esther to interfere with or be foolish with. Esther needed further assurance to win her case. So she bridled her tongue and held her peace until favor was strongly established. Esther would rather test the favor granted her than make a hasty petition that would jeopardize her life.

> **Esther 5:7-8**
> Then answered Esther, and said, *My petition and my request is; If I have found favour in the sight of the king, and if it please the king to grant my petition, and to perform my request, let the king and Haman come to the banquet that I shall prepare for them, and I will do tomorrow as the king hath said.*

Prayer Points

- *That I would not make hasty presentation that will jeopardize my life*
- *That I would know how to apply wisdom in all matters that concerns my deliverance*
- *That the Lord would grant me unlimited and unconditional favor*

Haman's Anger Destroys his Prosperity

Anger is a destroyer of destiny and hatred is a manufacturer of disaster. Wherever there is anger, a life is frustrated. Wherever there is hatred, a destiny is threatened. Even as light and darkness can never dwell together, so anger and joy cannot be a joint force for peace. When light comes, darkness must disappear because the presence of light is righteousness and Jesus is the Light of the World.

Haman was a man of darkness whose heart harbored iniquity. Haman was an entity of destruction that had no fear of God, yet he occupied a high position of authority as the prime minister of Persia. So he had the opportunity to harness spiritual wickedness in high places as an agent of Satan who related with the powers and principalities of darkness.

Haman may probably be possessed and controlled by one of the princes of Persia who hindered the spiritual atmosphere during the days of Daniel's prayer in Babylon.

Due to the wickedness of Haman's heart, he could not know joy. Both joy and gladness represent the fruit of the Spirit (as we are told in the New Testament in Galatians 5:22), so Haman could not retain them for too long because his heart was full of evil.

Even his wealth, promotion, and the multitude of his children could not fetch him a sense of joy or peace, because of his spiritual poverty.

Spiritual Poverty Haunts Haman's Prosperity

Haman was materially very rich and physically prosperous, but lacked spiritual wealth. He was poor in spirit and in truth. He lacked the fruit of the Spirit because material wealth could not satisfy his soul and spirit being. Haman had no relationship with Jehovah God and lacked the fear of God in his natural self. Hence he says, in verse 13, **"Yet all this availeth me nothing, so long as I see Mordecai the Jew sitting at the king's gate."**

Haunted by the Guilt of Evil

Wow! This is scary! How can a man be so poor in spirit that he could not retain a piece of joy in his heart after such a great and meritorious acquisition of wealth and status? Haman was haunted by the guilt of the evil that he had plotted against the Jews. An evil man runs even when no one pursues him. Haman was living under the torment of wickedness. Nothing else pleased Haman than the work of evil. So he was happy to erect a gallows for human destruction.

> **Esther 5:9-14**,
>
> *Then went Haman forth that day joyful and with a glad heart: but when Haman saw Mordecai in the king's gate, that he stood not up, nor moved for him, he was full of indignation against Mordecai.* Nevertheless Haman refrained himself: and when he came home, he sent and called for his friends, and Zeresh his wife. And *Haman told them of the glory of his riches, and the multitude of his children, and all the things wherein the king had promoted him*, and *how he had advanced him above the princes and servants of the king.* Haman said moreover, *Yea, Esther the queen did let no man come in with the king unto the banquet that she had prepared but myself; and tomorrow am I invited unto her also with the king. Yet all this availeth me nothing, so long as I see Mordecai the Jew sitting at the king's gate.* Then said Zeresh his wife and all his friends unto him, *Let a gallows be made of fifty cubits high, and tomorrow speak*

thou unto the king that Mordecai may be hanged thereon*:** then ***go thou in merrily **with the king unto the banquet.** *And the thing pleased Haman; and he caused the gallows to be made.*

Prayer Points

- *That the enemy of my life will never know peace*
- *That joy and gladness will be missing from the heart of the evil conspirators against my life*
- *That those who conspire against me shall never rest or know peace*
- *That the devisors or evil shall lack joy and gladness*

Songs of Inspiration
We Have an Anchor

Words: Priscilla J. Owens, 1882.
Music: William J. Kirkpatrick

Will your anchor hold in the storms of life,
When the clouds unfold their wings of strife?
When the strong tides lift and the cables strain,
Will your anchor drift, or firm remain?

Refrain

We have an anchor that keeps the soul
Steadfast and sure while the billows roll,
Fastened to the Rock which cannot move,
Grounded firm and deep in the Savior's love.
It is safely moored, 'twill the storm withstand,
For 'tis well secured by the Savior's hand;
And the cables, passed from His heart to mine,
Can defy that blast, thro' strength divine.

Refrain

It will surely hold in the Straits of Fear—
When the breakers have told that the reef is near;
Though the tempest rave and the wild winds blow,
Not an angry wave shall our bark o'erflow.

Refrain

> It will firmly hold in the Floods of Death—-
> When the waters cold chill our latest breath,
> On the rising tide it can never fail,
> While our hopes abide within the Veil.

Refrain

> When our eyes behold through the gath'ring night
> The city of gold, our harbor bright,
> We shall anchor fast by the heav'nly shore,
> With the storms all past forevermore.

Refrain

Application

In order to achieve effective results in fasting, it is important that you identify the particular problems that need solution. Use the reflective questions provided to map out strategic solutions to the problems that affect your family members, environment, or anyone whom you intend to help besides yourself.

1. **List 3-5 lesson points that you have learned from today's reading.**

   _____
   _____
   _____
   _____
   _____

2. **Identify how the lesson affects you positively in 3-5 points.**

   _____
   _____
   _____
   _____
   _____

3. **Identify how you intend to use the lesson from today's passage to resolve your problem in 3-5 points.**

   _____
   _____
   _____
   _____
   _____

Strategic Deliverance Prayer

The Problem

Need wisdom to go before the authorities with my petition

The Situation

Need to know how to approach the king with an important matter
Need wisdom to make petition without creating
an offence that would nullify my petition
Need to test the authourities' favor to establish my request

The Goal

That the king will hear my heart's cry before I present my petition;
That the king will encourage me constantly
until my victory is established;
That the enemy of my life will never know peace;
That joy and gladness will be missing from the heart
of the evil conspirators against my life;
That those who conspire against me shall not know rest or peace;
That the devisors of evil shall lack joy and gladness;
That I will not make a hasty presentation that would jeopardize my life;
That I will know how to apply wisdom in all
matters that concern my deliverance;
That the Lord will grant me unlimited and unconditional favor;
That the Lord will hear my cry even before my petition is presented;
That my petition will be respected and honored with a sense of urgency;
That I will know how to position myself to attract the authority's attention;
That my personal appearance and countenance
will attract favor of love and acceptance.

Authority of Scripture

Esther 5:6

And the king said unto Esther at the banquet of wine, *What is thy petition*? And *it shall be granted thee*: and *what is thy request? even to the half of the kingdom it shall be performed.*

Prayer in Action

My Father in Heaven, Hallowed be Thy name;
You are Jehovah Raah—My great Shepherd;
The One who watches over my life;
You are Jehovah Tsidkenu—the God of Righteousness;
The One who clothes me with mercy and grace;
You are Jehovah Shammah—The Ever-present One;
The One who surrounds me with divine favor
And hears me when I call.
Blessed be Your name and the works of Your hand.
O Lord, hear my petition this day,
Even as you heard the cry of Queen Esther
And granted her favor before the authority.
O Lord, attend unto my prayer, that the enemy
of my life will never know peace until he has
turned away from plotting evil against me.
O Lord, take over my battle,
That joy and gladness will be missing from the
hearts of those who threaten my life until the
conspirators of evil are swallowed in poverty.
O Lord, dismantle the strongholds of iniquity that the
devisers of evil shall not prosper in doing evil.
O Lord, grant me wisdom, that I will not make a hasty
presentation that would jeopardize my request and favor.
O Lord, teach me how to apply wisdom in all matters
that concern my deliverance, and grant me unlimited
and unconditional favor in my daily endeavors.
O Lord, let your mercy prevail over my life, and cause the
authority to feel my heart even before I ask, so that my petition
will be respected and honored with a sense of urgency.
O Lord, teach me to position myself to attract the authority's
attention, that my personal appearance and countenance
will attract favor of love and acceptance. Amen!

Deliverance Warfare

In the name of Jesus and with the authority in the blood of Jesus, I stand on the authority of the Word of God to raise a standard against the powers and principalities of darkness in the air, on the land and in the sea. In the name and authority in the blood of Jesus, I command that any satanic stronghold that conspires against me shall not prosper. In the name and by the authority in the blood of Jesus, I command that the workers of iniquity and the conspirators of evil shall not rest and never know peace or joy in their lives until they have repented from doing evil. In the name of Jesus and by the authority in the blood of Jesus, let the conspirators of evil be scattered and let their works be consumed in the fire of destruction. In the name of Jesus and by the authority in the blood of Jesus, let the stronghold of the workers of iniquity be uprooted and cast into the sea of destruction. In the name of Jesus I uproot and cast out the spirit of depression and oppression, Therefore I shall not perish, but shall have long life and prosperity, in Jesus's name. In the name of Jesus, I cover my life and destiny with the blood of Jesus that was shed for me on the cross of Calvary. In the name of Jesus, I build a hedge of protection around my life with the fire of the Holy Ghost. The arrows that fly by day and the terror by night shall not come after me nor interfere with me. There shall be no enchantment or divination against me, in the name of Jesus Christ my Lord and Savior. Amen!

Breaking and Uprooting Curses: Curses of False Accusation

In the name of Jesus, and with the authority in the blood of Jesus, I bind and uproot the tree of curses planted against my life. I speak to the tree of **false accusation** that affects my life. You shall not prosper against my destiny. I command you, curse of **false accusation** to be uprooted out of my destiny right now. In the name of Jesus, you tree of **false accusation** shall not prosper in my life. Be uprooted out of my life and destiny right now, in the name of Jesus. Be cast out into the sea of destruction right now, in the name of Jesus. I shall not see you, tree of **false accusation** again and you shall not come by me, in Jesus's name. I shall not invite you, tree of **false accusation** again, and you shall not harass me, in Jesus's name I shall not entertain you, tree of **false accusation** again, and you shall not terrorize my life, in Jesus's name. Let the blood of Jesus separate me from the curse of **false accusation** that steals the joy of my salvation. Let the fire of the Holy Ghost destroy the root of **false accusation** that afflicts me. The tree of **false accusation** shall no longer have access to me, in Jesus's name. The tree of **false accusation** shall no longer manifest within and around me again, in Jesus's name. I am washed and cleansed by the blood of Jesus Christ my Lord and Savior. I am covered and sealed in the name of Jesus. I am protected and guarded by the fire of the Holy Ghost. Amen!

Declaration

In the name of Jesus and with the authority in the blood of Jesus, I stand on the authority in the word of the Lord to declare and decree favor upon my life and destiny.
Even as it is written in the book of Esther 5:6**, that "the king said unto Esther at the banquet of wine,** *What is thy petition?* **And** *it shall be granted thee*: **and** *what is thy request? even to the half of the kingdom it shall be performed."*
So shall it be, that I shall receive a double portion of the favor that the Lord granted unto Queen Esther and her people, in the name of Jesus Christ my Lord and Savior.
Therefore, I declare and decree that the king shall love and accept me, in Jesus's name. Amen!
I declare and decree that the workers of iniquity shall not prosper in their conspiracy, in Jesus's name.
I declare and decree that the king will hear my heart's cry before I present my petition, in Jesus's name.
I declare and decree that the king will encourage me constantly until my victory is established, in Jesus's name.
I declare and decree that the king will hear my heart's cry before I present my petition, in Jesus's name.
I declare and decree that the king will encourage me constantly until my victory is established, in Jesus's name.
I declare and decree that the enemy of my life will never know peace, in Jesus's name.
I declare and decree that joy and gladness will be missing from the heart of the conspirators of my life, in Jesus's name.
I declare and decree that those who conspire against me shall be poor in spirit, in Jesus's name.

I declare and decree that the devisers of evil shall lack joy and gladness, in Jesus's name.
I declare and decree that I will not make a hasty presentation that will jeopardize my life, in Jesus's name.
I declare and decree that I will know how to apply wisdom in all matters that concern my deliverance, in Jesus's name.
I declare and decree that the Lord will grant me unlimited and unconditional favor, in Jesus's name.
I declare and decree that the Lord will hear my cry even before my petition is presented, in Jesus's name.
I declare and decree that my petition will be respected and honored with a sense of urgency, in Jesus's name.
I declare and decree that I will know how to position myself to attract the king's attention, in Jesus's name.
I declare and decree that my personal appearance and countenance will attract favor of love and acceptance, in Jesus's name. Amen!

Prayer Observations and Experiences

You may remember your dreams and some past occurrences while doing this prayer. You may also receive a revelation. It's important that you make notes for future reference.

Experiences

_____
_____
_____
_____
_____
_____

Observations

_____
_____
_____
_____
_____
_____

Revelations

_____
_____
_____
_____
_____
_____

CHAPTER ELEVEN

Sixth Chapter of Esther

Esther 6:1-14

On that night could not the king sleep, and he commanded to bring the book of records of the chronicles; and they were read before the king. And it was found written, that Mordecai had told of Bigthana and Teresh, two of the king's chamberlains, the keepers of the door, who sought to lay hand on the king Ahasuerus. And the king said, What honour and dignity hath been done to Mordecai for this? Then said the king's servants that ministered unto him, There is nothing done for him.

And the king said, Who is in the court? Now Haman was come into the outward court of the king's house, to speak unto the king to hang Mordecai on the gallows that he had prepared for him. And the king's servants said unto him, Behold, Haman standeth in the court. And the king said, Let him come in. So Haman came in. And the king said unto him, What shall be done unto the man whom the king delighteth to honour? Now Haman thought in his heart, To whom would the king delight to do honour more than to myself? And Haman answered the king, For the man whom the king delighteth to honour, Let the royal apparel be brought which the king useth to wear, and the horse that the king rideth upon, and the crown royal which is set upon his head: And let this apparel and horse be delivered to the hand of one of the king's most noble princes, that they may array the man withal whom the king delighteth to honour, and bring him on horseback through the street of the city, and proclaim before him, Thus shall it be done to the man whom the king delighteth to honour. Then the king said to Haman, Make haste, and take the apparel and the horse, as thou hast said, and do even so to Mordecai the Jew, that sitteth at the king's gate: let nothing fail of all that thou hast spoken. Then took Haman the apparel and the horse, and arrayed Mordecai, and brought him on horseback through the street of the city, and proclaimed before him, Thus shall it be done unto the man whom the king delighteth to honour.

And Mordecai came again to the king's gate. But Haman hasted to his house mourning, and having his head covered. And Haman told Zeresh his wife and all his friends every thing that had befallen him. Then said his wise men and Zeresh his wife unto him, If Mordecai be of the seed of the Jews, before whom thou hast begun to fall, thou shalt not prevail against him, but shalt surely fall before him. And while they were yet talking with him, came the king's chamberlains, and hasted to bring Haman unto the banquet that Esther had prepared.

Day Thirteen:
The Struggle with Generational Curses

The Struggle between Esau and Jacob

The struggle between the twin brothers continued as Esau vowed to kill Jacob. Esau's raging anger for Jacob deepened with hatred and bitterness that had germinated and grown to become an evil tree bearing satanic fruits from generation to generation. The anger and hatred from Esau was transferred to his descendants, the Amalekites. Thousands of years after the death of Esau, his descendant, Haman the Agagite of Amalek, who was not conceived at the time of the offence, was raging with bitterness towards the Jews, Jacob's descendants.

Protracted anger is one of the major roots of generational curses. Therefore, unresolved issues should not be appeased with gifts without dealing with the problem. Instead of dealing with the misunderstanding between Esau and himself, Jacob tried to pacify Esau with gifts, which he refused initially.

> **Genesis 32:20, 33:9-11**
> And say ye moreover, Behold, thy servant Jacob is behind us. For he said, *I will appease him with the present that goeth before me, and afterward I will see his face; peradventure he will accept of me* ...
>
> And Esau said, I have enough, my brother; *keep that thou hast unto thyself.* And Jacob said, Nay, I pray thee, *if now I have found grace in thy*

> *sight, then receive my present at my hand:* **for therefore I have seen thy face, as though I had seen the face of God, and thou wast pleased with me.** *Take, I pray thee, my blessing that is brought to thee;* **because God hath dealt graciously with me, and because I have enough.** *And he urged him, and he took it.*

Jacob had to persuade him to accept the gift because he was afraid for his life since Esau's plan was to kill him after the death of their father Isaac. Meanwhile Isaac was still alive, at this very moment when Jacob was returning to Padan Aram. Following a long moment of persuasion, Esau accepted the gift as Jacob begged for favor, but the discussion that would have led to reconciliation was not mentioned. *The root of the matter was not dealt with so the conflict between Jacob and Esau was never resolved.* Therefore, Jacob was still afraid for his life after Esau had accepted the peace offering.

> **Genesis 33:12-15**
> **And he said, Let us take our journey, and let us go, and I will go before thee. And he said unto him,** *My lord knoweth that the children are tender,* **and the flocks and herds with young are with me: and** *if men should overdrive them one day, all the flock will die.* **Let my lord, I pray thee, pass over before his servant: and** *I will lead on softly,* **according as the cattle that goeth before me and** *the children be able to endure,* **until I come unto my lord unto Seir. And Esau said, Let me now leave with thee some of the folk**

that *are* with me. And he said, *What needeth it? let me find grace in the sight of my lord.*

Esau did not understand the implication of trading his birthright for a red stew of pottage.

The offence remained fresh in the heart of Esau and Jacob because it was not dealt with, spoken about, or discussed for it to be uprooted. Rather, Jacob tried to cover up the offence with a peace offering (Genesis 32:20).

Ironically, soon after Jacob had purposed to appease Esau's anger, he went into an encounter in which he wrestled with the Lord. It's been ages now since the root of anger was planted into the relationship of the twin brothers, yet even today the descendants of Jacob are still wrestling with their cousins in the Middle East. Hence, the war between the twin brothers was still looming in the days of Queen Esther, as rage exhibited in Haman the Agagite against Mordecai and the Jews.

Application

In order to achieve effective results in fasting, it is important that you identify the particular problems that need solution. Use the reflective questions provided to map out strategic solutions to the problems that affect your family members, environment, or anyone whom you intend to help besides yourself.

1. **List 3-5 lesson points that you have learned from today's reading.**

   _____
   _____
   _____
   _____
   _____

2. **Identify how the lesson affects you positively in 3-5 points.**

   _____
   _____
   _____
   _____
   _____

3. **Identify how you intend to use the lesson from today's passage to resolve your problem in 3-5 points.**

   _____
   _____
   _____
   _____
   _____

Day Fourteen: Causes of Generational Curse

When a misunderstanding is not ironed out and erased totally from existence, it settles down to develop into a seed of evil. The negative reaction that develops from that offence or misunderstanding empowers a seed to germinate and grow up to become a fruit-bearing tree. If the tree is not identified and uprooted, it will become a stronghold in a person's life and later on develop into a family tree that is passed on for inheritance. Unfortunately, some trees do not bear fruit in their early years of existence. In the age of maturation, when the tree has been well groomed by the individual's behavior, *that offensive tree begins to blossom with demonic fruits that represent a curse.*

A curse is the result of an evil that was planted or embossed into a place, a thing, or a person's life, behavior, character, and destiny. A curse is a problem that defies solution until it is uprooted and cast into an acid of destruction. In **Matthew 7:17-20**, Jesus had this to say: "**Even so every good tree bringeth forth good fruit; but a corrupt tree bringeth forth evil fruit. A good tree cannot bring forth evil fruit, neither can a corrupt tree bring forth good fruit. Every tree that bringeth not forth good fruit is hewn down, and cast into the fire. Wherefore by their fruits ye shall know them**".

A curse is a seed that germinates into a tree that bears fruit of evil. "**If Mordecai be of the seed of the Jews, before whom thou hast begun to fall, thou shalt not prevail against him, but shalt surely fall before him**" **(Esther 6:13)**.

If a curse is broken and not properly discarded, it will find its way back into existence. If the branches of the tree of a curse are trimmed or cut off, it will grow up stronger than ever before, because the stump of the tree is still standing and the root is having a stronghold in the source of its existence.

For instance, if you pray that God would heal you from anger, then you would also have to plan to uproot it from your life by making a conscious effort to discard the behavior and attitude that attracts the manifestation of anger. Your response and reaction to situations will either empower the spirit of anger to have a stronghold on your life or dispel it from your life. If you consciously control your reaction to situations, the spirit of anger will not be able to influence your response to offences in order to create a curse. Likewise, if you do not caution yourself and watch over your character and behavior as you pray, the enemy will fight against your prayer and wrestle with you to discourage you so that your Christian faith may be affected.

Impact of the Curse on the King

The king was affected as the war of curses loomed over his environment and kingdom. The support of the king was needed to uproot the generational curse which affected the family of Esther and her people. The king became part of the instrument of deliverance to play the role of a mediator. The Lord would use him to rescue the descendants of Jacob, the Jews, from perishing in the hands of Esau's descendant—Haman the Agagite from Amalek origin.

Uprooting the Curse

The case at hand was treacherous. Before the matter could be resolved, Esther needed to die to herself. She needed to confess her sins with prayer and supplication in order to attract the presence of the Most High God. Having been in the presence of God with fasting, Esther gathered wisdom on how to make her petition before the king. Esther exercised patience as she watched over the favor she had gained from her prayer and fasting. Esther gave God the fullness of time to intervene in the matter in His own way.

Esther started her journey into the king's heart on the third day of her fast, after she had received empowerment from the realms of fasting. By the third day of her appearance and persuasive invitation to her royal banquet, the Lord had begun to melt the heart and soul of the king, so much so that he lost sleep.

Instead of requesting music to drive him to sleep as royalty demands, the king requested the chronicles of events be read to him. Once again, the Lord would stir up the events in the chronicles so that the matter under petition would be revealed to the king through divine orchestration. Hence, the issue of Mordecai's deliverance was preceded by a royal honor and promotion.

Evidence of Uprooting a Curse

- When a curse is being uprooted, the authority's heart will be stirred up for your sake.
- When a curse is being uprooted, the king's sleep will be troubled for your sake.
- When a curse is being uprooted, the king will remember you.
- When a curse is being uprooted, the king will honor you.

Esther 6:1-3
***On that night could not the king sleep*, and he commanded to bring the book of records of the**

chronicles; and they were read before the king. And it was found written, that Mordecai had told of Bigthana and Teresh, two of the king's chamberlains, *the keepers of the door, who sought to lay hand on the king Ahasuerus.* And the king said, *What honour and dignity hath been done to Mordecai for this?* Then said the king's servants that ministered unto him, *There is nothing done for him.*

Prayer Points

- *That the authority shall not sleep for your sake*
- *That every good thing you have done will be recorded in your name*
- *That you shall be rewarded in due season*
- *That the king himself shall speak for you*

Esther 6:4-12

And the king said, *Who is in the court?* Now Haman was come into the outward court of the king's house, to speak unto the king to hang Mordecai on the gallows that he had prepared for him. And the king's servants said unto him, Behold, Haman standeth in the court. And the king said, Let him come in. So Haman came in. And the king said unto him, *What shall be done unto the man whom the king delighteth to honour?* Now Haman thought in his heart, To whom would the king delight to do honour more than to myself? And Haman answered the king, For the man whom the king delighteth to honour, *let the royal apparel be brought which the king useth to wear, and the horse that the king rideth upon, and the crown royal which is set upon his head: and let this apparel and horse be delivered to the hand of one of the king's most noble princes, that they may array the man withal whom the king delighteth to honour, and bring him on horseback through the street of the city, and proclaim before him, Thus shall it be done to the man whom the king delighteth to honour.* Then the king said to Haman, *Make haste, and take the apparel and the horse, as thou hast said, and do even so to Mordecai the Jew, that sitteth at the king's gate: let nothing fail of all that thou hast spoken.*

Then took Haman the apparel and the horse, and arrayed Mordecai, and brought him on horseback through the street of the city, and proclaimed before him, Thus shall it be done unto the man whom the king delighteth to honour. And Mordecai came again to the king's gate. But *Haman hasted to his house mourning, and having his head covered.*

Prayer Points

- *That the Lord will cause my enemy to bow down at my feet*
- *That the Lord will cause my enemy to respect and honor me*

- *That the Lord will reverse the elements of destruction that the conspirators plot against me*
- *That the Lord will cause the workers of iniquity to raise my banner of celebration before the public*
- *That the Lord will command my enemy to serve me*
- *That the Lord will embarrass and disgrace those who stand up against me*

Esther 6:13-14

And Haman told Zeresh his wife and all his friends everything that had befallen him. Then said his wise men and Zeresh his wife unto him, *If Mordecai be of the seed of the Jews, before whom thou hast begun to fall, thou shalt not prevail against him, but shalt surely fall before him.* **And while they were yet talking with him, came the king's chamberlains, and hasted to bring Haman unto the banquet that Esther had prepared.**

Prayer Points

- *That I will not cherish evil in my heart against other persons*
- *That I will not consider myself better than other persons*
- *That I will not debase and despise others to promote myself*
- *That I will not plot destruction of another person's destiny while seeking personal promotion*

Songs of Inspiration
Victory in Jesus

Eugene Monroe Bartlett 1939

I heard an old, old story, how a Savior came from glory
How He gave His life on Calvary to save a wretch like me
I heard about His groaning, of His precious blood's atoning
Then I repented of my sins and won the victory
Chorus:
Oh victory in Jesus (victory in Jesus), my Savior (my Savior) forever (forever)
He sought me and He bought me with His redeeming blood (He bought me with His blood)
(He loved me 'ere I knew Him) He loved me 'ere I knew Him (and all my love is due Him) and all my love is due Him
He plunged me to victory beneath the cleansing flood
I heard about His healing, of His cleansing power revealing
How He made the lame to walk again and He caused the blind to see
(I cried out, "Dear Jesus") And then I cried, "Dear Jesus, (come and heal my broken spirit) come and heal my broken spirit"
I then obeyed His blest command and gained the victory
Repeat Chorus
I heard about a mansion He has built for me in glory
And I heard about the street of gold beyond the crystal sea (beyond the crystal sea)
(The angels singing) About the angels singing (the old redemption story) and the old redemption story
Oh and some sweet day I'll sing up there the song of victory
Repeat Chorus (x2)

Application

In order to achieve effective results in fasting, it is important that you identify the particular problems that need solution. Use the reflective questions provided to map out strategic solutions to the problems that affect your family members, environment, or anyone whom you intend to help besides yourself.

1. **List 3-5 lesson points that you have learned from today's reading.**

   _____
   _____
   _____
   _____
   _____

2. **Identify how the lesson affects you positively in 3-5 points.**

   _____
   _____
   _____
   _____
   _____

3. **Identify how you intend to use the lesson from today's passage to resolve your problem in 3-5 points.**

   _____
   _____
   _____
   _____
   _____

Strategic Deliverance Prayer

The Problem

Need to uproot any curse in my life and
reverse my situation for good

The Situation

My works and efforts have not been identified or recognized.
I feel something is blocking my promotion.
I am overdue for honor and promotion.
I feel oppressed and suppressed on my job and in my life.

The Goal

That the authority over my life shall not sleep for my sake
That every good thing I have done will be recorded in my name
That I shall be rewarded in due season
That the king himself shall speak for me
That the Lord will cause my enemy to bow down at my feet
That the Lord will cause my enemy to respect and honor me
That the Lord will reverse the elements of destruction
that the conspirators plot against me
That the Lord will cause the workers of iniquity to
raise my banner of celebration before the public
That the Lord will command my enemy to serve me
That the Lord will embarrass and disgrace
those who stand up against me
That I will not cherish evil in my heart against other persons
That I will not consider myself better than other persons
That I will not debase and despise others to promote myself
That I will not plot destruction of another person's
destiny while seeking personal promotion

Authority of Scripture

Esther 6:1-3

On that night could not the king sleep, **and he commanded to bring the book of records of the chronicles; and they were read before the king. And it was found written, that Mordecai had told of Bigthana and Teresh, two of the king's chamberlains,** *the keepers of the door, who sought to lay hand on the king Ahasuerus.* **And the king said,** *What honour and dignity hath been done to Mordecai for this?* **Then said the king's servants that ministered unto him,** *There is nothing done for him.*

Prayer in Action

O Lord my Father in Heaven,
Glory, power, honor and majesty be unto You.
You are indeed Jehovah El ha Gibbor—the
Great Warrior who fights my battles.
O Lord God, You are my Hero and Conqueror.
Be thou exalted and uplifted above all
others, Great God of Wonders.
You are worthy to be praised and adored, Jehovah Adon Olam.
Thank you, Lord, for taking over my battles.
You are Jehovah Boreh—the Creator of mankind.
The hearts of kings are in your hands,
For You are the One who stirs up solution in the heart of kings.
Great God of Wonders, I worship and adore
You for the works of Your hand,
For You have done great things. Amen!

Deliverance Warfare

In the name of Jesus and with the authority in the blood of Jesus, I stand on the authority of the Word of God to raise a standard against the powers and principalities of darkness in the air, on the land, and in the sea. For the Word of God states in **Esther 6:3**, that *"On that night could not the king sleep,* **and *he commanded to bring the book of records of the chronicles; and they were read before the king.* And it was found written, that Mordecai had told of Bigthana and Teresh, two of the king's chamberlains,** *the keepers of the door, who sought to lay hand on the king Ahasuerus.* **And the king said,** *What honour and dignity hath been done to Mordecai for this?* **Then said the king's servants that ministered unto him,** *There is nothing done for him."*

In the name of Jesus Christ my Lord and Redeemer, I stand on the righteous word of the Most High God to dismantle the kingdom of darkness and scatter the workers of iniquity in the spiritual realm, in the physical realm, in the material realm, in the emotional realm, in the secular realm, and every realm of my life endeavors.

In the name of Jesus, I uproot and cast out any judgment written against me.

Therefore, the counsel of the iniquitous plotted against my life and destiny shall not prosper, and the iniquitous shall not find rest in evil doing, in Jesus's name.

In the name of Jesus, I uproot the spirit of stagnancy and demotion,

Therefore, the authory shall not sleep until my favor is established and my promotion is manifested.
In the name of Jesus and with the authority in the blood of Jesus, I uproot and cast out any evil report that has been embossed into my record.
Therefore, let every good thing I have done be recorded in my name right now, in Jesus's name.
In the name of Jesus, I uproot and cast out the spirit of forgetfulness and rejection.
Therefore the king shall speak for me and I shall be rewarded in due season, in the name of Jesus.
In the name of Jesus, I uproot and cast out the spirit of poverty from my life.
Therefore, my enemy shall bow down at my feet with respect and honor, in Jesus's name.
In the name of Jesus, I uproot and cast out any curse that has been planted against my blessing.
Therefore, I reverse the elements of destruction that the conspirators plotted against me, in Jesus's name.
In the name of Jesus I uproot and cast out the spirit of shame, disgrace and embarrassment from my life.
Therefore, I will not be debased or despised, in Jesus's name.
In the name of Jesus, I uproot and cast out the spirit of murder and destruction of life.
Therefore I shall not be killed or murdered under any situation or circumstance, in Jesus's name.
In the name of Jesus the destroyers of destiny shall not dig any pit of death or grave for me.
Therefore, I reverse the conspiracy of the destroyers of destiny that they shall be destroyed by the works of their own hands, in Jesus's name.

In the name of Jesus, I uproot and cast out the
spirit of depression and oppression.
Therefore, I shall not perish, but shall have long
life and prosperity, in Jesus's name.
In the name of Jesus, I cover my life and destiny with the
blood of that was shed for me on the cross of Calvary.
In the name of Jesus, I build a hedge of protection
over my life with the fire of the Holy Ghost.
The arrows that fly by day and the terror by night
shall not come after me nor interfere with me.
There shall be no enchantment or divination against me,
in the name of Jesus Christ my Lord and Savior. Amen!

Breaking and Uprooting Curses: Curses of Delay and Denial that Affect Prosperity

In the name of Jesus, and with the authority in the blood of Jesus I bind and uproot the tree of curses planted against my life.
I speak to the tree of **delay and denial that affects prosperity** that affect my life.
You shall not prosper in my destiny.
I command you, curse of **delay and denial that affects prosperity** to be uprooted out of my destiny right now.
In the name of Jesus, you tree of **delay and denial that affects prosperity** shall not prosper in my life.
Be uprooted out of my life and destiny
right now, in the name of Jesus.
Be cast out into the sea of destruction right now, in the name of Jesus.
I shall not see you, tree of **delay and denial that affects prosperity** again and you shall not come by me, in Jesus's name.
I shall not invite you, tree of **delay and denial that affects prosperity** again and you shall not harass me, in Jesus's name
I shall not entertain you, tree of **delay and denial that affects prosperity** again and you shall not terrorize my life, in Jesus's name.
Let the blood of Jesus separate me from the curse of **delay and denial that affects prosperity** that steals the joy of my salvation.
Let the fire of the Holy Ghost destroy the root of **delay and denial that affects prosperity** that afflicts me.
The tree of **delay and denial that affects prosperity** shall no longer have access to me, in Jesus's name.
The tree of **delay and denial that affects prosperity** shall no longer manifest within and around me again, in Jesus's name.
I am washed and cleansed by the blood of Jesus Christ my Lord and Savior.
I am covered and sealed in the name of Jesus.
I am protected and guarded by the fire of the Holy Ghost. Amen!

Declaration

In the name of Jesus and with the authority in the blood of Jesus, I stand on the authority in the word of the Lord to declare and decree favor upon my life and destiny. Even as it is written in **Esther 6:1-3:**
"*On that night could not the king sleep,* and *he commanded to bring the book of records of the chronicles; and they were read before the king.* And it was found written, that Mordecai had told of Bigthana and Teresh, two of the king's chamberlains, *the keepers of the door, who sought to lay hand on the king Ahasuerus.* And the king said, *What honour and dignity hath been done to Mordecai for this*? Then said the king's servants that ministered unto him, *There is nothing done for him.*"

I declare and decree that the king shall not sleep for my sake, in Jesus's name.

I declare and decree that every good thing that I have done shall be attributed to my name, in Jesus's name.

I declare and decree that I shall be rewarded in due season, in Jesus's name.

I declare and decree that the king himself shall speak for me, in Jesus's name.

I declare and decree that the Lord will cause my enemy to bow down at my feet, in Jesus's name.

I declare and decree that the Lord will cause my enemy to respect and honor me, in Jesus's name.

I declare and decree that the Lord will reverse the elements of destruction that the conspirators plot against me, in Jesus's name.

I declare and decree that the Lord will cause the workers of iniquity to raise my banner of celebration before the public, in Jesus's name.
I declare and decree that the Lord will command my enemy to serve me, in Jesus's name.
I declare and decree that the Lord will embarrass and disgrace those who stand up against me, in Jesus's name.
I declare and decree that I shall not cherish evil in my heart against other persons, in Jesus's name.
I declare and decree that I shall not consider myself better than other persons, in Jesus's name.
I declare and decree that I shall not debase and despise others to promote myself, in Jesus's name.
I declare and decree that I shall not plot destruction of another person's destiny while seeking my personal promotion, in Jesus's name. Amen!

Prayer Observations and Experiences

You may remember your dreams and some past occurrences while doing this prayer. You may also receive a revelation. It's important that you make notes for future reference.

Experiences

_____
_____
_____
_____
_____
_____

Observations

_____
_____
_____
_____
_____
_____

Revelations

_____
_____
_____
_____
_____
_____

CHAPTER TWELVE

Seventh Chapter of Esther

Esther 7:1-10

So the king and Haman came to banquet with Esther the queen. And the king said again unto Esther on the second day at the banquet of wine, Whatis thy petition, queen Esther? and it shall be granted thee: and what is thy request? and it shall be performed, even to the half of the kingdom. Then Esther the queen answered and said, If I have found favour in thy sight, O king, and if it please the king, let my life be given me at my petition, and my people at my request: For we are sold, I and my people, to be destroyed, to be slain, and to perish. But if we had been sold for bondmen and bondwomen, I had held my tongue, although the enemy could not countervail the king's damage. Then the king Ahasuerus answered and said unto Esther the queen, Who is he, and where is he, that durst presume in his heart to do so? And Esther said, The adversary and enemy is this wicked Haman.

Then Haman was afraid before the king and the queen.

And the king arising from the banquet of wine in his wrath went into the palace garden: and Haman stood up to make request for his life to Esther the queen; for he saw that there was evil determined against him by the king. Then the king returned out of the palace garden into the place of the banquet of wine; and Haman was fallen upon the bed whereon Esther was. Then said the king, Will he force the queen also before me in the house? As the word went out of the king's mouth, they covered Haman's face. And Harbonah, one of the chamberlains, said before the king, Behold also, the gallows fifty cubits high, which Haman had made for Mordecai, who had spoken good for the king, standeth in the house of Haman. Then the king said, Hang him thereon. So they hanged Haman on the gallows that he had prepared for Mordecai. Then was the king's wrath pacified.

Day Fifteen:
Favor for Support to Uproot Curses

Now, in the third session of meeting with Esther, the king was bound by the promise he had pronounced on the various occasions during the previous meetings they had with Haman the destroyer.

Having been encouraged by the king's persuasion, Queen Esther decided to open the carnage. All along, the queen had exercised caution as the matter was highly delicate, with regards to the king's royal seal and the destruction of lives. Although the king was aware of the matter, he had not given it deep thought. The king had also not considered the consequences and the repercussions that the matter would have on both the present and future generations.

Haman Preys on King Ahasuerus's Weakness

The king trusted his prime-minister Haman without an iota of doubt. The king did not think it was necessary to examine Haman's suggestions or proposals. The king felt very comfortable with Haman's decisions and did not bother to cross-check the details or challenge the motive behind Haman's request to destroy a people.

- Haman took advantage of the king's trust for him, and began to meddle with the king's intellectual ability.
- Haman exploited the king's drunkenness to suppress his decision making.
- Haman also used a monetary gift to buy the king's favor in order to imprison his intellectual abilities.

- Although King Ahasuerus was a great and powerful authority who ruled over a huge kingdom of nations that spanned from India to Ethiopia, Haman managed to prey upon his royal throne, and manipulated the king to become his wine-drinking buddy.
- Haman used drunkenness to detonate the king's governmental consciousness.
- Haman used liquor to maliciously influence King Ahasuerus to empower him to plot the annihilation of a people.

Since the king was intoxicated with liquor, he foolishly consented to the ploy without consideration. Hence, he released his signet ring and all the necessary materials required for Haman to pursue his deadly attack on Mordecai and the Jews. But God in heaven would intervene and quell the atrocity connived against His people.

Spiritual Enhancement

The people of the world (non-Christians and ordinary churchgoers) do not make decisions without consulting a spiritual power. People in governmental authority, royal authorities (kings and princes), politicians, business giants, and professional executives, and business owners often belong to secret societies or cults where they conjure powers to motivate and enhance their secular ventures. Some of these people often consult spiritualists, botanicals, palm readers, astrologers, magicians, and all manner of soothsayers to forecast their omens on a regular basis.

King Ahasuerus consulted with the wise men (fortune tellers) to predict the times and season when Queen Vashti disappointed him (Esther 1:13). Haman also consulted oracles (*powers and principalities of darkness*) to strengthen his bid to manipulate the king and the public to support his devilish attack against Mordecai and the Jews (Esther 3:7-8).

While the people of the world consulted demonic entities and the powers of darkness, Esther sought the counsel of the Most High God with fasting and supplication. The God of Esther is the King of kings and the Lord of lords. Esther served and worshipped the Great God of Wonders who has the power to make and unmake kings, and the power to turn the heart of kings and their decisions around.

Having waited on Jehovah God for divine direction and intervention, Queen Esther finally mustered courage to speak out. The queen shocked the king with the kind of petition that she presented. The king was probably expecting Esther to ask for wealth, honor, or assistance for somebody, but it was none of those. Rather, the queen was petitioning the king for the preservation of her life and that of her brethren from destruction. Queen Esther's words and presentation were sharp, precise, strong, and straightforward.

> **Esther 7:3 -4**
>
> **Then Esther the queen answered and said, If I have found favour in thy sight, O king, and if it please the king,** *let my life be given me at my petition, and my people at my request*: **For we are sold,** *I and my people, to be destroyed, to be slain, and to perish.* **But if we had been sold for bondmen and bondwomen, I had held my tongue, although the enemy could not countervail the king's damage.**

Her petition was the least of all requests that the king ever expected in his kingdom. Meanwhile, the situation was due to the king's flaws—he was a drunk. He was easily influenced by the power of alcohol. Each time he was tipsy with liquor, he committed grave mistakes that affected his kingdom. Even Esther knew that she could not present herself to the king without inviting him to a banquet of wine. However, Esther used prayer and fasting to get the king's attention. She did not manipulate the king as Haman did.

On the third day of the banquet, as the king moved on to persuade the queen once again, Esther uttered these statements: **"For we are sold, both life and freedom of the Jews were sold. We are sold to be destroyed, to be slain, and to perish"** as she referred to the decree which Haman had written and published with the king's approval against the Jews in **Esther 3:9**.

Thus a whole nation had been sold to satisfy the pride of one person who was seeking revenge to please his ego.

Haman Sold the Jews as Esau Sold His birthright

The root of the revenge goes back to the time when Esau sold his birthright to Jacob for the red stew pottage. Unconscious of the implication of selling his birthright, Esau became bitter and swore to kill Jacob after the death of his father Isaac. Although Esau was pacified with gifts and the matter was never discussed, the Amalekites have since sought revenge *on behalf of Esau their ancestral parent.*

Therefore in revenge for the sold birthright, Haman also sold Jacob's descendants for the sum of ten thousand pieces of silver. **Esther 3:8-11** states thus:

> **And Haman said unto king Ahasuerus, There is a certain people scattered abroad and**

> dispersed among the people in all the provinces of thy kingdom; and their laws *are* diverse from all people; neither keep they the king's laws: therefore it *is* not for the king's profit to suffer them. If it please the king, *let it be written* that they may be destroyed: and *I will pay ten thousand talents of silver to the hands of those that have the charge of the business, to bring it into the king's treasuries.* And the king took his ring from his hand, and gave it unto Haman the son of Hammedatha the Agagite, the Jews' enemy. And the king said unto Haman, *The silver is given to thee, the people also, to do with them as it seemeth good to thee.*

Esther stated that *both life and freedom of the Jews were sold.* **"For we are sold, I and my people, to be destroyed, to be slain, and to perish (7:4)"** Just like Esau sold his birthright, Haman also sold Mordecai and the Jews for ten thousand pieces of silver.

The king was further shocked upon realizing that his signature had been used to perpetrate evil apart from his right frame of mind—because he acted while in drunken stupor, in a totally wrong frame of mind. Unconscious of the harm that he had signed and sealed, the king asked Esther the queen, **"Who is he, and where is he, that durst presume in his heart to do so?"** (Esther 7:5)

What could have caused anyone to desire to slaughter the queen and her people? If it were to be easy, Esther would have stated that Haman did so with the support of the king himself, as the king was guilty and in the heart of the matter. If the king had thoughtfully considered Haman's request, he would not have empowered such an atrocity in his kingdom.

However, when a generational curse is looming, no one can stop it until it has been uprooted and cast into the sea of destruction. Cutting off the branches does not stop the tree of an ancestral curse from flourishing or bearing fruit of iniquity.

Prayer Points

- *That we will not be so ignorant to support the workers of iniquity foolishly*
- *That we will not stupidly dip our hands into the destruction of other persons*

Esther 7:1-2

So the king and Haman came to banquet with Esther the queen. And the king said again unto Esther on the second day at the banquet of wine, ***What is thy petition, queen Esther? and it shall be granted thee: and what is thy request? and it shall be performed, even to the half of the kingdom.***

Prayer Points

- *That our leaders will be consistent in their hearts to do good*
- *That I will be consistent in my decision making and promises*

Application:

In order to achieve effective results in fasting, it is important that you identify the particular problems that need solution. Use the reflective questions provided to map out strategic solutions to the problems that affect your family members, environment, or anyone whom you intend to help besides yourself.

1. **List 3-5 lesson points that you have learned from today's reading.**

   _____
   _____
   _____
   _____
   _____

2. **Identify how the lesson affects you positively in 3-5 points.**

   _____
   _____
   _____
   _____
   _____

3. **Identify how you intend to use the lesson from today's passage to resolve your problem in 3-5 points.**

   _____
   _____
   _____
   _____
   _____

Day Sixteen: Request for Protection and Preservation of Life

For hundreds of years, Esau's descendants harassed and tormented Jacob's descendants constantly and consistently. It was as though there would never be a help to end the torment. Many centuries later, even Adolf Hitler tried annihilating the Jews with the promulgation of the holocaust.

The Power of Intensive Prayer Fast

Fasting with intensive prayer is a powerful weapon for warfare and confrontation against the enemy of our souls. Whenever intensive prayer is supported with fasting, every knee shall bow and every tongue shall confess that Jesus Christ is Lord and Jehovah God intervenes in the affairs of the righteous.

Just as Jacob appeased Esau for the protection and preservation of his life, Esther appealed to the king for same. Esther's three days' intensive prayer fast and appeal turned around to jeopardize Haman's wicked plot to annihilate the Jews. Esther's prayer fast heaped coals of fire upon the head of Haman and his own plot tumbled over him. Instead, Haman suffered the consequences of his own plot.

> Esther 7:3-5:
> ***Then Esther the queen answered and said, If I have found favour in thy sight, O king, and***

if it please the king, let my life be given me at my petition, and my people at my request: For we are sold, I and my people, to be destroyed, to be slain, and to perish. But if we had been sold for bondmen and bondwomen, I had held my tongue, although the enemy could not countervail the king's damage. Then the king Ahasuerus answered and said unto Esther the queen, Who is he, and where is he, that durst presume in his heart to do so?

Prayer Points

- *That I will not be partakers of the works of iniquity*
- *That I will not be implicated with atrocities*

Haman's Curse Reversed against Him

Does an evil person fear the same kind of destruction that he/she plotted against another person? Why was Haman afraid to die? If so then,

- Do not curse or plan evil against another person.
- Do not speak negatively about anyone if you do not want anybody to say evil things about you.
- Refrain from doing evil if you really dread evil and do not want to fall into a similar pit.

When Haman was plotting evil against a people, he did not realize that he could suffer the same consequences of the evil he planned against another person. Now the curse he released had turned into a pruning hook as the judgment that he had set up would later become his fate.

Haman Invited the Spirit of Death

Haman had invited the spirit of death and mass destruction when he sold the Jews for annihilation. *He invited the spirit of death to come, but he did not prepare to meet with Mr. Death, or to entertain Mr. Death in a banquet of wine.* Be that as it may, Mr. Death honored Haman's invitation, yet Haman was not ready to receive Mr. Death. Unexpectedly, Haman meets with Mr. Death face to face at the banquet of wine and said, *"You invited me to come so I am here,"* but Haman was afraid. **"Haman stood up to make request for his life to Esther the queen; for he saw that there was evil determined against him by the king"** (Esther 7:7).

Legal Grounds for Death to Operate

Since Haman decreed and signed a pact for the invitation of Mr. Death, of course Mr. Death had legal grounds to operate in the Persian Empire. Death had been given a legal invitation that was signed and sealed with the signature of the highest authority in the Persian Kingdom. The principalities in charge of destruction of lives received an open invitation for mass destruction. The nation's gate was legally opened to the spirit of mass destruction. The king and his prime minister gave the principality of annihilation freedom to visit the kingdom with sorrow and pain.

Satan is a legalist. Since the proposal of destruction was established with the king's authority and decreed on legal terms, the reversal of the invitation to destroy was not completely removed, but was reversed and redirected to another destination. This time, the blood of the lamb had covered the Jews through prayer and fasting, so the first stop was made at Haman, and the next move was directed towards the enemies of the Jews.

In view of the Abrahamic Covenant promise, the Jews were saved and the curse was uprooted from among the Jews as it is written in **Genesis 12:2-3, "And I will make of thee a great nation, and I will bless thee, and make thy name great; and thou shalt be a blessing: And I will bless them that bless thee, and curse him that curseth thee: and in thee shall all families of the earth be blessed."**

Therefore, the curse rested on Haman and his people. It is a dangerous thing to invite the spirit of death under any circumstances. Since Satan is a legalist, once invited, evil comes and hangs around till he gets a hold on a legal ground to operate. Do not invite Satan and his cohorts into a situation; otherwise you have to honor that invitation with the life of an innocent person if not your own life. Therefore stop cursing or wishing someone evil. The destruction that followed the invitation from Haman's conspired atrocities was probably worse than he had plotted.

> **Esther 7:6-7**
> And Esther said, *The adversary and enemy is this wicked Haman.* Then Haman was afraid before the king and the queen. And the king

arising from the banquet of wine in his wrath *went* into the palace garden: and *Haman stood up to make request for his life to Esther the queen*; for he saw that there was evil determined against him by the king.

Prayer Points

- *That my enemy will be paid back with his own coin by divine intervention*
- *That I will not fight the battles that confront me with the arm of flesh but by the power of the Most High God*
- *That the Lord will cause my enemy to fall before me*

Curse Uprooted

Do not play with death. Do not entertain the spirit of death. Do not call upon death when you are not ready to die. Do not plan to destroy anyone no matter their offence. Do not determine in your heart to hurt anyone, even if you do not like their ways. Do not swear to avenge an offence, even if it's painful. Do not indulge innocent people in your wrongdoing, it may bounce back. Do not plant evil against anybody; it will affect the posterity of many generations ahead. At this point, Haman's wife, Zeresh, and his wise men (fortune-tellers) who initially conjured omens to support his satanic ambition could no longer stand with him but rather warned him to refrain from touching a Jewish man, as we see in **Esther 6:13-14**:

And Haman told Zeresh his wife and all his friends everything that had befallen him. Then said *his wise men and Zeresh his wife* unto him, *If Mordecai be of the seed of the Jews, before whom thou hast begun to fall, thou shalt not prevail against him, but shalt surely fall before him.* And while they were yet talking with him, came the king's chamberlains, and hasted to bring Haman unto the banquet that Esther had prepared.

Uprooted Curse Hits Haman

But it was too late. Before the warning could sink into Haman's thoughts, the adversity that he planted had already shifted toward him. The destruction he had planted as a result of an ancestral curse was *returning to sender* with the highest speed on the expressway to Haman's house. *The curse that was uprooted from Esther's people destroyed Haman.* The king's vexation exceeded Haman's anger and bitterness against the people of God.

In the initial covenant that was given to Abraham, the Almighty God promised to curse anyone who curses Abraham and his descendants (Genesis 12:3). Zeresh and the soothsayers called Haman's attention to it. Unknown to his wife and friends, the war in the heart of Haman was aimed at repossessing the birthright of Esau which was linked to the Abrahamic Covenant blessing. Until the matter was resolved, there was no going back to revoke what had been written. Jacob was the rightful owner of the Abrahamic Covenant blessing from the conception, but Isaac was going to give it to Esau. The promise is for Jacob, and so it is to this day. No matter the war that was ever initiated against the descendants of Jacob, it is written in Numbers 23:22-24: **"God brought them out of Egypt; he hath as it were the strength of an unicorn. *Surely there is no enchantment against Jacob, neither is there any divination against Israel:* according to this time it shall be said of Jacob and of Israel, *What hath God wrought!* Behold, the people shall rise up as a great lion, and lift up himself as a young lion: he shall not lie down until he eat of the prey, and drink the blood of the slain."**

Haman's Judgment and Death Sentence

Do not judge or condemn other people to death if you don't expect to be sentenced to death. The king did not pronounce judgment on Haman. Rather, the very people that Haman had incited against Mordecai and the Jews pronounced his judgment as they showed the king the gallows that Haman had erected on which to hang Mordecai. More so, judgment was written by Haman against the Jews and now the judgment was being reversed to take hold of the perpetrator himself. So the king sanctioned the judgment that sentenced Haman to death.

> **Esther 7:8-10:**
> **Then the king returned out of the palace garden into the place of the banquet of wine; and *Haman was fallen upon the bed whereon Esther was.* Then said the king, *Will he force the queen also before me in the house?* As the word went out of the king's mouth, they covered Haman's face. And Harbonah, one of the chamberlains, said before the king, *Behold also, the gallows***

fifty cubits high, which Haman had made for Mordecai, who had spoken good for the king, standeth in the house of Haman. Then the king said, Hang him thereon. So they hanged Haman on the gallows that he had prepared for Mordecai. Then was the king's wrath pacified.

Song of Inspiration
Guide Me O Thou Great Jehovah

Words: William Williams, Halleluiah (Bristol, England: 1745) (Arglwydd, arwain trwy'r anialwch). Translated from Welsh to English by Peter Williams, Hymns on Various Subjects (Carmarthen, Wales: 1771); Williams published another English translation in Lady Huntingdon's Collection, circa 1772.

Music: Cwm Rhondda, John Hughes, 1907. Hughes wrote this tune in Tonteg (near Pontypridd), Wales, to commemorate a music festival held in nearby Capel Rhondda, Hopkinstown. It was first performed November 1 that year to Welsh words by Ann Griffiths; in the early days it was simply known as Rhondda, but within a year he changed the name to Cwm Rhondda, used Peter Williams' translation, and the rest is history Alternate tunes (some use slightly different endings to the lyrics):

This hymn was sung, in Welsh, in the Academy Award winning movie *How Green Was My Valley* (1941). It was sung in English at the funeral of Diana, Princess of Wales, in Westminster Abbey, London, September 6, 1997.

Guide me, O Thou great Jehovah,
[*or* Guide me, O Thou great Redeemer…]
Pilgrim through this barren land.
I am weak, but Thou art mighty;

Hold me with Thy powerful hand.

Bread of Heaven, Bread of Heaven,
Feed me till I want no more;
Feed me till I want no more.

Open now the crystal fountain,
Whence the healing stream doth flow;
Let the fire and cloudy pillar
Lead me all my journey through.

Strong Deliverer, strong Deliverer,
Be Thou still my Strength and Shield;
Be Thou still my Strength and Shield.

Lord, I trust Thy mighty power,
Wondrous are Thy works of old;
Thou deliver'st Thine from thralldom,
Who for naught themselves had sold:

Thou didst conquer, Thou didst conquer,
Sin, and Satan and the grave,
Sin, and Satan and the grave.

When I tread the verge of Jordan,
Bid my anxious fears subside;
Death of deaths, and hell's destruction,
Land me safe on Canaan's side.

Songs of praises, songs of praises,
I will ever give to Thee;

I will ever give to Thee.

Musing on my habitation,
Musing on my heav'nly home,
Fills my soul with holy longings:
Come, my Jesus, quickly come;
Vanity is all I see;

Lord, I long to be with Thee!
Lord, I long to be with Thee!

Application:

In order to achieve effective results in fasting, it is important that you identify the particular problems that need solution. Use the reflective questions provided to map out strategic solutions to the problems that affect your family members, environment, or anyone whom you intend to help besides yourself.

1. **List 3-5 lesson points that you have learned from today's reading.**

   _____
   _____
   _____
   _____
   _____

2. **Identify how the lesson affects you positively in 3-5 points.**

   _____
   _____
   _____
   _____
   _____

3. **Identify how you intend to use the lesson from today's passage to resolve your problem in 3-5 points.**

   _____
   _____
   _____
   _____
   _____

Strategic Deliverance Prayer

The Problem

That my prayer and fasting will attract divine intervention
so that my petition will receive instant attention and solution.

The Situation

The enemy has written a false allegation against me.
The enemy has incited the public against my progress and prosperity.
The enemy is interfering with my status and relationship.
The enemy has traded my life for death.

The Goal

Need to gain total favor before God and man
Need my petition to be granted without an iota of doubt
Need instant intervention against the conspirator of destruction
Need to uproot any curse planted against me
Need to destroy the instrument of wickedness
Need to scatter the workers of iniquity
That I will not be too ignorant to support the workers of iniquity foolishly
That I will not stupidly dip my hands into the destruction of other persons
That our leaders will be consistent in their hearts to do good
That I will be consistent in keeping promises and in decision making
That my enemy will be paid back with his or
her own coin by divine intervention
That I will not fight the battles that confront me with the
arm of flesh but by the power of the Most High God
That the Lord will cause my enemy to fall before me

Authority of Scripture

Esther 7:3-4

Then Esther the queen answered and said, If I have found favour in thy sight, O king, and if it please the king, let my life be given me at my petition, and my people at my request: For we are sold, I and my people, to be destroyed, to be slain, and to perish. But if we had been sold for bondmen and bondwomen, I had held my tongue, although the enemy could not countervail the king's damage.

Prayer in Action

Jehovah God, My Lord and Father,
Great is Thy faithfulness.
Great is Thy loving kindness.
O Lord, You are so good and so kind.
O Lord, You are gracious and merciful.
O Lord, You are worthy to be praised and adored.
O Lord, You are the protector and preserver of life.
Thank You for delivering me from evil.
Thank You for nullifying the works of evil planted against me.
Thank You for hearing and answering my cry.
Thank You for providing solutions to my problems.
In Jesus's name, I render my gratitude and appreciation
Unto the great God of divine intervention. Amen!
O Lord, salvation and deliverance belong to You.
Hear my cry even before I pray,
And intervene in all matters that concern me.
O Lord, You are the Great and Mighty Warrior.
You are able to fight my battles for me.
O Lord, protect and preserve the life of my people and myself,
And halt the assault that the enemy has
plotted against my people and me.
O Lord, set confusion into the camp of
those who conspire evil against me.
O Lord, scatter their gathering and turn
their counsel into foolishness,
And destroy the foundation of their
stronghold, in Jesus's name. Amen!

Deliverance Warfare

In the name of Jesus, and with the authority in the
blood of Jesus Christ my Lord and Savior,
I come against the powers and principalities of
darkness in the air, the land, and the sea.
In the name of Jesus Christ, I raise a standard against
rulers of darkness and their human cohorts with the
blood that was shed on the cross of Calvary.
In the name of Jesus, the powers of darkness shall not hinder
or interfere with the favor upon my life and destiny.
In the name of Jesus, the workers of iniquity shall not hinder or
interfere with the petition that I make at any time or any day.
In the name of Jesus, I uproot and cast out the
conspirators of destruction from my life and destiny.
Those who conspire against my life and destiny shall not
prosper and their works shall fail, in the name of Jesus.
In the name of Jesus, I uproot and cast out any curse planted
against me in the spiritual realm, in the physical realm,
in the emotional realm, and in the material realm.
I command that no curse planted against me shall prosper, and
every tongue that shall pronounce a curse against me shall be
consumed by the fire of the Holy Ghost, in Jesus's name.
In the name of Jesus, I uproot and cast out any instrument of
wickedness planted against me in the spiritual realm, in the
physical realm, in the material realm, and in the emotional realm.
I command the fire of the Holy Ghost to consume any form of
enchantment or divination enacted against me, in Jesus's name.
I command the fire of the Holy Ghost to scatter any form of
satanic counsel uttered against me and confuse the gathering
of evil mounted against me, in the name of Jesus. Amen!

Breaking and Uprooting Curses: Curse of Rejection and Dejection

In the name of Jesus, and with the authority in the blood of Jesus,
I bind and uproot the tree of curses planted against my life,
I speak to the tree of **rejection and dejection** that affects my life.
You shall not prosper against my destiny.
I command you, curse of **rejection and dejection**
to be uprooted out of my destiny right now.
In the name of Jesus, you tree of **rejection and dejection** shall not prosper in my life.
Be uprooted out of my life and destiny right now, in the name of Jesus.
Be cast out into the sea of destruction right now, in the name of Jesus.
I shall not see you, tree of **rejection and dejection** again
and you shall not come by me, in Jesus's name.
I shall not invite you, tree of **rejection and dejection**
again and you shall not harass me, in Jesus's name.
I shall not entertain you, tree of **rejection and dejection**
again and you shall not terrorize my life, in Jesus's name.
Let the blood of Jesus separate me from the curse of **rejection and dejection** that steals the joy of my salvation.
Let the fire of the Holy Ghost destroy the root of
rejection and dejection that afflicts me.
The tree of **rejection and dejection** shall no
longer have access to me, in Jesus's name.
The tree of **rejection and dejection** shall no longer
manifest within and around me again, in Jesus's name.
I am washed and cleansed by the blood of
Jesus Christ my Lord and Savior.
I am covered and sealed in the name of Jesus.
I am protected and guarded by the fire of the Holy Ghost. Amen!

Declaration

In the name of Jesus Christ my Lord and Savior, and with the authority in the blood of Jesus Christ that was shed on the cross of Calvary, I declare and decree that whatever I bind on earth shall be bound in heaven and whatever I loose on earth shall be loosed in heaven.
Therefore, I stand on the authority of the Word of God written in the book of **Esther 7:3** that says, *"If I have found favour in thy sight, O king, and if it please the king, let my life be given me at my petition, and my people at my request:"*
I declare and decree the favor of the Most High God upon my life, and I command that the favor of the Lord shall surround me and go before me in the spiritual realm, physical realm, material realm, and emotional realm, in Jesus's name.
I declare and decree that the favor of the Lord shall cause men and women to hear and consider my petition with honor and respect, in Jesus's name.
I declare and decree that I shall gain total favor before God and man so that my petition shall be granted without an iota of doubt, in Jesus's name.
I declare and decree that I shall experience instant intervention against those who conspire against me, in Jesus's name.
I declare and decree that any curse planted against me shall be uprooted and cast into the sea of destruction, in Jesus's name.
I declare and decree that the power of Holy Spirit shall consume the instrument of wickedness fashioned against me, in Jesus's name.
I declare and decree that the power of the Holy Ghost shall scatter the workers of iniquity, in Jesus's name.

I declare and decree that I shall not be too ignorant to support the workers of iniquity foolishly, in Jesus's name.
I declare and decree that I shall not stupidly dip my hands into the destruction of other persons, in Jesus's name.
I declare and decree that the authorities over me shall be consistent in their hearts to do good and not evil, in Jesus's name.
I declare and decree that my enemy shall be paid back with his or her own coin by divine intervention, in Jesus's name.
I declare and decree that I shall not fight the battles that confront me with the arm of flesh but by the power of the Most High God in Jesus's name.
I declare and decree that the Lord will cause my enemy to fall before me, in Jesus's name. Amen!

Prayer Observations and Experiences

You may remember your dreams and some past occurrences while doing this prayer. You may also receive a revelation. It's important that you make notes for future reference.

Experiences

_____
_____
_____
_____
_____
_____

Observations

_____
_____
_____
_____
_____
_____

Revelations

_____
_____
_____
_____
_____
_____

CHAPTER THIRTEEN

Eighth Chapter of Esther

Esther 8:1-17:

On that day did the king Ahasuerus give the house of Haman the Jews' enemy unto Esther the queen. And Mordecai came before the king; for Esther had told what he was unto her. And the king took off his ring, which he had taken from Haman, and gave it unto Mordecai. And Esther set Mordecai over the house of Haman.

And Esther spake yet again before the king, and fell down at his feet, and besought him with tears to put away the mischief of Haman the Agagite, and his device that he had devised against the Jews. Then the king held out the golden sceptre toward Esther. So Esther arose, and stood before the king, And said, If it please the king, and if I have found favour in his sight, and the thing seem right before the king, and I be pleasing in his eyes, let it be written to reverse the letters devised by Haman the son of Hammedatha the Agagite, which he wrote to destroy the Jews which are in all the king's provinces: For how can I endure to see the evil that shall come unto my people? or how can I endure to see the destruction of my kindred? Then the king Ahasuerus said unto Esther the queen and to Mordecai the Jew, Behold, I have given Esther the house of Haman, and him they have hanged upon the gallows, because he laid his hand upon the Jews. Write ye also for the Jews, as it liketh you, in the king's name, and seal it with the king's ring: for the writing which is written in the king's name, and sealed with the king's ring, may no man reverse. Then were the king's scribes called at that time in the third month, that is, the month Sivan, on the three and twentieth day thereof; and it was written according to all that Mordecai commanded unto the Jews, and to the lieutenants, and the deputies and rulers of the provinces which are from India unto Ethiopia, an hundred twenty and seven provinces, unto every province according to the writing thereof, and unto every people after their language, and to the Jews according to their writing, and according to their language. And he wrote in the king Ahasuerus' name, and sealed it with the king's ring, and sent letters by posts on horseback, and riders on mules, camels, and young dromedaries: Wherein the king granted the Jews which were in every city to gather themselves together, and to stand for their life, to destroy, to slay, and to cause to perish, all the power of the people and province that would assault them, both little ones and women, and to take the spoil of them for a prey, upon one day in all the provinces of king Ahasuerus, namely, upon the thirteenth day of the twelfth month, which is the month Adar. The copy of the writing for a commandment to be given in every province was published unto all people, and that the Jews should be ready against that day to avenge themselves on their enemies. So the posts that rode upon mules and camels went out, being hastened and pressed on by the king's commandment. And the decree was given at Shushan the palace.

And Mordecai went out from the presence of the king in royal apparel of blue and white, and with a great crown of gold, and with a garment of fine linen and purple: and the city of Shushan rejoiced and was glad. The Jews had light, and gladness, and joy, and honour. And in every province, and in every city, whithersoever the king's commandment and his decree came, the Jews had joy and gladness, a feast and a good day. And many of the people of the land became Jews; for the fear of the Jews fell upon them.

Day Seventeen: Repossession of Royal Destiny

Benjamin was the brother of Joseph and the last son of Rachel, the wife of Jacob. Rachel died in the process of giving birth to Benjamin. Rachel had two sons. When Jacob was told that Joseph was dead, not knowing that his brothers had sold him into slavery, he held onto Benjamin as though he were his only son. Benjamin's family was one of the twelve tribes of Israel. Kish the father of Saul was a descendant of Benjamin. Saul the Benjamite was the first king of Israel. Saul's descendants could not inherit the kingdom of royalty that the Lord had given to the Benjamite because Saul disobeyed God's command to utterly eliminate King Agag and the Amalekites.

Although Saul spared King Agag, who was later killed in order to fulfill the Lord's commandment, the Amalekites were angry with the Israelites. Consequently, the Amalekites and the family of Agag have since sought revenge for the misunderstanding that ensued from the days of Esau. The matter also led to the Amalekites' attack against Israel in the wilderness while they were on their way from the land of slavery in Egypt. This incident finally resurfaced between Haman the Agagite of Amalek and Mordecai the Israelite.

Royal Inheritance: Result of the Fast

Just as Jacob got the blessing of Esau which originally belonged to him, Esther inherited the royal position of Haman and turned it over to Mordecai. The king gave Haman's house to Esther, and she transferred it to Mordecai.

After the Hamanic Curse was uprooted and cast into the sea of destruction, both Esther and Mordecai were promoted to a higher authority in the kingdom of Ahasuerus.

In the first promotion, Mordecai was honored publicly in royal apparel, during which Haman was made to sing the praise of Mordecai his enemy. The king also gave his signet ring which was taken from Haman to Mordecai. We read in **Esther 8:1-2**, "On that day did *the king Ahasuerus give the house of Haman the Jews' enemy unto Esther the queen.* **And** *Mordecai came before the king*; for Esther had told what he was unto her. *And the king took off his ring, which he had taken from Haman, and gave it unto Mordecai. And Esther set Mordecai over the house of Haman.*"

Prayer Points

- *That the material wealth of the wicked shall be transferred to me (the righteous)*
- *That the royal status of the ungodly shall be given to me*

Esther's Second Petition

Despite the honor that she had gained which resulted in the hanging of Haman on the gallows, Esther did not take the king for granted. Esther pressed further for mercy as she humbled herself at the feet of the king to make an appeal to revoke Haman's scheme against the Jews. Haman was dead, but the curse that he had written against Mordecai and the Jews was still alive. The curse was in a state of maturation and ready to explode like a time bomb (handwriting of ordinances). As long as the curse of annihilation that Haman had brought upon the Jews was still alive and in place, Esther and Mordecai's new status was useless. Their elevation was without peace or joy as long as the plot had not been cancelled or withdrawn from action. There was a need to mount up another strategy that would cause the king to honor his words, so that the Hamanic curse would be totally uprooted, eradicated, and cast into the sea of destruction, never to be revoked again in the Persian kingdom.

This kind of situation can be described as part of the purpose of the death of our Lord and Savior Jesus Christ on the cross of Calvary. Scripture states in the New Testament that the blood of Jesus Christ was shed for the redemption of our soul as in **Colossians 2:14-15,**

> **Blotting out the handwriting of ordinances that was against us, which was contrary to us, and took it out of the way, nailing it to his cross; "and having spoiled principalities and powers, he made a shew of them openly, triumphing over them in it."**

Esther's Humble Strategy

Humility is a fruit of the Spirit. Humility is a deep expression of the fear of God. Humility is a weapon against the enemy and an instrument for winning favor. Esther applied humility as a strategy to further gain more favor from the king. Unlike Vashti who had exhibited pride while the king expressed love and affection that was rejected, Esther demonstrated respect for her favor as she fell at his feet. Esther's humility and tears spoke louder as she wet the king's feet with the shedding of her tears. The king was touched by Esther's humility and sympathized with her. Making a difference between the dethroned Vashti, who was a symbol of pride, and Esther who replaced the arrogant Vashti, the king was moved to grant Esther's second petition.

> **Esther 8:3-5**
> And ***Esther spake yet again before the king, and fell down at his feet,*** and ***besought him with tears to put away the mischief of Haman the Agagite,*** and ***his device that he had devised against the Jews.*** Then the king held out the golden sceptre toward Esther. So Esther arose, and stood before the king, And said, If it please the king, and ***if I have found favour in his sight,*** and ***the thing seem right before the king,*** and ***I be pleasing in his eyes, let it be written to reverse the letters devised by Haman*** the son of Hammedatha the Agagite, ***which he wrote to destroy the Jews*** which are in all the king's provinces:

Prayer Points

- *That my tears will not be in vain but attract mercy*
- *That the authority will listen to my petition*
- *That my humility will be respected*
- *That my request will be specific*
- *That any mischief devised against me and my people shall be reversed*
- *That any destructive letter written against me shall be reversed*

Application

In order to achieve effective results in fasting, it is important that you identify the particular problems that need solution. Use the reflective questions provided to map out strategic solutions to the problems that affect your family members, environment, or anyone whom you intend to help besides yourself.

1. **List 3-5 lesson points that you have learned from today's reading.**

   _____
   _____
   _____
   _____
   _____

2. **Identify how the lesson affects you positively in 3-5 points.**

   _____
   _____
   _____
   _____
   _____

3. **Identify how you intend to use the lesson from today's passage to resolve your problem in 3-5 points.**

   _____
   _____
   _____
   _____
   _____

Day Eighteen:
The Empowerment of Esther and Mordecai

A specific prayer will receive a specific answer according to how it is presented and expected. Esther's request was specific. She had prayed and trusted God, yet at the same time she transformed her prayer into reality. Although she had fasted and trusted the Lord to intervene, she also needed the human kingdom to work with her so that the reality of her request would be manifested in the natural realm. Esther plugged herself into the throne of grace through fasting and connected herself to the heart of the King of kings in glory so that God's authority would rule on earth. Whatever is sanctioned in the spiritual realm in heaven will be manifested in the physical realm on earth as it says in **Matthew 16:19, "And I will give unto thee the keys of the kingdom of heaven: and whatsoever thou shalt bind on earth shall be bound in heaven: and whatsoever thou shalt loose on earth shall be loosed in heaven."**

Esther's prayer and petition were focused on just one thing—that the curse of annihilation written against the Jews would be reversed so that the lives of the Jews would be spared. The king not only granted her petition but also empowered her and Mordecai to uproot the curse from the land and also protect themselves against the enemies of the Jews.

Specific Solution Granted to Reverse a Generational Curse

- The royal accommodation that Haman occupied as prime minister of the land was turned over to Esther and Mordecai.
- Haman was hanged on the gallows that he had selfishly prepared for Mordecai's death.
- The royal authority that was once conferred unto Haman the enemy of the Jews was taken away and presented to Mordecai.
- The same royal seal which Haman used as weapon of destruction to eliminate the Jews turned around to become an instrument of deliverance.

Esther 8:6-8

For how can I endure to see the evil that shall come unto my people? or how can I endure to see the destruction of my kindred? Then the king Ahasuerus said unto Esther the queen and to Mordecai the Jew, Behold, I have given Esther the house of Haman, and him they have hanged upon the gallows, because he laid his hand upon the Jews. *Write ye also for the Jews, as it liketh you, in the king's name, and seal it with the king's ring: for the writing which is written in the king's name, and sealed with the king's ring, may no man reverse.*

Prayer Points

- *That no man will reverse my blessings and divine protection*
- *That my prosperity will be established and sealed forever*
- *That no one or situation will tamper with my favor*

Esther 8:9-14

Then were the king's scribes called at that time in the third month, that is, the month Sivan, on the three and twentieth *day* thereof; *and it was written according to all that Mordecai commanded unto the Jews, and to the lieutenants, and the deputies and rulers of the provinces which are from India unto Ethiopia*, an hundred twenty and seven provinces, unto every province according to the writing thereof, and *unto every people after their language*, and *to the Jews according to their writing, and according to their language.* And he wrote in the king Ahasuerus's name, and sealed *it* with the king's ring, and sent letters by posts on horseback, *and* riders on mules, camels, *and* young dromedaries: Wherein the king granted the Jews which *were* in every city to gather themselves together, and *to stand for their life, to destroy, to slay, and to cause to perish, all the power of the people and province that would assault them, both little ones and women, and to take the spoil of them for a prey*, upon one day in all the provinces of king Ahasuerus, namely, upon the thirteenth *day* of the twelfth month, which *is* the month Adar. The copy of the writing for a commandment to be given in every province was published unto all people, and *that the Jews should be ready against that day to avenge themselves on their enemies. So* the posts that rode upon mules and camels went out, being hastened and pressed on by the

king's commandment. And the decree was given at Shushan the palace.

Prayer Points

- *That my favor will be published in the nations*
- *That my promotion will be recognized before kings and princes in the nations*
- *That the law of the lands shall be in my favor*
- *That favor of love and acceptance would be decreed for my destiny*

Esther 8:15-17

And *Mordecai went out from the presence of the king in royal apparel of blue and white, and with a great crown of gold, and with a garment of fine linen and purple: and the city of Shushan rejoiced and was glad.* The Jews had *light, and gladness, and joy, and honour.* **And in every province, and in every city,** *whithersoever the king's commandment and his decree came, the Jews had joy and gladness, a feast and a good day.* **And many of the people of the land became Jews; for the fear of the Jews fell upon them.**

Prayer Points

- *That the nations would be glad and rejoice over me*
- *That I will have light, gladness, joy, and honor wherever I go*

Songs of Inspiration
Onward, Christian Soldiers

Words: Sabine Baring-Gould, in Church Times, 1865. This hymn was sung at the end of the Academy Award-winning movie, Mrs. Miniver (1942).

Music: St. Gertrude, Arthur S. Sullivan, 1871

Baring-Gould wrote about this hymn:

> "Whit-Monday is a great day for school festivals in Yorkshire. One Whit-Monday, thirty years ago, it was arranged that our school should join forces with that of a neighboring village. I wanted the children to sing when marching from one village to another, but couldn't think of anything quite suitable; so I sat up at night, resolved that I would write something myself. "Onward, Christian Soldiers" was the result. It was written in great haste, and I am afraid some of the rhymes are faulty. Certainly nothing has surprised me more than its popularity. I don't remember how it got printed first, but I know that very soon it found its way into several collections. I have written a few other hymns since then, but only two or three have become at all well-known."

According to reports, "This hymn was sung at the funeral of American president Dwight Eisenhower at the National Cathedral, Washington, DC, March 1969." www.cyberhymnal.org.

Onward, Christian soldiers, marching as to war,
With the cross of Jesus going on before.
Christ, the royal Master, leads against the foe;
Forward into battle see His banners go!

Refrain

Onward, Christian soldiers, marching as to war,
With the cross of Jesus going on before.
At the sign of triumph Satan's host doth flee;
On then, Christian soldiers, on to victory!
Hell's foundations quiver at the shout of praise;
Brothers lift your voices, loud your anthems raise.

Refrain

Like a mighty army moves the church of God;
Brothers, we are treading where the saints have trod.
We are not divided, all one body we,
One in hope and doctrine, one in charity.

Refrain

What the saints established that I hold for true.
What the saints believèd, that I believe too.
Long as earth endureth, men the faith will hold,
Kingdoms, nations, empires, in destruction rolled.

Refrain

Crowns and thrones may perish, kingdoms rise and wane,

But the church of Jesus constant will remain.
Gates of hell can never gainst that church prevail;
We have Christ's own promise, and that cannot fail.

Refrain

Onward then, ye people, join our happy throng,
Blend with ours your voices in the triumph song.
Glory, laud and honor unto Christ the King,
This through countless ages men and angels sing.

Refrain

Application

In order to achieve effective results in fasting, it is important that you identify the particular problems that need solution. Use the reflective questions provided to map out strategic solutions to the problems that affect your family members, environment, or anyone whom you intend to help besides yourself.

1. **List 3-5 lesson points that you have learned from today's reading.**

   _____
   _____
   _____
   _____
   _____

2. **Identify how the lesson affects you positively in 3-5 points.**

   _____
   _____
   _____
   _____
   _____

3. **Identify how you intend to use the lesson from today's passage to resolve your problem in 3-5 points.**

   _____
   _____
   _____
   _____
   _____

Strategic Deliverance Prayer

The Problem

Need to reverse and destroy any curse written against me and my people

The Situation

Satanic verses have been decreed against me and my people
The enemy has proposed to oppress and suppress my destiny
The enemy has been interfering with my wealth and prosperity

The Goal

That my tears will not be in vain but attract mercy
That the king will listen to my petition
That my humility will be respected
That my request will be specific
That any mischief devised against me and my people shall be reversed
That any destructive letter written against me shall be reversed
That the material wealth of the wicked shall
be transferred to me (the righteous)
That the royal status of the ungodly shall be given to me
That no man will reverse my blessings and divine protection
That my prosperity would be established and sealed forever
That no one or situation will tamper with my favor
That my favor will be published in the nations
That my promotion will be recognized before
kings and princes in the nations
That the law of the lands shall be in my favor
That the nations would be glad and rejoice over me
That I will have light, gladness, joy and honor wherever I go

Authority of Scripture

Esther 8:3-5

And *Esther spake yet again before the king, and fell down at his feet,* and *besought him with tears to put away the mischief of Haman the Agagite,* and *his device that he had devised against the Jews. Then the king held out the golden sceptre toward Esther. So Esther arose, and stood before the king,* And said, If it please the king, and *if I have found favour in his sight,* and *the thing seem right before the king,* and *I be pleasing in his eyes, let it be written to reverse the letters devised by Haman* the son of Hammedatha the Agagite, *which he wrote to destroy the Jews* which *are* in all the king's provinces:

Prayer in Action

Our Father in heaven, the Great God of Wonders,
Jehovah Adonai, our Lord and Master,
Hallowed be thy name—You are the Most High God.
You are worthy to be praised—Jehovah El Shaddai.
You are Jehovah Boreh—the God of unconditional favor.
You are Jehovah El Gibbor—the Great and Mighty Warrior.
You are Jehovah Adir—the Strong One who fights my battles.
You deserve the glory, the honor, and adoration.
You are the Rock of Ages—the rescuer of my life.
You are my Fortress—the protector of my life and destiny.
Blessed be thy name, O Lord and my God.
Thank You for the great deliverance from the works of iniquity.
Thank You for the great protection from
the conspirators of destruction.
Thank You for the great intervention from
the devisers of wickedness.
Thank You, Almighty God, for everything. Amen!

Deliverance Warfare

In the name of Jesus and with the authority in the blood of Jesus, I stand on the authority in the Word of God to raise a standard against Satan and his cohorts. Listen to me, Satan, Jesus died to shed His blood for the remission of my sins, Therefore you have no accusation against me and your cohorts shall not hold anything against me. In the name of Jesus, I bind and uproot any form of accusation written against my favor. In the name of Jesus, I bind and uproot any curse of destruction published against my destiny. In the name of Jesus, I reverse any handwriting of ordinances published against my name. In the name of Jesus, I reverse any satanic counsel plotted against my status. Let the blood of Jesus Christ that was shed on the cross of Calvary erase every stain of evil published against my name and destiny. Let the fire of the Holy Ghost consume the document of destruction written and published against my name and destiny. Let the blood of Jesus build a wall of protection around my life and destiny. Let the fire of the Holy Ghost build a fortress of protection around my life and destiny. I command the evils that are cast out to go into the sea of destruction right now, in Jesus's name. They shall not see me again and I shall not invite them, in Jesus's name. Amen!

Breaking and Uprooting Curses: Curse of Stagnation and Destruction

In the name of Jesus, and with the authority in the blood of Jesus,
I bind and uproot the tree of curses planted against my life.
I speak to the tree of **stagnation and destruction** that affects my life,
You shall not prosper against my destiny.
I command you, curse of **stagnation and destruction**
to be uprooted out of my destiny right now.
In the name of Jesus, you tree of **stagnation and destruction** shall not prosper in my life.
Be uprooted out of my life and destiny right now, in the name of Jesus.
Be cast out into the sea of destruction right now, in the name of Jesus.
I shall not see you tree of **stagnation and destruction**
again and you shall not come by me, in Jesus's name.
I shall not invite you tree of **stagnation and destruction**
again and you shall not harass me, in Jesus's name
I shall not entertain you tree of **stagnation and destruction**
again and you shall not terrorize my life, in Jesus's name.
Let the blood of Jesus separate me from the curse of **stagnation and destruction** that steals the joy of my salvation.
Let the fire of the Holy Ghost destroy the root of
stagnation and destruction that afflicts me.
The tree of **stagnation and destruction** shall no
longer have access to me, in Jesus's name.
The tree of **stagnation and destruction** shall no longer
manifest within and around me again, in Jesus's name.
I am washed and cleansed by the blood of
Jesus Christ my Lord and Savior.
I am covered and sealed in, the name of Jesus.
I am protected and guarded by the fire of the Holy Ghost. Amen!

Declaration

In the name of Jesus and with the authority
in the Word of the Lord,
I declare and decree the counsel and purpose of the
Most High God upon my life and destiny.
Whatever I bind on earth shall be bound in heaven,
And whatever I loose on earth shall be loosed in heaven.
Therefore I declare divine favor upon my life to uproot
the curses that have been published against my life
and destiny as it is written in **Esther 8:3-5:**
"And Esther spake yet again before the king, and fell down at his feet, and besought him with tears to put away the mischief of Haman the Agagite, and his device that he had devised against the Jews. Then the king held out the golden sceptre toward Esther. So Esther arose, and stood before the king, And said, If it please the king, and if I have found favour in his sight, and the thing seem right before the king, and I be pleasing in his eyes, let it be written to reverse the letters devised by Haman the son of Hammedatha the Agagite, which he wrote to destroy the Jews which are in all the king's provinces."
Even as Esther found favor before the king, I
declare and decree that my tears shall not be in
vain but attract mercy, in Jesus's name.
I declare and decree that the king will listen
to my petition, in Jesus's name.
I declare and decree that my humility shall
be respected, in Jesus's name.

I declare and decree that my request shall
be specific, in Jesus's name.
I declare and decree that any mischief devised against
me and my people shall be reversed, in Jesus's name.
I declare and decree that any destructive letter written
against me shall be reversed, in Jesus's name.
I declare and decree that the material wealth of the wicked
shall be transferred to me (the righteous), in Jesus's name.
I declare and decree that the royal status of the
ungodly shall be given to me, in Jesus's name.
I declare and decree that no one shall reverse my
blessing and divine protection, in Jesus's name.
I declare and decree that my prosperity shall be
established and sealed forever, in Jesus's name.
I declare and decree that no one or situation shall
tamper with my favor, in Jesus's name.
I declare and decree that my favor shall be
published in the nations, in Jesus's name.
I declare and decree that my promotion shall be recognized
before kings and princes in the nations, in Jesus's name.
I declare and decree that the law of the lands
shall be in my favor, in Jesus's name.
I declare and decree that the nations shall be
glad and rejoice over me, in Jesus's name.
I declare and decree that *I shall have light, gladness, joy
and honor wherever I go*, in Jesus's name. Amen!

Prayer Observations and Experiences

You may remember your dreams and some past occurrences while doing this prayer. You may also receive a revelation. It's important that you make notes for future reference.

Experiences

_____
_____
_____
_____
_____
_____

Observations

_____
_____
_____
_____
_____
_____

Revelations

_____
_____
_____
_____
_____
_____

CHAPTER FOURTEEN

Ninth Chapter of Esther

Esther 9:25-32

Now in the twelfth month, that is, the month Adar, on the thirteenth day of the same, when the king's commandment and his decree drew near to be put in execution, in the day that the enemies of the Jews hoped to have power over them, (though it was turned to the contrary, that the Jews had rule over them that hated them;) The Jews gathered themselves together in their cities throughout all the provinces of the king Ahasuerus, to lay hand on such as sought their hurt: and no man could withstand them; for the fear of them fell upon all people. And all the rulers of the provinces, and the lieutenants, and the deputies, and officers of the king, helped the Jews; because the fear of Mordecai fell upon them. For Mordecai was great in the king's house, and his fame went out throughout all the provinces: for this man Mordecai waxed greater and greater. Thus the Jews smote all their enemies with the stroke of the sword, and slaughter, and destruction, and did what they would unto those that hated them. And in Shushan the palace the Jews slew and destroyed five hundred men. And Parshandatha, and Dalphon, and Aspatha, And Poratha, and Adalia, and Aridatha, And Parmashta, and Arisai, and Aridai, and Vajezatha, The ten sons of Haman the son of Hammedatha, the enemy of the Jews, slew they; but on the spoil laid they not their hand. On that day the number of those that were slain in Shushan the palace was brought before the king. And the king said unto Esther the queen, The Jews have slain and destroyed five hundred men in Shushan the palace, and the ten sons of Haman; what have they done in the rest of the king's provinces? now what is thy petition? and it shall be granted thee: or what is thy request further? and it shall be done. Then said Esther, If it please the king, let it be granted to the Jews which are in Shushan to do to morrow also according unto this day's decree, and let Haman's ten sons be hanged upon the gallows. And the king commanded it so to be done: and the decree was given at Shushan; and they hanged Haman's ten sons. For the Jews that were in Shushan gathered themselves together on the fourteenth day also of the month Adar, and slew three hundred men at Shushan; but on the prey they laid not their hand. But the other Jews that were in the king's provinces gathered themselves together, and stood for their lives, and had rest from their enemies, and slew of their foes seventy and five thousand, but they laid not their hands on the prey, On the thirteenth day of the month Adar; and on the fourteenth day of the same rested they, and made it a day of feasting and gladness. But the Jews that were at Shushan assembled together on the thirteenth day thereof, and on the fourteenth thereof; and on the fifteenth day of the same they rested, and made it a day of feasting and gladness. Therefore the Jews of the villages, that dwelt in the unwalled towns, made the fourteenth day of the month Adar a day of gladness and feasting, and a good day, and of sending portions one to another.

And Mordecai wrote these things, and sent letters unto all the Jews that were in all the provinces of the king Ahasuerus, both nigh and far, To stablish this among them, that they should keep the fourteenth day of the month Adar, and the fifteenth day of the same, yearly, as the days wherein the Jews rested from their enemies, and the month which was turned unto them from sorrow to joy, and from mourning into a good day: that they should make them days of feasting and joy, and of sending portions one to another, and gifts to the poor. And the Jews undertook to do as they had begun, and as Mordecai had written unto them; because Haman the son of Hammedatha, the Agagite, the enemy of all the Jews, had devised against the Jews to destroy them, and had cast Pur, that is, the lot, to consume them, and to destroy them; but when Esther came before the king, he commanded by letters that his wicked device, which he devised against the Jews, should return upon his own head, and that he and his sons should be hanged on the gallows. Wherefore they called these days Purim after the name of Pur. Therefore for all the words of this letter, and of that which they had seen concerning this matter, and which had come unto them, The Jews ordained, and took upon them, and upon their seed, and upon all such as joined themselves unto them, so as it should not fail, that they would keep these two days according to their writing, and according to their appointed time every year; and that these days should be remembered and kept throughout every generation, every family, every province, and every city; and that these days of Purim should not fail from among the Jews, nor the memorial of them perish from their seed. Then Esther the queen, the daughter of Abihail, and Mordecai the Jew, wrote with all authority, to confirm this second letter of Purim. And he sent the letters unto all the Jews, to the hundred twenty and seven provinces of the kingdom of Ahasuerus, with words of peace and truth, To confirm these days of Purim in their times appointed, according as Mordecai the Jew and Esther the queen had enjoined them, and as they had decreed for themselves and for their seed, the matters of the fastings and their cry. And the decree of Esther confirmed these matters of Purim; and it was written in the book.

Day Nineteen: Maintenance of Royal and Divine Destiny

Reinforcement and Maintenance of Deliverance

This chapter reveals how Mordecai had used Queen Esther's marriage to King Ahasuerus to seek deliverance from generational curses, and how they both emphasized reinforcement and maintenance of their deliverance after the ancestral curses had been uprooted.

Both Queen Esther and Mordecai wrote and published the continuation of an annual fast and prayer to build reinforcements against regermination and revenge of the curses that had been uprooted. The Jews had suddenly been empowered to uproot their enemies from the foundation of the earth, but there was need for a strategy that would prevent revenge, or reoccurrence of the past hatred from emerging with a higher force in the near future.

Although Mordecai had escaped and cheated death from the hands of the wicked and nefarious Haman, wisdom implied that he should use his position to build a stronghold of protection for the future generation of Jews around the world. Hence, Mordecai used his position to decree a law of protection and preservation of lives for the Jews. Queen Esther backed up Mordecai's writing to establish a total breakthrough that ought to be recognized beyond the kingdom of her husband King Ahasuerus. Queen Esther also appended a seal that established the decree forever.

Matthew 12:43-45 says, "**When the unclean spirit is gone out of a man, he walketh through dry places, seeking rest, and findeth none. Then he saith, I will return into my house from whence I came out; and when he is come, he findeth it empty,** swept, and garnished. Then goeth he, and taketh with himself seven other spirits more wicked than himself, and they enter in and dwell there: and the last state of that man is worse than the first. Even so shall it be also unto this wicked generation."

Maintaining Deliverance on Legal Grounds

By appending a royal seal on the decree, Queen Esther established legal grounds for the protection and preservation of the Jews against the manifestation of the ancestral curse.

- Curses may be uprooted but if legal grounds are not established, the curse may resurface again.
- When a curse is uprooted, the root must be destroyed from existence and the mark must be erased from recognition.
- Curses are easily planted but difficult to be uprooted.
- The process of uprooting curses is risky and demanding.
- The process of uprooting curses also requires moral and legal support as seen in the process established in the case of Esther.
- After uprooting curses, all doors must be shut and sealed against future invasion.

Esther 9:1-2

Now in the twelfth month, that *is,* the month Adar, on the thirteenth day of the same, when the king's commandment and his decree drew near to be put in execution, in the day that the enemies of the Jews hoped to have power over them, (though it was turned to the contrary, that

the Jews had rule over them that hated them;) *The Jews gathered themselves together in their cities throughout all the provinces of the king Ahasuerus, to lay hand on such as sought their hurt*: and *no man could withstand them; for the fear of them fell upon all people.*

Prayer Points

- *That my enemies will not be able to touch me*
- *That those who hate me shall fear to hurt me*
- *The fear of me shall fall upon people*
- *Those who devise evil shall not be able to withstand me*

Mordecai Gained Governmental Support

Mordecai worked out his salvation with fear and trembling. He also worked hard to ensure that his prayer and fasting was not in vain. He watched as he prayed. He respected and honored Esther's instructions. Hence, both of them experienced joint victories that opened door for their royal destiny to be fulfilled.

Esther 9:3-4

And *all the rulers of the provinces, and the lieutenants, and the deputies, and officers of the king, helped the Jews; because the fear of Mordecai fell upon them. For Mordecai was great in the king's house, and his fame went out throughout all the provinces: for this man Mordecai waxed greater and greater.*

Prayer Points

- That I shall gain governmental support in my daily endeavors
- That I shall be great in all realms of my existence
- That everyone shall be willing to bless me

Uprooting and Destroying Conspirators of Destiny:

In order to ensure that the enemies of the Jews do not rise up against them to revenge the uprooting of Hamanic evil conspiracy, both Queen Esther and Mordecai applied wisdom to their strategies. They did not celebrate victory without making sure that the conspirators did not attack them unexpectedly. All doors were shut and locked against unexpected assault, harassment, and terrorism from weapons of revenge. Hence, it sufficed that Haman's family was annihilated as he had plotted against the Jews. Otherwise the generational curse of revenge would continue with Haman's children against the Jews.

> **Esther 9:5-10**
> Thus *the Jews smote all their enemies with the stroke of the sword, and slaughter, and destruction, and did what they would unto those that hated them. And in Shushan the palace the Jews slew and destroyed five hundred men. And Parshandatha, and Dalphon, and Aspatha, And Poratha, and Adalia, and Aridatha,*

And Parmashta, and Arisai, and Aridai, and Vajezatha, the ten sons of Haman the son of Hammedatha, the enemy of the Jews, slew they; but on the spoil laid they not their hand.

Prayer Points

- *That the pipeline of curses would be disconnected from my life and destiny*
- *That the generations of the iniquitous would be uprooted and wiped away*
- *That those who conspire false allegations would not survive the fire of consumption*
- *That those who devise evil against me shall be consumed in their evil plot*

The King Increased Esther's Favor

1. Fasting and prayer generates power that exhumes and consumes the works of iniquity.
2. Fasting and prayer illuminate light and consumes darkness.
3. Fasting and prayer empower the righteous to pull down satanic strongholds.
4. Fasting and prayer release authority to dismantle the foundation of curses.
5. Fasting and prayer produce power that destabilizes the conspirators of evil.
6. Fasting and prayer uproot the evil planted against the people's destinies.

7. Fasting and prayer is the master key for shutting the doors of evil and opening the doors of favor to fulfill divine destiny.

Esther 9:11-12
On that day the number of those that were slain in Shushan the palace was brought before the king. And *the king said unto Esther the queen, the Jews have slain and destroyed five hundred men in Shushan the palace, and the ten sons of Haman; what have they done in the rest of the king's provinces? now what is thy petition? and it shall be granted thee: or what is thy request further? and it shall be done.*

Prayer Points

- *That my favor will be increased*
- *That my favor will have no limitation*
- *That the king will be willing to grant me unconditional favor without limit*

Uprooting Haman's Descendants to Prevent Revenge

Esther 9:13-14
Then said Esther, If it please the king, let it be granted to the Jews which *are* in Shushan to do to morrow also *according unto this day's decree,* and *let Haman's ten sons be hanged upon the gallows.* And *the king commanded it so to be*

***done:* and the decree was given at Shushan;** *and they hanged Haman's ten sons.*

Prayer Points

- *That the descendants of evil devisers shall not plot revenge against me*
- *That the descendants of satanic conspirators will not gain access to my descendants for destruction*
- *That the tree of evil that has been uprooted shall not spring up again*
- *That the root of the curse of revenge shall not rise up against my generation and descendants*

Application

In order to achieve effective results in fasting, it is important that you identify the particular problems that need solution. Use the reflective questions provided to map out strategic solutions to the problems that affect your family members, environment, or anyone whom you intend to help besides yourself.

1. **List 3-5 lesson points that you have learned from today's reading.**

   _____
   _____
   _____
   _____
   _____

2. **Identify how the lesson affects you positively in 3-5 points.**

   _____
   _____
   _____
   _____
   _____

3. **Identify how you intend to use the lesson from today's passage to resolve your problem in 3-5 points.**

   _____
   _____
   _____
   _____
   _____

Day Twenty: Rest from Ancestral Enmity and Generational Curse

There is a time to war and a time to rest. Don't give up until the battle is won and it is over. The battle may be won but not over until you have established your legal grounds to sustain your victory.

> **Esther 9:15-22**
>
> For the Jews that were in Shushan gathered themselves together on the fourteenth day also of the month Adar, and slew three hundred men at Shushan; but on the prey they laid not their hand. But the other Jews that were in the king's provinces gathered themselves together, and stood for their lives, *and had rest from their enemies*, and slew of their foes seventy and five thousand, but they laid not their hands on the prey, on the thirteenth day of the month Adar; and on the fourteenth day of the same rested they, and made it a day of feasting and gladness. But the Jews that were at Shushan assembled together on the thirteenth day thereof, and on the fourteenth thereof; and on the fifteenth *day of the same they rested, and made it a day of feasting and gladness.* Therefore the Jews of the villages, that dwelt in the unwalled towns, made the fourteenth day of the month Adar *a day of*

gladness and feasting, and a good day, and of sending portions one to another.

And Mordecai wrote these things, and sent letters unto all the Jews that were in all the provinces of the king Ahasuerus, both nigh and far, to stablish this among them, that they should keep the fourteenth day of the month Adar, and the fifteenth day of the same, yearly, as *the days wherein the Jews rested from their enemies*, and the month which was turned unto them *from sorrow to joy*, and *from mourning into a good day*: that they should make them *days of feasting and joy, and of sending portions one to another, and gifts to the poor*.

Prayer Points

- *That the season of sorrow shall be turned into joy*
- *That the season of mourning shall be turned into a good day*
- *That a season of rejection shall be turned into gladness and feasting*

Haman's Wicked and Satanic Device Returned unto Him and His Family

- Do not curse anyone if you do not want to be cursed.
- Do not devise evil against anybody if you do not want anyone to plot destruction of your life.

- Give just what you need and want for your prosperity and so shall it be done to you.
- Haman plotted evil and was paid back by his own written document that he designed against Mordecai and the Jews.
- The people who supported Haman's wicked plot inherited the curse of destruction.

Esther 9:23-25

And the Jews undertook to do as they had begun, and as Mordecai had written unto them; because Haman the son of Hammedatha, the Agagite, the enemy of all the Jews, had devised against the Jews to destroy them, and had cast Pur, that *is*, the lot, to consume them, and to destroy them; but when Esther came before the king, *he commanded by letters that his wicked device, which he devised against the Jews, should return upon his own head, and that he and his sons should be hanged on the gallows.*

Prayer Points

- *That I shall never indulge in devising satanic verses*
- *That I shall never be involved in conspiring destruction of anybody*
- *That I shall not plot evil against anybody*
- *That I shall never plant a curse against anyone*
- *That those who rise up against me shall be destroyed by their own evil plots*

Recording and Establishing the Victory over Generational Curses

Both Queen Esther and Mordecai planted and established their victories to be implemented as a law all over the world.

- Do not take your victory today for granted; tomorrow may not be the same.
- Do not despise others when you have successfully accomplished a mission; your enemy may take advantage of your celebration and plot revenge when you might forget.
- Create a memorial that will remind you of your victory from generation to generation.

Esther 9:26-32

Wherefore they called these days Purim after the name of Pur. Therefore for all the words of this letter, and of that which they had seen concerning this matter, and which had come unto them, the Jews ordained, and took upon them, and *upon their seed*, and upon all such as joined themselves unto them, so as it should not fail, *that they would keep these two days according to their writing, and according to their appointed time every year; that these days should be remembered and kept throughout every generation, every family, every province, and every city; and that these days of Purim should not fail from among the Jews, nor the memorial of them perish from their seed. Then Esther the queen, the daughter of Abihail, and*

Mordecai the Jew, wrote with all authority, to confirm this second letter of Purim. **And he sent the letters unto all the Jews,** **to the hundred twenty and seven provinces of the kingdom of Ahasuerus,** *with words of peace and truth,* **to confirm these days of Purim in their times** *appointed,* **according as Mordecai the Jew and Esther the queen had enjoined them, and** *as they had decreed for themselves and for their seed, the matters of the fastings and their cry.* **And the decree of Esther confirmed these matters of Purim; and it was written in the book.**

Prayer Points

- *That I will establish a memorial of victory against the enemy of my destiny*
- *That I will celebrate victory over the devisers of evil*
- *That a decree shall be established to celebrate the preservation of my destiny*
- *That my seed and descendants shall recognize the victory of uprooting generational curses from our lives*
- *That my seed and descendants shall not inherit the evil and repercussion of generational curses*

Songs of Inspiration
Rock of Ages, Cleft for Me

Words: Augustus M. Toplady, 1776.
Music: Toplady, Thomas Hastings, 1830 (MIDI, score). Alternate tunes:

- Cuyler, J. Hyatt Brewer (1851-1931) (MIDI, score)
- Redhead, Richard Redhead, 1853

Sir William Henry Wills, in a letter to Dean Lefroy, published in the [London] Times in June, 1898, says "Toplady was one day overtaken by a thunderstorm in Burrington Coombe, on the edge of my property, Blagdon, a rocky glen running up into the heart of the Mendip range, and there, taking shelter between two massive piers of our native limestone rock, he penned the hymn, "Rock of Ages, cleft for me, Let me hide myself in Thee."

There is a precipitous crag of limestone a hundred feet high, and right down its centre is the deep recess in which Toplady sheltered." Telford, p. 257

This hymn was sung at the funeral of William Gladstone in Westminster Abbey, London, England. Prince Albert of Britain asked it be sung to him as he lay dying. In Hymns That Have Helped, W. T. Stead stated: …when the London went down in the Bay of Biscay, January 11, 1866, the last thing which the last man who left the ship heard as the boat pushed off from the doomed vessel was the voices of the passengers singing "Rock of Ages."

In another story:

A missionary … complained of the slow progress made in India in converting the natives on account of explaining the teachings of Christianity so that the ignorant people could understand them. Some of the most beautiful passages in the Bible, for instance are destroyed by translation. He attempted to have [Rock of Ages] translated into the native dialect, so that the natives might appreciate its beauty. The work was entrusted to a young Hindu Bible student who had the reputation of being something of a poet. The next day he brought his translation for approval, and his rendering, as translated back into English, read like this: *"Very old stone, split for my benefit, Let me absent myself under one of your fragments."*

Jones: "The hymn was also reportedly sung at the funeral of American President Benjamin Harrison because it was his favorite hymn, and the only one he ever tried to sing." www.cyberhymnal.org.

Rock of Ages, cleft for me,
Let me hide myself in Thee;
Let the water and the blood,
From Thy wounded side which flowed,
Be of sin the double cure;
Save from wrath and make me pure.

Not the labor of my hands
Can fulfill Thy law's demands;
Could my zeal no respite know,
Could my tears forever flow,

All for sin could not atone;
Thou must save, and Thou alone.

Nothing in my hand I bring,
Simply to the cross I cling;
Naked, come to Thee for dress;
Helpless look to Thee for grace;
Foul, I to the fountain fly;
Wash me, Savior, or I die.

While I draw this fleeting breath,
When mine eyes shall close in death,
[*originally* When my eye-strings break in death]
When I soar to worlds unknown,
See Thee on Thy judgment throne,

Rock of Ages, cleft for me,
Let me hide myself in Thee.

Application:

In order to achieve effective results in fasting, it is important that you identify the particular problems that need solution. Use the reflective questions provided to map out strategic solutions to the problems that affect your family members, environment, or anyone whom you intend to help besides yourself.

1. **List 3-5 lesson points that you have learned from today's reading.**

   _____
   _____
   _____
   _____
   _____

2. **Identify how the lesson affects you positively in 3-5 points.**

   _____
   _____
   _____
   _____
   _____

3. **Identify how you intend to use the lesson from today's passage to resolve your problem in 3-5 points.**

   _____
   _____
   _____
   _____
   _____

Strategic Deliverance Prayer

The Problem

Need to uproot and stop the flow of ancestral curses from my life and descendants
Need to cut off and block the pipeline of generational curses in my life and in the destiny of my descendants

The Situation

The descendants of evil devisers have often plotted destruction against my life.
The descendants of my enemies want to plot revenge against my destiny and that of my posterity.
The enemies of my ancestors are hunting my prosperity.

The Goal

That my enemies will not be able to touch me
That those who hate me shall fear to hurt me
The fear of me shall fall upon people
Those who devise evil shall not be able to withstand me
That my favor will be increased
That my favor will have no limitation
That the king will be willing to grant me unconditional favor without limit
That the descendants of evil devisers shall not plot revenge against me

That the descendants of satanic conspirators will not
gain access to my descendants for destruction
That the tree of evil that has been uprooted
shall not spring up again
That the root of the curse of revenge shall not rise
up against my generation and descendants
That my season of sorrow shall be turned into joy
That my season of mourning shall be turned into a good day
That a season of rejection shall be turned
into gladness and feasting
That I shall never indulge in devising satanic verses
That I shall never be involved in conspiring destruction of anybody
That I shall not plot evil against anybody
That I shall never plant a curse against anyone
That those who rise up against me shall be
destroyed by their own evil plots
That I will establish a memorial of victory
against the enemy of my destiny
That I will celebrate victory over the devisers of evil
That a decree shall be established to celebrate
the preservation of my destiny
That my seed and descendants shall recognize the victory
of uprooting generational curses from our lives
That my seed and descendants shall not inherit the
evil and repercussion of generational curses

Authority of Scripture

Esther 9:12-14

And *the king said unto Esther the queen, The Jews have slain and destroyed five hundred men in Shushan the palace, and the ten sons of Haman; what have they done in the rest of the king's provinces? now what is thy petition? and it shall be granted thee: or what is thy request further? and it shall be done.* said Esther, If it please the king, let it be granted to the Jews which *are* in Shushan to do to morrow also *according unto this day's decree,* and *let Haman's ten sons be hanged upon the gallows.* And *the king commanded it so to be done*: and the decree was given at Shushan; *and they hanged Haman's ten sons.*

Prayer in Action

O Lord and My Father,
The Rock of Ages and the Ancient of Days,
Jehovah God and the King of Glory,
My God, my Deliverer and my Fortress,
What shall I render to You, my Lord and Redeemer?
There are no words to express the depth of my appreciation
For the great and mighty works that you have performed in my life.
O Lord and my God, You deserve the glory, the honor and adoration.
Blessed Redeemer and Living Word,
There are no tongues holy and pure enough to worship and adore You
For the grace and mercy that You have shown me.
Yes, Lord, there are no expressions that can
explain the unconditional favor
That you have poured upon my life and destiny.
O Lord my Fortress, thank You for
deliverance from generational curses.
O Lord my Deliverer, thank You for saving
me from the hand of the devourer.
O Lord my Savior, thank You for releasing me from the pangs of death.
O Lord my Redeemer, thank You for hiding
me from the storm of destruction.
You are worthy of our praise and worthy to be adored.
Thank You, Lord God Almighty.
Thank You for the preservation and protection of my life and destiny.
Thank You for uprooting and blocking ancestral
curses from afflicting my descendants.
Thank You for destroying the seed of ancestral
vengeance from my descendants' destiny.
Thank You, Jehovah God! Amen!

Deliverance Warfare

In the name of Jesus and with the authority in the
blood of Jesus Christ our Lord and Savior,
I stand on the authority in the blood that Jesus
shed for me on the cross of Calvary,
To declare a war against Satan and his powers and principalities
of darkness in the air, on the land, and in the sea.
In the name of Jesus, I bind and uproot the stronghold
of revenge from my life and my descendants'
destinies and cast it into the sea of destruction.
In the name of Jesus, I bind and uproot the ancestral
spirit of revenge from my environment and descendants
and cast it into the sea of destruction.
In the name of Jesus, I bind and uproot the generational
trees of curses planted since the era of my ancestors
and cast them into the fire of destruction.
In the name of Jesus, I bind and uproot the pipeline
of curses flowing from the era of my ancestor to my
generation and cast them into the fire of destruction.
In the name of Jesus, I command the link of generational
curses to be broken off me right now and never to flow again.
In the name of Jesus, I command the influence of ancestral curses
affecting the destiny of my extended
families and future generations
to cease manifesting in our lives.
Let the blood that was shed for my redemption nullify the
existence of any ancestral curse that hunts my life, in Jesus's name.
Let the fire of the Holy Ghost destroy the root of every
generational curse infiltrating my life, in Jesus's name.

Breaking and Uprooting Curses: Curse of Revenge and Ancestral Contamination

In the name of Jesus, and with the authority in the blood of Jesus I bind and uproot the tree of curses planted against my life.
I speak to the tree of **revenge and ancestral contamination** that affects my life.
You shall not prosper in my destiny.
I command you, curse of **revenge and ancestral contamination** to be uprooted out of my destiny right now.
In the name of Jesus, you tree of **revenge and ancestral contamination** shall not prosper in my life.
Be uprooted out of my life and destiny right now, in the name of Jesus.
Be cast out into the sea of destruction right now, in the name of Jesus.
I shall not see you, tree of **revenge and ancestral contamination** again, and you shall not come by me, in Jesus's name.
I shall not invite you, tree of **revenge and ancestral contamination** again, and you shall not harass me, in Jesus's name
I shall not entertain you, tree of **revenge and ancestral contamination** again, and you shall not terrorize my life, in Jesus's name.
Let the blood of Jesus separate me from the curse of **revenge and ancestral contamination** that steals the joy of my salvation.
Let the fire of the Holy Ghost destroy the root of **revenge and ancestral contamination** that afflicts me.

The tree of **revenge and ancestral contamination** shall no longer have access to me, in Jesus's name.
The tree of **revenge and ancestral contamination** shall no longer manifest within and around me again, in Jesus's name.
I am washed and cleansed by the blood of
Jesus Christ my Lord and Savior.
I am covered and sealed in the name of Jesus.
I am protected and guarded by the fire of the Holy Ghost. Amen!

Declaration

In the name of Jesus and by the authority in the
blood of Jesus Christ my Lord and Savior,
I stand on the written Word of God to declare and
decree favor to destroy the affliction of ancestral
curses that affect my life and destiny.
According to the book of **Esther 9:12-14** that states,
"**And** *the king said unto Esther the queen, The Jews
have slain and destroyed five hundred men in Shushan
the palace, and the ten sons of Haman; what have
they done in the rest of the king's provinces? now
what is thy petition? and it shall be granted thee: or
what is thy request further? and it shall be done.*
**Then said Esther, If it please the king, let it be
granted to the Jews which** *are* **in Shushan to do to
morrow also** *according unto this day's decree,* **and** *let
Haman's ten sons be hanged upon the gallows.*
And *the king commanded it so to be done*: **and the decree
was given at Shushan;** *and they hanged Haman's ten sons.*"
Therefore, I declare and decree that my enemies
will not be able to touch me, in Jesus's name.
I declare and decree that those who hate me
shall fear to hurt me, in Jesus's name.
I declare and decree that the fear of me shall
fall upon people, in Jesus's name.
I declare and decree that those who devise evil shall
not be able to withstand me, in Jesus's name.
I declare and decree that my favor will
be increased, in Jesus's name.

I declare and decree that my favor will have
no limitation, in Jesus's name.
I declare and decree that the king will be willing to grant
me unconditional favor without limit, in Jesus's name.
I declare and decree that the descendants of evil devisers
shall not plot revenge against me, in Jesus's name.
I declare and decree that the descendants of
satanic conspirators will not gain access to my
descendants for destruction, in Jesus's name.
I declare and decree that the tree of evil that has been
uprooted shall not spring up again, in Jesus's name.
I declare and decree that the root of the curse of revenge shall not
rise up against my generation and descendants, in Jesus's name.
I declare and decree that the season of sorrow
shall be turned into joy, in Jesus's name.
I declare and decree that the season of mourning shall be
turned into a good season of celebration, in Jesus's name.
I declare and decree that a season of rejection shall be
turned into gladness and feasting, in Jesus's name.
I declare and decree that I shall never indulge in
devising satanic verses, in Jesus's name.
I declare and decree that I shall never be involved in
conspiring destruction of anybody, in Jesus's name.
I declare and decree that I shall not plot evil
against anybody, in Jesus's name.
I declare and decree that I shall never plant a
curse against anyone, in Jesus's name.
I declare and decree that those who rise up against me shall
be destroyed by their own evil plots, in Jesus's name.
I declare and decree that I will establish a memorial of
victory against the enemy of my destiny, in Jesus's name.

I declare and decree that I will celebrate victory over the devisers of evil, in Jesus's name.
I declare and decree that a decree shall be established to celebrate the preservation of my destiny, in Jesus's name.
I declare and decree that my seed and descendants shall recognize the victory of uprooting generational curses from our lives, in Jesus's name.
I declare and decree that my seed and descendants shall not inherit the evil and repercussions of generational curses, in Jesus's name.

Prayer Observations and Experiences

You may remember your dreams and some past occurrences while doing this prayer. You may also receive a revelation. It's important that you make notes for future reference.

Experiences

_____
_____
_____
_____
_____

Observations

_____
_____
_____
_____
_____

Revelations

_____
_____
_____
_____
_____

CHAPTER FIFTEEN

Tenth Chapter of Esther

Esther 10:1-3

And the king Ahasuerus laid a tribute upon the land, and upon the isles of the sea. And all the acts of his power and of his might, and the declaration of the greatness of Mordecai, whereunto the king advanced him, are they not written in the book of the chronicles of the kings of Media and Persia? For Mordecai the Jew was next unto king Ahasuerus, and great among the Jews, and accepted of the multitude of his brethren, seeking the wealth of his people, and speaking peace to all his seed.

Day Twenty-One:
Proclamation of Final Conquest and Victory

It is one thing to declare a war and it is another thing to win the war against the enemy in order to proclaim total victory. It is dangerous to initiate a war that you are not prepared to fight. It is an absurdity to lead an aggression when you are not prepared to face the consequences thereof.

For over a year, Haman premeditated and plotted a war to annihilate Mordecai and the Jews. In the long run, the war turned around against him when he least expected or prepared for it. Although he had indulged in the consultation of divination and worked out diabolical strategies, and also manipulated the king in the bid of his wickedness, all the atrocities he ever plotted worked out against him.

In the long run, the people he hated were stronger than him spiritually and physically. Haman and his conspirators were uprooted and the generational curse of struggles and aggression against the Jews was also eliminated. Consequently, the enemies of the Jews were destroyed along with Haman the deviser of wickedness.

Finally, the curse was uprooted and the intention of it was reversed and cast into the sea of destruction. In the reversal, the position of prime minister of the Persian Empire that Haman had occupied was turned over to Mordecai. The massive wealth and prosperity that Haman had acquired was also transferred to Mordecai.

Queen Esther was also empowered and elevated to a powerful position in the kingdom. The Jews gained liberation to live and operate freely in the kingdom. More so, they gained superiority above the natives of the territories wherever they dwelt.

Destroying the Pipeline of Curses Uprooted

It is very critical that when a curse has been uprooted, one maintains a covering of sustenance and protection against the emergence of that affliction. A curse is influenced by an evil spirit and germinated like a seed that is planted to bear evil fruit, as we see in **Matthew 7:15-20**:

> **Beware of false prophets, which come to you in sheep's clothing, but *inwardly they are ravening wolves.* Ye shall know them by their fruits. Do men gather grapes of thorns, or figs of thistles? Even so every good tree bringeth forth good fruit; but a corrupt tree bringeth forth evil fruit. A good tree cannot bring forth evil fruit, neither can a corrupt tree bring forth good fruit. Every tree that bringeth not forth good fruit is hewn down, and cast into the fire. Wherefore by their fruits ye shall know them.**

The Seed of the Unborn Generation – Posterity

Mordecai took serious notice of the fact that the curse emanating from Esau had flowed in the pipeline of many generations until it was uprooted. But caution must be taken to avoid a reoccurrence of that which has been uprooted and destroyed.

The fact is that any problem or misunderstanding that is never discussed or resolved is likely to turn into a seed of evil that infiltrates and interferers with us and our future generations of innocent people. Sweeping an issue under the carpet or ignoring an issue and avoiding touching it is dangerous to the realms of truth and spiritual prosperity. If truth must ever be honored, then one needs to be sincere with the foundation of our Christianity. Confession and repentance must be made with forgiveness coming from the depth of our hearts. It is not good to retain evil in our hearts and thoughts; it will affect future generations and cause them undeserved pains at a price to a sin that Christ Jesus has already paid for.

The book of Esther ended with Mordecai speaking and decreeing peace to the seed of Israel—the Jews and the descendants of Jacob as he stated thus: **"For Mordecai the Jew was next unto king Ahasuerus, and great among the Jews, and accepted of the multitude of his brethren, seeking the wealth of his people, and speaking peace to all his seed"** (Esther 10:3). The seed of Mordecai refers to all the Jews who are his brethren and the future generations of the children of Israel.

Esther 10:1 And the king Ahasuerus laid a tribute upon the land, and *upon* the isles of the sea. And all the acts of his power and of his might, and the declaration of the greatness of Mordecai, whereunto the king advanced him, *are* they not written in the book of the chronicles of the kings of Media and Persia? *For Mordecai the Jew was next unto king Ahasuerus, and great among the Jews, and accepted of the multitude of his brethren, seeking the wealth of his people, and speaking peace to all his seed.*

Prayer Points

- *That my seed will not inherit any evil that afflicts me*
- *That my seed will be free from generational curses*
- *That my seed will inherit my blessings and prosperity*
- *That whatever has been uprooted will never resurface in my descendants.*

Songs of Inspiration
Now Thank We All Our God

Words: Martin Rinkart, circa 1636 (Nun danket alle Gott); first appeared in Praxis Pietatis Melica, by Johann Crüger (Berlin, Germany: 1647); translated from German to English by Catherine Winkworth, 1856.

Music: Nun Danket, attributed to Johann Crüger, 1647; harmony by Felix Mendelssohn, 1840 (MIDI, score). Though the tune is found Crüger's Praxis Pietatis Melica, and is attributed to Crüger, Catherine Winkworth believed Martin Rinkart wrote the tune in 1644.

"Martin Rinkart, a Lutheran minister, was in Eilenburg, Saxony, during the Thirty Years' War. The walled city of Eilenburg saw a steady stream of refugees pour through its gates. The Swedish army surrounded the city, and famine and plague were rampant. Eight hundred homes were destroyed, and the people began to perish. There was a tremendous strain on the pastors who had to conduct dozens of funerals daily. Finally, the pastors, too, succumbed, and Rinkart was the only one left—doing 50 funerals a day. When the Swedes demanded a huge ransom, Rinkart left the safety of the walls to plead for mercy. The Swedish commander, impressed by his faith and courage, lowered his demands. Soon afterward, the Thirty Years' War ended, and Rinkart wrote this hymn for a grand celebration service. It is a testament to his faith that, after such misery, he was able to write a hymn of abiding trust and gratitude toward God." www.cyberhymnal.org.

Now thank we all our God, with heart and hands and voices,
Who wondrous things has done, in Whom this world rejoices;
Who from our mothers' arms has blessed us on our way
With countless gifts of love, and still is ours today.

O may this bounteous God through all our life be near us,
With ever joyful hearts and blessèd peace to cheer us;
And keep us in His grace, and guide us when perplexed;
And free us from all ills, in this world and the next!

All praise and thanks to God the Father now be given;
The Son and Him Who reigns with Them in highest Heaven;
The one eternal God, whom earth and Heaven adore;
For thus it was, is now, and shall be evermore.

Application

In order to achieve effective results in fasting, it is important that you identify the particular problems that need solution. Use the reflective questions provided to map out strategic solutions to the problems that affect your family members, environment, or anyone whom you intend to help besides yourself.

1. **List 3-5 lesson points that you have learned from today's reading.**

   _____
   _____
   _____
   _____
   _____

2. **Identify how the lesson affects you positively in 3-5 points.**

   _____
   _____
   _____
   _____
   _____

3. **Identify how you intend to use the lesson from today's passage to resolve your problem in 3-5 points.**

   _____
   _____
   _____
   _____
   _____

Strategic Deliverance Prayer

The Problem

My challenges will propel me into my destiny
for promotion and I shall be established.

The Situation

The Lord God has heard my cry.
My petition has been granted.
My favor has been established.
God has blessed me, no one can curse me.

The Goal

That my favor will be established forever
That my descendants will inherit my blessings
from generation to generation
That no curse will affect me and my descendants
That my descendants will never depart from the fear of God
That my descendants will serve the Lord forever
That my descendants will appreciate the Great God of Wonders

Authority of Scripture

Esther 10:3

For Mordecai the Jew was next unto king Ahasuerus, and great among the Jews, and accepted of the multitude of his brethren, seeking the wealth of his people, and speaking peace to all his seed.

Prayer in Action

Great God of Wonders—Jehovah is Your name.
You are the immortal and invisible God—
the One who knows all things.
You are the Almighty Father—the King
of kings and the Lord of all.
You are the Rock of Ages and the Ancient of Days.
You deserve all the glory and adoration.
Blessings and honor be unto You, O Lord our God.
Who is like unto thee, O Lord?
Who is comparable to thee, Jehovah God?
You are Jehovah Jireh—the Great Provider,
The One who sends the dew of heaven to water the earth.
You are Jehovah Boreh—the Creator of heaven and earth,
Who made the sun to shine and the rain to fall upon the earth.
Hallowed be thy name, Great God of Wonders.
For the works of Your hands shall praise You,
As the heavens tell of Your glory and the earth exalt Your name,
Wonderful, glorious and majestic are Your names.
O let the waters of the sea storm and spread Your
name abroad to the ends of the earth.
O let the shout of praise rise above the mountains
and penetrate the skies into the heavens.
O let the branches of trees wave symbolic
praises unto the King of Glory.
O let the birds of the air sing hosanna unto the
Great God of Wonders beyond the skies.
O let everything that has breath exalt the Lord our God and
worship at Your footstool, for holy and worthy are You.

Halleluiah, Glory be to God in the highest!
Hosanna to the King of Glory!
Glory, glory, glory, halleluiah be unto the Ancient of Days!
Thank You, Lord for all that You have done to deliver me.
Thank You, Lord, for all that You have done to preserve my life.
Thank You, Lord, for all that You have
done to establish me in prosperity.
Thank You, Jehovah God!
Thank You, Jesus Christ our Lord and Redeemer. Amen!

Deliverance Warfare

In the name of Jesus and with the authority in the
blood of Jesus Christ our Lord and Savior,
I stand on the authority in the blood that Jesus
shed for me on the cross of Calvary,
To declare a war against Satan and his powers and
principalities of darkness in the air, on the land, and in the
sea, and to raise a standard against the concoction of evil;
In the name of Jesus, I bind and uproot the stronghold of curses
from my life, from my descendants, and from our destiny;
I cast them into the sea of destruction right now, in Jesus's name.
In the name of Jesus, I bind and uproot ancestral curses that
operate in my environment that would affect my descendants;
I cast them into the sea of destruction right now, in Jesus's name.
In the name of Jesus, I bind and uproot the generational
trees of curses planted since the ages of my ancestors;
I cast them into the fire of destruction right now, in Jesus's name.
In the name of Jesus, I bind and uproot the pipeline of curses
flowing from the days of my ancestors to my generation;
I cast them into the fire of destruction right now, in Jesus's name.
In the name of Jesus, I bind and uproot the generational curses
of sicknesses and diseases planted since the ages of my ancestors;
I cast them into the fire of destruction right now, in Jesus's name.
In the name of Jesus, I bind and uproot the generational curses
of lack and poverty planted since the ages of my ancestors;
I cast them into the fire of destruction right now, in Jesus's name.
In the name of Jesus, I bind and uproot the generational curses of
accidents and early death planted since the age of my ancestors;
I cast them into the fire of destruction right now, in Jesus's name.

In the name of Jesus, I bind and uproot the generational curses of struggle and pain planted since the ages of my ancestors; I cast them into the fire of destruction right now, in Jesus's name. In the name of Jesus, I bind and uproot the generational curses of broken homes and dysfunctional marriages planted since the age of my ancestors; I cast them into the fire of destruction right now in Jesus's name. In the name of Jesus, I bind and uproot the generational curses of demonic attacks and satanic interference planted since the ages of my ancestors; I cast them into the fire of destruction right now, in Jesus's name. In the name of Jesus, I command the link of generational curses to be broken from me right now and never to flow again. In the name of Jesus, I command the influence of ancestral curses affecting the destiny of my generational families to cease manifesting right now in our lives. Let the blood that was shed for my redemption nullify and void the existence of any ancestral curse that hunts my life right now, in Jesus's name. Let the fire of the Holy Ghost destroy the root of every generational curse infiltrating into my life right now, in Jesus's name. The blood of Jesus sets me free from evil right now. The blood of Jesus releases me from all manner of spiritual oaths and promises right now. The blood of Jesus liberates me from satanic verses written or published against me right now. Amen!

Breaking and Uprooting Curses: Curses that Hinders Destiny Promotion and Establishment

In the name of Jesus, and with the authority in the blood of Jesus,
I bind and uproot the tree of curses planted against my life.
I speak to the tree of **curses that hinders destiny promotion and establishment**
that affects my life,
You shall not operate in my destiny, in Jesus's name.
I command you, tree of **curses that hinders destiny promotion and establishment** to be uprooted out
of my destiny right now, in Jesus's name.
In the name of Jesus, you tree of **curses that hinders destiny promotion and establishment** shall not prosper against my life.
Be uprooted out of my life and destiny
right now, in the name of Jesus.
Be cast out into the sea of destruction
right now, in the name of Jesus.
I shall not see you, tree of **curses that hinders destiny promotion and establishment** again and
you shall not come by me, in Jesus's name.
I shall not invite you, tree of **curses that hinders destiny promotion and establishment** again and
you shall not harass me, in Jesus's name.
I shall not entertain you, tree of **curses that hinders destiny promotion and establishment** again and
you shall not terrorize my life, in Jesus's name.

Let the blood of Jesus separate me from the tree of **curses that hinders destiny promotion and establishment** that steals the joy of my salvation.
Let the fire of the Holy Ghost destroy the root of **curses that hinders destiny promotion and establishment** that afflicts me.
The tree of **curses that hinders destiny promotion and establishment** shall no longer have access to me, in Jesus's name.
The tree of **curses that hinders destiny promotion and establishment** shall no longer manifest within and around me again, in Jesus's name.
I am washed and cleansed by the blood of Jesus Christ my Lord and Savior.
I am covered and sealed in, the name of Jesus.
I am protected and guarded by the fire of the Holy Ghost. Amen!

Declaration

In the name of Jesus and with the authority in the
blood of Jesus Christ my Lord and Savior,
I stand on the written Word of God to declare and decree favor to destroy the affliction of ancestral curses that affect my life and destiny.
I stand to declare and decree the manifestation of my
blessings and prosperity right now in the name of Jesus.
Even as Esther and Mordecai uprooted the ancestral curses
that were intended to annihilate them, I also stand on the
authority of the Word of God to uproot and destroy all
manner of curses that oppress and suppress my destiny.
It is written in **Esther 10:3** that,
"For Mordecai the Jew was next unto king Ahasuerus, and great among the Jews, and accepted of the multitude of his brethren, seeking the wealth of his people, and speaking peace to all his seed."
So shall be my portion, in Jesus's name.
I declare and decree that my favor will be
established forever, in Jesus's name.
I declare and decree that my descendants will inherit my
blessings from generation to generation, in Jesus's name.
I declare and decree that no curse will affect me
and my descendants, in Jesus's name.
I declare and decree that my descendants will never
depart from the fear of God, in Jesus's name.
I declare and decree that my descendants will
serve the Lord forever, in Jesus's name.
I declare and decree that my descendants will appreciate
the Great God of Wonders, in Jesus's name. Amen!

Songs of Inspiration
Immortal Invisible God Only Wise God

Words: Walter C. Smith, Hymns of Christ and the Christian Life, 1876.

Music: St. Denio, Welsh melody, from Canaidau y Cyssegr, by John Roberts, 1839 (MIDI, score).

Immortal, invisible, God only wise,
In light inaccessible hid from our eyes,
Most blessèd, most glorious, the Ancient of Days,
Almighty, victorious, Thy great Name we praise.

Unresting, unhasting, and silent as light,
Nor wanting, nor wasting, Thou rulest in might;
Thy justice, like mountains, high soaring above
Thy clouds, which are fountains of goodness and love.

To all, life Thou givest, to both great and small;
In all life Thou livest, the true life of all;
We blossom and flourish as leaves on the tree,
And wither and perish—but naught changeth Thee.
Great Father of glory, pure Father of light,
Thine angels adore Thee, all veiling their sight;
But of all Thy rich graces this grace, Lord, impart
Take the veil from our faces, the vile from our heart.

All laud we would render; O help us to see
'Tis only the splendor of light hideth Thee,
And so let Thy glory, Almighty, impart,
Through Christ in His story, Thy Christ to the heart.

Prayer Observations and Experiences

You may remember your dreams and some past occurrences while doing this prayer. You may also receive a revelation. It's important that you make notes for future reference.

Experiences

_____
_____
_____
_____
_____
_____

Observations

_____
_____
_____
_____
_____
_____

Revelations

_____
_____
_____
_____
_____
_____

Reflection

The purpose of this book is to enable readers to make amendments wherever they have made some mistakes that have caused them to slump into a state of stagnancy, retrogression, and depression. For a person to gain full recovery and start off on a progressive pathway, it is important to reflect on the notes that one has jotted down in each chapter of this book. It is also important to do some specific reflections, because a general reflection may be productive but not effective. Reflection is a process of examining the lessons that you learned from reading or studying this book. For instance, it is wise to answer the questions below in order to experience the effectiveness of this book, as you may be expecting a real makeover in your life.

What have you learned?

_____
_____
_____
_____
_____
_____

How will you apply the lesson learned to your life?

_____
_____
_____
_____

How will you use the lesson learned to assist others?

_____
_____
_____
_____
_____
_____

What are the challenges or hindrances you are encountering?

_____
_____
_____
_____
_____

Find out if God has ever spoken to you. What did God say, and what did you hear?

_____
_____
_____
_____
_____

Are you in the right profession? Are you in the right place?

_____
_____
_____
_____
_____

What is solution to you? Can you identify the solutions to some specific problems in your life?

_____
_____
_____
_____
_____

Do you understand deliverance? What level of deliverance have you experienced so far?

_____
_____
_____
_____
_____

What have you discovered about yourself?

_____
_____
_____

What are the specific instructions and strategies that you want to adopt in order to overcome the ancestral challenges that confront some members of your family and yourself?

_____
_____
_____
_____
_____

Asking for a deliverance solution means you want the Lord to intervene in matters that concern you. Do you really want His perfect will or permissive will for your daily endeavors?

_____
_____
_____
_____
_____

What are the areas in which you need deliverance intervention?

_____
_____
_____
_____
_____

Identify your challenges.

_____
_____
_____
_____
_____

Identify your weak points and shortcomings.

_____
_____
_____
_____
_____

Do you have a teachable spirit?

_____
_____
_____
_____
_____

How often have you changed relationship because of hurt or anger?

_____
_____
_____
_____
_____

Whenever you come across stagnancy in the course of an aspiration, do you withdraw from active duty? What do you do to effect corrections in order not to fail again?

___

How do you react when someone points out your errors or weaknesses?

___

Do you often get angry, or do you work toward change?

___

How has the message in this book affected your life?

___

Give a brief summary on what reading of this book meant to you.

_____
_____
_____
_____
_____

Would you recommend the contents of this book to somebody?

_____
_____
_____
_____
_____

Send your comments about how you feel about this book to the author. You may include the response to the questions answered above. Your words could be a healing balm to somebody in another part of the world.

_____
_____
_____
_____

About the Author

Pauline Walley-Daniels, PhD, is an ordained prophetic deliverance apostle who teaches the Word of God with dramatic demonstrations. She is the president of Pauline Walley Evangelistic Ministries and Christian Communications and is the CEO of the Pauline Walley Deliverance Bible Institute, as well as the Prophetic Deliverance Training and Theological Institute, which includes the School of Intensive Training for Leadership and the School of Deliverance, in New York.

Dr. Pauline is affiliated with the Christian International Ministries Network and is the vice-president of Fellowship of Ministers International. Dr. Pauline serves on the Christian Life Educators Network board of regency. She is affiliated with International Coalition of Apostles and is a member of Morris Cerullo World Evangelism's Global Prayer Strike Force team.

She holds a master's degree in journalism and a PhD in pulpit communications and expository preaching. Dr. Pauline is the author of twenty books and is married to Rev. Frederick Daniels of Overcomers' House Prophetic Deliverance Church in the Bronx, New York.

Bibliography

MacArthur, John. *MacArthur Study Bible. New King James Version.* Nashville:Thomas Nelson, 1997.

Matthew Henry's Commentary on the Whole Bible. Peabody, MA: Hendrickson Publishers, 1992.

Rodgers, Bob. *The 21 Day Fast: 21 Days That Will Revolutionize Your Life*! Louisville, KY: Bob Rodgers Ministries.***

Thompson Chain Reference Study Bible, New King James Version. Indianapolis: Thomas Nelson, 1997.

Oxford Dictionary and Thesaurus. New York: Oxford University Press, 1996.

Walley, Pauline. *School of Deliverance I: Receive and Maintain Your Deliverance on Legal Grounds.* New York: Xulon Press, 2005.

Walley, Pauline. *School of Deliverance II: Pulling Down Satanic Strongholds.* New York: Xulon Press, 2006.

Walley, Pauline. *Strategic Prayer Tactics I: Effective Communications with Aromatic Expressions.* New York: Xulon Press, 2006.

Walley, Pauline. *Strategic Prayer Tactics II: Effective Deliverance Prayer Tactics—Warfare and Confrontations.* New York: Xulon Press, 2006.

Walley, Pauline. *Strategic Prayer Tactics I: Effective Prayer Communications with Aromatic Expressions.* New York: Xulon Press, 2007.

www.aish.com
www.answers.yahoo.com.
www.bereanadvocate.com.
www.buzzle.com.
www.ca.anwers.yahoo.com
www.cyberhymnal.org.
www.e-sword.software.informer.com.
www.freechristianresources.org.
www.faithcycleministries.org.
www.hymnlyrics.org.
www.hymnsite.com.
www.jewishencyclopedia.com.
www.messianictemplebethel.org.
www.middletownbiblechurch.org.
www.moodyministries.net.
www.rastawifeline.blogspot.com.
www.shechter.edu.
www.tfdixie.com.
www.jwa.org.
www.wikipedia.org.
www.unityinchrist.com.

Appendixes

Decision

If you have never surrendered your life to Jesus Christ, to accept him as your Lord and Savior, then it is important for you to do so right away. Otherwise, it will be difficult for you to conquer the enemy, and to overcome the negative spirits that rule your life. If you are willing to accept Jesus Christ as your Lord and Savior, then pray like this:

Lord Jesus, I come to You just as I am.
Forgive my sins and deliver me from all works of iniquity.
Deliver me from all the evil characteristics that affect my life.
Deliver me from all the behaviors that have kept me in bondage.
Set my soul and spirit free to worship You in spirit and in truth.
Come into my life and make me whole.
I need You, Lord.
I need You every hour unto eternity. Amen!

Rededication

If you have once made a decision to surrender your life to Christ Jesus but you have been struggling with the Christian life, then you need to rededicate your life in order to gain a reconnection with the Lord. Also, if you are somehow an active Christian, but are still struggling with some ungodly characteristics and behaviors, then you need to rededicate yourself to the lordship of Jesus Christ. Make a total surrender, so that the enemy will not have any form of control in your life.

You may pray like this:

> *Lord Jesus, teach me to surrender my total being to Your lordship and control, so that the enemy will no longer have a part in me.*
>
> *Teach me to abide in You so that You will also abide in me and dwell in my life.*
>
> *O Lord, teach me to study Your Word, and to make a conscious effort to apply it to my daily living.*
>
> *O Lord, wash me, cleanse me, and purify my spirit, soul, and body, so that I may be acceptable in Your sight.*
>
> *Thank You, Lord, for delivering me from the works of iniquity. Amen!*

Pauline Walley Deliverance Bible Institute & Prophetic-Deliverance Theological Training Institute (School of Intensive Training for Ministry and Leadership Equipment)

The Pauline Walley Deliverance Bible Institute is a school of intensive training that equips and empowers leaders, individuals, and church groups in the ministry. It is an intensive, practical training center where people are taught to build their images and personalities, to improve their ministry skills and abilities, develop their talents and gifts, and minister to family members, friends, churches, and/or fellowship members, and to themselves.

In the process of training, people learn how to receive ministration against the battle of life as it is in our daily endeavors.

The areas of study include the following:

- School of Deliverance
- School of Strategic Prayer
- School of Tactical Evangelism
- School of Mentoring and Leadership
- School of the Gifts of the Holy Spirit
- School of the Prophets
- School of Prophetic Deliverance
- School of Prophetic Intercession
- School of Ministerial Responsibilities and Church Administration

The School of Intensive Trainings is held in different parts of the world at various times. At seminar levels, one week or two weeks of intensive training help leaders and ministers, or church/fellowship groups to establish various arms of church ministry, and equip their members for such purposes.

Biweekly intensive training programs, the one-year certificate course and degree programs are readily available in the Bronx, New York, and other regions based on request. If you are interested in hosting any of these programs in your region, country, or church/ministry, please contact us. See details about our contact information and website on the back pages.

Christian Books by Dr. Pauline Walley (Dr. Pauline Walley-Daniels)

The Authority of an Overcomer: You Can Have It ... I Have It

The Authority of an Overcomer shares the real-life testimony of a day-to-day experience with the Lord Jesus Christ. It encourages you to apply the Word of God to every facet of your life, such as sleeping and waking with Jesus, walking and talking with Jesus, and dining with Him as you would with your spouse or a friend.

Somebody Cares ... Cares for You ... Cares for Me

Somebody Cares ... Cares for You ... Cares for Me talks about the care that the Lord God Almighty has for every one of us. It teaches you to care for other people through a type of mentoring. It enlightens you to how to exercise tolerance toward their shortcomings. You will learn the importance of self-mentoring, and the true meaning of love as you read this book.

Receive and Maintain Your Deliverance on Legal Grounds

Many people go from one prayer house to another, from the general practitioner to the specialist, from the minister to the bishop, seeking help to overcome a spiritual problem. Some others go from chapel to church with the same mission and expectation, yet never hit the target. Why? Many people lack the knowledge of how to maintain their healing and deliverance. This book, *Receive and Maintain Your Deliverance on Legal Grounds,* will educate you on the need for deliverance ministration, and how to maintain what you receive from God.

Anger: Get Rid of It ... You Can Overcome It

Anger is one of the many problems that many people seek to resolve, but for which they lack the solution. Many have resigned their fate to it, thinking that it is a natural phenomenon. *Anger: Get Rid of It ... You Can Overcome It* teaches about the causes of outburst of wrath, and how to uproot them out of your life.

The Power of the Spoken Word

There is a purpose for which we speak. When we speak, we expect something to happen so that the purpose of our utterance will be fulfilled. *The Power of the Spoken Word* teaches you to exercise your authority, so that the words you utter will be manifested effectively.

The Holy Spirit: The Uniqueness of His Presence

The presence of the Holy Spirit highlights the differences between the gifts of the Spirit, the presence of God, and the visitation of the Holy Spirit. In *The Holy Spirit: The Uniqueness of His Presence,* you will learn to enjoy the delightful presence of the Holy Spirit in your spiritual walk.

The Holy Spirit: Maintain His Presence in Trials and Temptations

The Holy Spirit: Maintain His Presence in Trials and Temptations educates you on how to maintain the presence of God, especially during trials and temptations. Oftentimes when Christians go through difficult situations, they think they are alone, but they need not feel that way. You can enter the presence of the Holy Spirit in difficult times, and witness His power to strengthen you in order to turn your situations around.

The Holy Spirit: Power of the Tongue

In recent times, many people have been seeking instant power and prophetic manifestations. Christians and ministers are indulging in all sorts of practices to demonstrate some special abilities to attract public attention. This book, *The Holy Spirit: Power of the Tongue,* discusses the various powers and anointing(s) at work. It will help you decipher between the Holy Spirit's power and satanic powers. It will also enlighten you about the various anointing(s) that exist, and how you can reach out for the genuine one.

Pulling Down Satanic Strongholds: War against Evil Spirits

Many Christians are under satanic attacks and influences, but very few people understand what the actual problems are. Some believe in God but have no idea that there is anything like the satanic realm; however, they are under satanic torments. This book, *Pulling Down Satanic Strongholds,* enlightens you on some of the operations of the devil. It will help you to know when an activity around you is of the devil. This knowledge will strengthen you in prayer and equip you against the wiles of the enemy.

When Satan Went to Church

Many people fear the devil more than they fear God. At the mention of Satan or demons, they are threatened to death. Yet they are complacent in their own ways and yield to sin easily. Let the fear of God grip you, and not the fear of Satan. *When Satan Went to Church* enlightens you about the activities of the enemy within, and around the church, the home, and the Christian community. It helps you identify battles and how to put on your armor of warfare against the enemy. It also encourages you to hold firmly the shield of faith. May the Lord enlighten your eyes of understanding as you read this book.

Solution: Deliverance Ministration to Self and Others

Since the death of Jesus Christ on the cross, humans have been given the opportunity to experience and encounter the joy of salvation. However, lack of knowledge has kept the world in the dark, and deprived it of the importance of Christianity. This book, *Solution: Deliverance Ministration to Self and Others,* portrays just what the title says. It educates you to understand the intricacies of deliverance ministration, and to avoid the dangerous practices that have discouraged others. Read it and you will be blessed as never before.

Strategic Prayer Tactics I: Effective Communications with Aromatic Expressions

This book, *Strategic Prayer Tactics I,* with its focus on the types and approaches to prayer, teaches you how to approach the throne of God with a specific need and the strategies to adopt for its presentation. It also teaches you to pray with Scripture as your legal authority. Read it and you will be blessed as never before.

Strategic Prayer Tactics II: Effective Deliverance Prayer Tactics. Warfare and Confrontations. Approach to Effective Communication in Prayer.

This book, *Effective Deliverance Prayer Tactics II,* teaches you how to separate your personal identity from demonic apparitions that emanate from ancestral curses. It also teaches you how to pull down satanic strongholds that interfere with your family by using Scripture as your legal authority. Read it and you will be blessed as never before.

School of Mentoring and Leadership I: The Act of Mentoring – Stirring Up, Activating, and Imparting Talents and Abilities for Effectiveness

We all have talents and abilities that need to be developed in order for us to achieve our ambitions. Many people are bedeviled by unfulfilled dreams and are wallowing in familiar oppression and depression. *School of Mentoring and Leadership I* will help you locate and choose a mentor who will help you discover and develop your abilities. It will lead you to the fulfillment of your ambition. This book will teach and draw you closer to your destiny. Stay blessed and enjoy the act of mentoring.

School of Mentoring and Leadership II: Progressive Achievement— Receive It, Maintain It. The Act of Self-Mentoring

This book, *Progressive Achievement: Receive It, Maintain It*, teaches you how to mentor yourself while you move in progression to overcome obstacles that would usually frustrate prosperity. It enlightens you about the various types of progress that may come your way and how to manage it. It also encourages you to overcome failure and disappointment. The book helps you to understand the concept of self-mentoring in the course of progressiveness as part of the characteristics of the Holy Spirit.

School of Prophetic Deliverance: Understand the Language, Interpretations, and Assignments

Everyone believes that he or she is a child of God. Unfortunately, not everyone hears the voice of the Father, and not all are close to Him; however, all are seeking His divine attention. *School of Prophetic Deliverance I* will teach the basic principles of the prophetic ministry, and also give you the basic understanding of the prophetic word and its operations. The understanding of the prophetic word will draw you closer to Him as never before. Stay blessed and enjoy the prophetic realm.

Destiny Solution Prayers: Lord, Make Me Over

Destiny Solution Prayers: Lord, Make Me Over is about how to get ahold of destiny. It discusses the various activities that connect one destination with another on the pathway to destiny. It teaches you how to recognize and respond to the voice of destiny. Each chapter provides you with a notepad for reflection, a prayer, and a motivational song that will encourage you to make over your life in order to fulfill your destiny with satisfaction. This book is a trip that guides you to walk the path of destiny with understanding and wisdom.

Progressive Solution Prayers for Fruitfulness and Fulfillment

Progressive Solution Prayers: Fruitfulness and Fulfillment is a prayer book that discusses the common problems that people face in everyday life and provides strategic solutions with the aid of Scripture-based intercessory and warfare prayers that teach you how to approach the throne of God in a focused and strategic manner. The book shows you how to apply different types of prayers to specific issues relating to you and your loved ones in order to achieve results.

Strategic Deliverance Solutions: Discover and Destroy Ancestral Curses

Strategic Deliverance Solutions: Discover and Destroy Ancestral Curses discusses the different types of curses that commonly exist in our daily lives and endeavors. The book shows us how to detect a curse from its roots. It enlightens us about the different kinds of solutions that could be applied to each type of curse. It also reveals the end result that each type of application would likely provide for a situation.

SUBSCRIPTION
Gospel Songs on Cassette
"Overcomers' Expression"
"Send Your Power"
"Vessels of Worship"
"Poetic Expression"

BOOKS
All the books listed are available in bookstores, and by order on line.

UNITED KINGDOM
Pauline Walley Christian Communications
P.O. Box 977, Aylesbury, Buckinghamshire, HP20 9HD
Tel: (+44) 7960-838-012

UNITED STATES
Pauline Walley Christian Communications
P.O. Box 250, Bronx, NY 10467
Tel: (718) 652-2916
Fax: (718) 405-2035
E-mail: admin@paulinewalley.org
Web site: www.school-of-deliverance.com
www.paulinewalley.org
www.paulinewalley.com
www.pwdi.org

About the Book

This book, *3-21 Days Esther's Progressive Prayer Fast* reveals how Esther led a people in an effective prayer fast that changed situations for life. The book shows you how to fast, and provides you with prayer points that could be applicable to your situation, and songs of inspiration to encourage you through each season of the fast. The insights and practical guidelines will enable you to break through the challenges and difficulties that confront your environment.

Made in the USA
San Bernardino, CA
21 January 2016